teens
@ the library
series

101+
Great Ideas
for
Teen Library
Web Sites

Miranda Doyle

BIBLIOTHÈQUES

uOttawa

LIBRARIES

Neal-Schuman Publishers, Inc.

New York   London

Published by Neal-Schuman Publishers, Inc.
100 William Street, Suite 2004
New York, NY 10038-4512

Printed and bound in the United States of America.

The paper used in this publication meets the minimum requirements of American National Standard for Information Sciences—Permanence of Paper for Printed Library Materials, ANSI Z39.48-1992.

ISBN-13: 978-1-55570-593-0
ISBN-10: 1-55570-593-6

Library of Congress Cataloging-in-Publication Data

Doyle, Miranda, 1972–
    101+ great ideas for teen library Web sites / Miranda Doyle.
       p. cm.—(Teens @ the library series)
    Includes bibliographical references and index.
    ISBN-13: 978-1-55570-593-0 (alk. paper)
    ISBN-10: 1-55570-593-6 (alk. paper)
  1. Library Web sites—Design. 2. Web sites for teenagers—Design. 3. Internet in young adults' libraries. 4. Libraries and teenagers. I. Title. II. Title: One hundred and one plus ideas for teen library Web sites.
Z674.75.W67D69 2007
027.62'6—dc22   2006039132

To my husband, Mark.
Thank you for all of your love and patience.

Contents

Figures List

Series Editor's Foreword

Do you remember the scope of service possibilities available to young adult librarians before the World Wide Web? We always strove to develop attractive, useful collections responsive to our teens' needs. We adopted the use of various new forms of media—including computers with access to the nascent Internet. We often promoted subscription databases to provide increased access to information. Although we took advantage of interlibrary loan, as well as regional and state-wide sharing programs, the talk of "libraries without walls"—as gates to the larger world of knowledge, as places of limitless learning and personal exploration without boundaries—seemed restricted to large, well-funded research libraries. The idea that the whole world would be available on-demand, anytime, from anywhere, for anyone was a dream for a distant "someday."

Welcome to "someday." Our dream has become their reality. The fact that today's teens and the World Wide Web were born at the same moment is reason enough for libraries to offer a lively and effective Web presence. As Miranda Doyle explains so clearly and cheerfully in *101⁺ Great Ideas for Teen Library Web Sites*, this sweeping shift compels all passionate professionals to improve the service we offer teens. She presents more than 100 ideas that range from the simple (install a counter so you learn more about how your site is being used) to cutting edge (vblogs and moblogs) and shows not just what can be done, but also how and why one should consider ways create, update, or expand your Web site. Citing successful examples from school and public libraries of all sizes, Doyle provides thoughtful guidance for those ready to take the next step. She explains in non-threatening, non-technical, easy-to-understand prose what one needs to know/learn, download/ buy to successfully develop the kind of Web sites teens will actively respond to and use.

Living in a media-saturated environment is another good reason to enliven Web sites. Librarians can only compete for teens' attention against the billions of advertising dollars spent by multinational corporations when we remember and apply the most basic psychological tenet of teendom. They are, have been, and will always be—social creatures. Teens are truly tribal as they hang together, bounce ideas off one another, create in concert, and then use their inventions as a group.

The Web, initially seen by many as isolating, lonely, and even alienating, has instead turned into the place teens meet and greet before they hit the street. Teens are social creatures who hammer out text and instant messages in incredible numbers and flock to so-called "social networking sites" to meet the same kinds of developmental needs that used to take place at the local drive-in or malt shop.

101⁺ Great Ideas shows how developing this interactive component in Web sites is the Holy Grail. Learn why chat rooms are *so* last century. Why teens like IM-ing better that e-mail. Why they prefer blogging over creating traditional Web pages and why RSS is even better than reading blogs. She does not stipulate that we immediately implement every innovative idea, but rather suggests that becoming more knowledgeable of the available digital smorgasbord, offers the freedom to intelligently design Web sites that meet our individual objectives and serve our young adult user's needs. It is less a technical manual than an idea cookbook. Test a recipe and see what gets cooking.

Doyle provides the information to move forward whether you are a beginner just testing the waters of Web site design or a veteran who wants to offer the newest ideas and cutting edge technologies. How many teens might we reach, taking just one idea from this book to implement on our library Web site? She offers the how and why. It is up to us to make it happen.

Joel Shoemaker
Teens@the Library Series Editor

Preface

As a librarian working with teens, you take exceptional care to create an appealing physical environment. Maybe you set aside a special area with comfy chairs, face-out books, and big, colorful signs. Perhaps you create themed book displays or hang your students' art work on the walls. You might keep up-to-date bulletin boards filled with news and activities. The purpose of constructing interesting and enticing surroundings is to send a visual message to young adults that the library welcomes them to explore all of the available resources offered. I designed *101+ Great Ideas for Teen Library Web Sites* to help make your organization's online presence equally distinctive. Your Web site is another one of your public "faces," the virtual counterpart to your physical space. It should be just as enticing, informative, and comfortable to use as your real-world facilities.

Even if you feel confident your site meets those measures, there is a new challenge to tackle. Simply designing a visually appealing site, even one packed with resources and links, is no longer enough. The term "Web 2.0" is a bit of a buzzword at the moment, but it accurately incorporates the idea that we are moving beyond the first generation of the Web—with its static photos, text, and lists of links. Today's users expect to participate actively in an online world where they can find gathering places, meet, socialize, share, and collaborate.

To construct virtual environments with real appeal, we need to look to controversial—but wildly successful—social networking sites like MySpace. These sites are popular because they offer an individual "corner" of the Web to decorate, voice thoughts and dreams, proclaim likes and dislikes, link up with friends, connect with others who share interests, put up photos, list favorite Web sites, write about innermost secrets, and express deeply held views. *101+ Great Ideas for Teen Library Web Sites* takes a cue from these well-liked features and translates them into possible additions to the classic library Web site.

Your pages should be the first place teens think to go when they want to

- rave about a book they read and loved,
- find other teens who worship their favorite author,
- post their reviews,

- argue over whether a book's ending was satisfying,
- add a comment to the young adult librarian's latest blog posting,
- ask a reference question or talk to a librarian.

The 101 individual ideas cover the areas of communications, information, and imagination. Each chapter also includes interviews with school and public librarians who have actually implemented some of these ideas. They describe how they did it and give advice on how to avoid potential pitfalls. Screenshots of the Web sites illustrate the final product. Many also tell how they incorporated teen participation into their sites. I also discuss two areas of serious concern for anyone working with minors: privacy and inappropriate content.

I hope this guide acts as a catalyst for your own unique take on these ideas or perhaps even ignites the fuse to a whole new invention. My focus here is definitely on the creative over the technical. Like most other YA librarians, I have succeeded with a game spirit, a hands-on approach, and ability to follow directions. You can easily find a great many "how-to" manuals that will present detailed instruction on HTML (Hypertext Markup Language, the codes used to create Web pages), Web site design, and the technical fine points of creating and maintaining a Web site. I do point out shortcuts and simple ways to implement the ideas—for example, using easy blogging Web sites rather than installing the necessary software on your own server.

ORGANIZATION

Part I, "Essential Web Site Know-How," lays the landscape with basic launching proficiencies for novices and expanding skills for the more experienced. The ideas begin with building Web site classics using logos, locations, links to catalogs, and aids for subject searching. A new level of tech skills adds elements like blogging, vlogs, moblogs, feeds, and instant and text messaging. It also looks at podcasting, video and vodcasting, wikis, and tagging.

Part II, "Communication," puts these basics into action with ideas that show sites that spotlight blogs for library news, feeds to keep current, e-mail newsletters, program reminders, podcasting, and more. Another area examines feedback features like surveys, suggestion forms, user polls, and ways to announce resources, mission statements, and policies. It also navigates online access to orientation, audio or video tours—even downloadable audio or e-books.

Part III, "Information," explores design ideas that delve into live reference and homework help, pathfinders, assignment links, college and career resources, search engine links, and assignment alerts. Online learning includes savvy ways to improve evaluation skills, avoid plagiarism, and construct correct citations. Other learning ideas include WebQuests, audio/video lectures, and faculty/student wikis. Readers' advisory possibilities include online lists of new books, blog reviews by teens and staff, audio/video booktalks, and virtual visits from authors.

Part IV, "Imagination, Inventiveness, and Ingenuity," highlights lots of entertaining and innovative endeavors like e-zines, creative writing forums, and poetry videos. Teen advisory boards can enhance and enlarge their Internet presence with a TAB page that features ways to apply online, declare a state mission, explain bylaws, and post meeting minutes. TAB blogs and TAB zines might initiate online discussion and offer book recommendations. You also learn ways to plug in your summer reading program with online sign ups, book reviews, and raffle entries. Other fun highlights include games and puzzles, breaking news, weather, and free content. It even considers methods to animate your site and load a photo gallery.

Part V, "Tech Companion Pages," is designed to help anyone unfamiliar with some of the technical terms in the book. This part provides an extensive glossary of key terms, defined and described as simply as possible. The glossary includes the many types of software mentioned in the interviews with librarians. Other technology support sections focus on results of teen surveys and cross-referenced lists of projects grouped by tool.

Part VI, "Help Pages: 101+ Great Ideas for Teen Library Web Sites," reviews the literature and books related to teen library Web sites, general Web design books, and directories of public library and school library teen Web sites, links and blogs for library Web masters and top inventive projects.

CREATING YOUR DREAM WEB SITE

In an ideal world, library Web sites for teens would engage users' interest, address their needs, and act as a "digital library" that extends far beyond the four walls of the library's physical building. A dream Web site for teens could become a place where teenagers linger to chat about books, where they meet others who share their passions, and where they become part of a vibrant community of young readers and writers. This Web site would also allow for easy participation and facilitate creative expression. It would connect teens instantly, wherever they might be, to a full range of library resources and to the expertise of the library staff.

While many Web sites are well on their way to fulfilling that dream, there is always room for improvement. The Internet has already moved from text and photos to audio and video—who knows what will be next? The ideas in this book are only a starting point.

My hope is that the ideas and interviews will inspire you to try something new with your Web site, whether it's as simple as adding a few book reviews written by teens or as innovative as offering podcasts, wikis, streaming video, or reference using instant messaging services. Whatever ideas you choose to use and adapt to your own needs and the needs of your teens, you will benefit from the advice and experience of librarians who have already tried it. If teens in your community respond with enthusiasm, you will know you've succeeded.

ACKNOWLEDGMENTS

I want to thank all of the public and school librarians who shared their invaluable expertise, experiences, and advice:

Doug Achterman, Vicki Builta, Meg Canada, Terese Chevalier, Patrick Delaney, Jessy Griffith, Will Haines, Gretchen S. Ipock, Annisha Jeffries, Thomas Kaun, Kathy Lussier, Sarah Kline Morgan, Ginger Nelms, Sandra Payne, Margo Schiller, Maggie Schmude, Kelli Staley, Mary Ellen Stasek, Emily M. Ugino, Ed Wilson, and Liz Zylstra.

Thank you, especially, to young adult librarian and author Patrick Jones, for sending journal articles and for your words of encouragement. I would also like to thank series editor Joel Shoemaker and Michael Kelley of Neal-Schuman for their hard work on this project.

Part I. Essential Web Site Know-How

Chapter 1

Launching or Expanding a Teen Library Web Site

OVERVIEW

Many of today's teens can barely imagine life without the Internet. It's often one of the first places they turn when they need information. However, to teens, the online world is much more than just a place to research homework topics—it's also the hub of their social life, as high on the list as their cell phones and iPods as a way to stay connected and entertained.

If these teens wonder what their local library has to offer, it's unlikely that they'll dig up a copy of the phone book and give their local librarian a call. Instead, they'll probably do a quick Google search for your library Web site. Hopefully, they will find at least a rudimentary page describing the library's teen services or providing access to the school library's catalog. If not, this book can help you get started. If you do already have a basic Web site for teen visitors to your library, this may be a good time to reassess it to find out whether it's meeting your users' needs.

Tips for Creating a Great Web Site

Focus on function, not just appearance. Yes, "cool" graphics do attract teens, but research shows that they prefer a clean, easy-to-use Web site over a glitzy one that's slow and confusing.

Balance your site with both text and graphics. When it comes to using the Web, teens are far less patient than adults. They also have less

---

sophisticated reading and research skills, and don't like to wade through vast quantities of written information.

Make your site interactive, not just informative. Teens want to "do something" on a Web site—fill out a form, take a quiz, submit a book review, play a game, post a message, or chat with a librarian.

Find out how your teens use technology. If they are obsessed with Instant Messaging, offer IM reference services. If they never go anywhere without their iPods, start a library podcast. If they're all into blogging, get them to contribute to a library blog. But don't use a new technology just to be cutting edge—first, have original content or an important service to offer.

Encourage teen participation. As you design your site, ask for ideas from teens along the way. Solicit book reviews, favorite links, creative writing and art, and other content. Better yet, put your student volunteers or Teen Advisory Council in charge of Web projects, so that they become honorary Webmasters.

Establish realistic goals. As you add new Web site features, those features will need to be monitored and updated regularly. Before you start and publicize a blog, online book club, or other service, think about the time commitment required and whether the benefits make it worthwhile.

Ensure privacy and plan for safety. If you want to post photos of teens online, or let them use their real names, be aware of any school or public library policies on doing so. It's generally better to use first names only, and to avoid posting information such as phone numbers or e-mail addresses.

Decide how much risk you can tolerate. Teens will want to participate actively on your Web site by posting messages to discussion forums, commenting on the library blog, or contributing to the library's wiki. You will need to weigh the risk of inappropriate postings against the benefits of an open exchange. A middle ground is to review comments and posts before they are added.

Choose tools and strategies to make your life easier. Learn to use Web design software such as Microsoft FrontPage or Macromedia Dreamweaver, both of which have tools that will make creating, organizing and uploading pages much simpler. While it's nice to know a little HTML—the code used to build Web pages—creating your entire Web site by hand would be quite tedious. Also, try using blogging software to make pages simple and quick to update. Finally, involve teens, other library staff members, teachers, and others in adding content to your page, so that you don't have to do it all yourself.

Experiment! Experiment! Experiment! There are many new and exciting opportunities for enhancing your library Web site. Stay current and try something cutting-edge. If you think it might improve your services to your patrons, think about adding audio and video content on your site, starting a library wiki, answering reference questions sent by cell phone, adding an RSS feed, or coming up with something no one has tried before. Your experiment might flop, but don't assume that it will unless you try.

EVALUATE YOUR SITE

The first step in assessing your library Web site is to decide what you would like to accomplish. Do you simply want to create a "face" to present to the world, with basic information about the library? Do you want to create a portal through which you can communicate with your patrons, providing help and guidance? Or do you aspire to create a true community of users?

Start your evaluation by determining which of the following categories your site falls into. Library Web sites for teens can be loosely grouped into three types:

1. Provides Static Information

Is the site primarily to provide information about the school or public library's services to teens? Many Web sites serve this function. They simply give the library a presence on the Web, and present facts, addresses, hours, contacts, and so on. Users are not invited to contribute or easily able to give feedback. This type of Web site is useful, but teens will probably visit it only occasionally, when they need the information on the site.

2. Provides Opportunities for Interaction

This type of site has all the basic information about the library, plus it offers opportunities for the user to interact with the Web site and with library staff. Users might visit the site to reserve books, check their library records, use a feedback form for comments and suggestions, submit reviews, fill out online applications, e-mail a librarian with a reference question, and so on.

This type of site is much more useful to patrons, since they can use it to connect with library staff and get their needs met. However, the communication is generally initiated by the users and moves only one way, between Web site users and library staff.

3. Creates a Community

This type of site is fully interactive. It provides information and opportunities to interact with library staff, but it also goes beyond that goal to provide a sense of community. Teens are able to contribute their comments, opinions, book suggestions, artwork, and much more. They are able to start a conversation with each other, not just with the adults who run the library. Librarians may provide content through blogs or online forums, but users have a chance to add their voices to the discussion as well. Because the site changes daily, users visit often to see what's new.

Boosting your Web site to this level requires work, regular maintenance, and a certain degree of risk, depending on how open you are to allowing teens to post unfiltered comments. However, it is also the type of site that will keep teens coming back, and give them a sense of belonging.

Where does your library Web site fall on that scale of 1 to 3? Where would you like it to be? This book is full of ideas to boost your site on that scale of interactivity and community building.

DETERMINE THE LEVEL OF TEEN PARTICIPATION

Look at where you are in terms of teen participation. As most librarians who work with teens already know, the best way to get teens to buy into and use your services is to make them a part of the process. Many libraries already do so, through teen advisory groups or other means.

Divide teen participation in Web site design and operation into three levels:

1. Sites Designed for Teens by Adults

This type of site is designed by librarians and technology staff. Library staff select the links, organizes the site, and write all of the content themselves, without consulting teens. While this may lead to a quicker and more efficient process, it may not result in a site that teens feel is "theirs."

2. Sites Designed with Input from Teens

This type of site is designed with input, advice, and opinions from teens. It may include links that teens have recommended, or teen book reviews, art work, writing and other creative contributions as features on the site.

3. Sites Designed by and for Teens

The most adventurous libraries turn over at least some parts of their site to teen advisory boards or to a group of students. In this scenario, teens (most likely with the oversight of an advisor) create pages of their own, as well as contributing content.

DECIDE WHAT YOU WANT TO ACCOMPLISH

Once you've determined where your Web site falls on these two scales, decide on your goals. Maybe you work in a large public library system and have very little control over the main teen Web pages. In that case, you might want to advocate for one or two new features, the ones you believe are most needed by your patrons. Maybe you are your own Webmaster, and want to make sweeping changes to your site.

Either way, the next step is to make sure you're choosing goals that fit the needs of your community. Perhaps you'll want to survey your teen patrons, your students, or your teen advisory board to decide on your priorities. You might also want to delve into psychology, using a list of developmental tasks that teens need to accomplish to make a successful transition to adolescence. Determine whether your site meets most or all of those needs. The American Library Association Web site includes many resources on this topic.

American Library Association
Professional Development Topics
Adolescent Development
Available at: www.ala.org/ala/yalsa/profdev/adolescentdevelopment.htm

WHAT RESEARCH SAYS ABOUT TEENS ON THE WEB

Many studies have looked at teens and their activities on the Web. A few of the most relevant are listed below:

The Digital Disconnect: The Widening Gap between Internet-savvy Students and Their Schools
Pew Internet & American Life, August 2002
Available at: www.pewinternet.org/PPF/r/67/report_display.asp

Generations Online
Pew Internet & American Life, January 2006
Available at: www.pewinternet.org/PPF/r/170/report_display.asp

Teenage Life Online: The Rise of the Networked Generation
Pew Internet & American Life, August 2003

Available at: www.pewinternet.org/PPF/r/8/presentation_display.asp

Teens and Technology: Youth Are Leading the Transition to a Fully Wired and Mobile Nation
Pew Internet & American Life, July 2005
Available at: www.pewinternet.org/PPF/r/162/report_display.asp
   Another interesting report, from the Horatio Alger Association, also looks at what kind of technology young people use, and what they use it for. The report is issued annually.

"State of Our Nation's Youth"
Horatio Alger Association
Available at: www.horatioalger.com/pubmat/surpro.cfm
   Many of these reports can be summarized briefly by pointing out that teens, more than any other group, use technology in a highly social way. They use it to connect to others. The most popular Web sites for teens are those that offer social networking and opportunities to share their photos, thoughts, and interests. Teens also seem to want to be connected at all times. They use instant messaging, text messaging, and cell phones to stay in constant contact with those they care about. Though many still do send e-mail, they much prefer instantaneous modes of communication.
   Teens also have some unique ways of using Web sites. A January 2005 study called "Usability of Web sites for Teenagers"—a summary is available at www.useit.com/alertbox/20050131.html—found that teens prefer sites that are easy to use, are not overloaded with text, and offer interactive features. The study also found that while teens use technology heavily, they are not necessarily "techno-wizards"—they often lack reading and research skills, as well as patience. This leads to frustration when they don't immediately find what they want. Their favorite sites have good visuals and less text, catering to the teens' shorter attention spans.
   However, the study also found that teens don't necessarily like Web sites just because they look "cool." They disliked sites with too much glitz, sound, graphics, and movement, because the special effects slowed the sites down and made them less functional.

HOW MUCH TIME WILL IT TAKE?

The next step in planning to create or upgrade your library Web site is to evaluate realistically how much time and energy you have to invest. Every Web site takes some minimal maintenance—links expire, or basic library information changes. However, some Web site offerings require more work than others. If you plan to feature one new book a month, you'll have to update that part of the site each month. If you add teen-submitted book reviews, they will probably require some editing, as well as a chunk of time for the task of adding them to a book review page and, perhaps, locating cover graphics for each review.

If you allow comments on your blog or offer open forums so that teens can start discussion, this will add an extra level of work. Comments may need to be reviewed before they are added to the site. If you choose to do so, this will need to be done in a timely manner. If you choose not to review comments in advance, you'll need to keep a close eye on your site to make sure no one posts inappropriate material.

One way to decide if certain areas of your Web site are worth the time you invest is to scrutinize your site statistics. Make sure you have access to software that will analyze the number of "hits," or visits, your site gets. Usually, you can determine roughly where these hits are coming from—your school computers, users at home, at the public library, in the U.S. or internationally—because the software will break down the hits for you. You will probably also be able to see how users are finding your site, whether they arrive from the school Web site, from a Google or other search engine query, or from a link on another site. Even more useful are the statistics on which part of your site draw the most hits. Most traffic analysis software will show you exactly which pages on your site are most popular. You should be able to see whether your booklists are used, whether students are accessing your research guides, and whether your blog is a big draw or rarely viewed.

If you pay to use a commercial server, most service providers also give you software that allows you to track Web site traffic. You can also download it for free or for a fee. Two free programs are StatCounter (available at: www.statcounter.com/) and Counted (available at: www.counted.com/), but there are many others. If you use Feedburner (available at: www.feedburner .com) for your podcasts, that site will tell you how many subscribers you have.

If you work at a public library system or school with its own server, ask the Webmaster if you can look at the statistics for your pages and files. If, after a few months or a year, you find that certain areas of your Web site are rarely used, it might be time to get rid of them.

Another thing you'll want to do regularly, especially if you make frequent changes, is make back-up copies your Web site. You probably already save duplicate copies of your important documents, but you should also do the same with your entire site. In cases of data loss, hacking, or simply cases where you accidentally delete some part of your site, you'll be glad you did.

Instead of doing this page by page, you can use tools that allow you to save a copy of the entire site in just a few minutes. If you use a Web hosting service for you site, they probably already provide site management tools for making back-ups. If something goes wrong, you'll be able to restore your site quickly and easily. If someone else manages your site, it's probably a good idea to ask how often they back up files. Whether you do it daily, weekly, or monthly is up to you, and should depend on how often your site changes and how much you would lose if the worst happened.

You can also cut down on time commitments by using technology to its best advantage. Blogging is a good example. Before blogs, Webmasters might have to do tedious HMTL coding by hand each time they added something new to a site. Now, blogging software does most of the hard work for you. For example, if you decide to feature one new book a month on your site, think about using a blog format. This way, you simply type your review, add a link, upload a graphic or two, and you've updated your site.

Blogs are one simple example of a content management system (CMS). Content management systems are software and Web applications that help organize information and allow users to work together to create documents. Blogs, wikis, online calendars or scheduling applications, software that facilitates online buying and selling, and systems that organize records, training documents, or instruction manuals could also fall under this category. Content management systems often allow authorized users to make changes to documents and contribute their own content to a Web site. Many libraries use content management systems to manage their Web sites and simplify routine tasks. For more on this subject, see the CMS Watch Web site, available at www.cmswatch.com.

Checking your site for "dead" or broken links—cases where the page you've linked to has moved or no longer exists—can also be tedious. Instead, use free software or Web sites that do it for you. Many Web services will allow you to enter the URL for your site and will then report back on any broken links. For instance, try the Web-based Dead Links site, available at www.dead-links.com. (Unfortunately, some firewalls will prevent you from using these and similar sites—ask your Webmaster or check with your Web hosting service for tools that might work for you.) If you use Microsoft FrontPage for Web design, note that the program has a tool called "Verify Hyperlinks" to help find broken links. (However, remember that automated link checkers can ensure that the link still works, but they can't tell you whether the content has changed.)

Last, but certainly not least, consider recruiting a team to help you. A teen advisory group can take over some of the duties. For example, you could assign each member a page to monitor for broken or outdated links.

Unlike automated link checkers, with a little training teens will also be able to tell you whether the sites are still offering useful information. Each teen advisory group member could also be responsible for contributing one item a month to the library's teen blog. Even better, put them to work creating original content, from audio programs or podcasts to video "newscasts," an online zine, or a blog that publishes poetry and creative writing. Not only will your site benefit, but teens will gain confidence, a creative outlet, and an investment in the library's Web site that will turn them into regular users.

In a school library, teachers might be willing to take charge of some elements of the library's Web page. For example, a science teacher might compile and monitor the science section of your homework help site.

POTENTIAL PITFALLS

As you begin to develop your Web site, you'll want to consider some areas where problems might arise. It's always a good idea to take a careful look at library and school policies before adding any feature to your site. If you have access to legal or public relations advice, consider getting a response to your plans, to spot possible issues before they arise. Some prime areas to think about include:

Privacy and Safety

Teen online safety is always a concern, with stories in the news about pedophiles and stalkers who find or meet their prey online. On the other hand, many Web site builders want to include photos, video, creative work, and other materials that might include identifying information. If your library or school does not have a policy already, a good rule of thumb is that teens should be identified by first name only, never their full names. Many schools have publicity authorization and release forms that parents must sign before images of their children are used, online or otherwise.

If teens are able to post directly to your Web site, consider including a warning advising them not to use their full names, and reminding them that they should never post their address, phone number, or other contact information.

Release Forms

Before you post student artwork, poetry, or other creative work, consider asking them (and/or their parents, assuming they are under eighteen) to sign a release form giving permission.

Responsibility for Content

What happens if a user posts a negative comment about a peer on your blog? What if inappropriate material turns up on a library discussion forum, or in a library wiki? Make sure you know the possible consequences and have a plan to deal with it.

Copyright

Where will you get the images and content you use on your site? How will you make sure you are using images and content legally? (See the introduction to Chapter 10 for information on using digital images of book covers.)

Outside Links

While most Web site designers check carefully to make sure the sites they link to are appropriate, it's impossible to monitor them constantly. A site you link to may add inappropriate content. A site you link to may then link to a site with adult content. Because you can't exercise total control over what happens outside your site, consider adding a disclaimer. A disclaimer could simply state that your library links to sites outside of the library's control, and cannot take responsibility for their content.

Some resources that may also help you keep out of trouble include:

Keeping It Legal: Questions Arising out of Web Site Management
By Jamie McKenzie
Available at: http://fno.org/jun96/legal.html

Web Design That Won't Get You in Trouble
Computers in Libraries
Available at: www.infotoday.com/cilmag/jun01/kennedy.htm

COMMENTS AND DISCUSSION FORUMS

Most library Web sites do not allow users to post their comments. If they offer blogs, for example, the comments option is disabled. This decision protects the library site from inappropriate posts, but it also discourages the sense of participation and community that most libraries hope to build. It's the safer, easier option, and it's an understandable choice. Most of us are far too busy to monitor the library's Web site constantly.

Still, Internet users are coming to expect the chance to express their opinions freely. People who visit Amazon.com's Web site want to comment on the book they've just read or the product they just bought. They also want to find out what other readers or buyers thought. People frequently visit discussion boards to discuss politics or get advice on their personal problems. They review hotels, movies, and Web sites. They take turns editing articles on the online encyclopedia Wikipedia.

The explosion in the use of blogs has also changed expectations. Blog readers expect to be able to comment, to trade links, and otherwise interact. Some newspapers and many online magazines allow readers to post comments about each story they publish. Web site users generally want to join the discussion, rather than act only as passive readers.

Since study after study shows that teens, in particular, go online to socialize, not just to gather information, it makes sense that sites catering to teens would offer interactivity. How can we do that without jeopardizing our libraries? How much responsibility do we have to make sure that there are no problematic posts? How much risk are we willing to shoulder in order to make our teen sites more relevant?

The answers to those questions depend on your particular community and your willingness to experiment. However, if you aren't able to offer completely open forums, there is some middle ground and there are some ways to head off trouble. For example, you can:

Post Rules and Policies on Your Web Site

If certain types of posts are not permitted, state this clearly. If offensive posts will be removed, say so. For school libraries, describe the consequences for students who violate the rules.

Require Forum Users to Register Using a Library Card Number

You can also allow only your school's students to post—several libraries are using this option. This way, you keep random people who find your site online from stirring up trouble. Require that those who register use their real names (but don't publish them online, of course).

Review Comments before Allowing Them to Go "Live" on Your Site

Most blogging software offers this option. Bloggers can read the comments first, then choose whether or not to add them to the blog. If you offer a discussion forum, look at the administration options to see if you can review posts first. (Of course, this puts librarians in the role of censor, a position most of us would rather avoid. It also slows down the pace of discussions and comments.)

Password-protect Your Wiki

Give the password only to authorized users. This may mean giving it out to students in a particular class, so that they can work on a project, or to the members of your teen advisory board so that they can add to booklists. Limiting access will mean less chance of vandalism. You can also require wiki users to register and give a valid e-mail address, which will help discourage vandals, Or ask for a library card number. Of course, the more barriers you erect, the fewer the users who will be willing to jump through your hoops.

Consider Using a Paid Site Designed for Educators with Safeguards Built in

Many companies are creating software and Web sites that are designed to help teachers and librarians monitor teen activity while still giving them space to express themselves. Gaggle.net, available at http://gaggle.net is one example. In a closed, more easily monitored system, teens can use e-mail, blogs, and wikis, produce podcasts, and create MySpace-like personal pages that are accessible by others at their school but not to the outside world. Because teachers and librarians oversee the content, this kind of service will never be as popular with teens as the uncensored Web. Still, they will at least have a chance to use these tools for learning and socializing in a more sheltered environment.

Always Include a Disclaimer

A warning about possible inappropriate content should also appear somewhere on your site, in case something troublesome does slip by.

It's to be hoped that more libraries will find ways around the pitfalls and begin allowing comments and discussion by Web site users. The benefits are so obvious; it's difficult to build a community online unless that community can interact freely, not just with library staff but with each other.

Teen librarian Kathryn Olson, a colleague of mine at San Francisco Public Library, recently attended a workshop about emerging technologies at the library, including blogs, wikis, virtual reference, social/networking sites and taxonomies, gaming, and instant messaging. She described the latest trends this way:

> Today, successful sites combine some if not all of these tools to keep users coming back. I came away from the group with the idea that interactivity is the key to staying relevant in today's technology-savvy climate.

Not only do people want to be part of or contributors to their environment, but, in doing so, they want to create their environment and community. . . . The established hegemony was one of dictation, modeling, hierarchies, and subordination. Today, our environments are more about community, creation and reciprocity. (Personal communication, May 1, 2006)

To develop this kind of environment, your teen Web site will need to become a place users can gather to talk about books, the library, and whatever it is that interests them most. If the library Web site becomes a gathering place and an ever-evolving community, it remains relevant, vibrant, and alive. Otherwise, it risks becoming obsolete.

A Note for Smaller Libraries

Big library systems and schools may have ample resources for creating their sites—professional Webmasters, access to slick graphics, huge servers—but small libraries should not despair. In some ways, you have an advantage. In large library systems, bureaucracy often slows the pace of innovation. New ideas may have to go through committees, gain approval from tech staff, and clear other hurdles before they are implemented.

As you'll see from many of the examples in this book, small libraries often lead the way. I've noticed that it is often at smaller library systems and schools where librarians are creating their own blogs, offering reference through instant messaging services, using podcasting and RSS feeds, creating wikis, and more. It's the solo school librarian or teen librarian in a small library who just wants to try something new—and doesn't need to form a committee to study the issue—who will often be on the cutting edge.

TWELVE GREAT PUBLIC AND SCHOOL LIBRARY WEB SITES FOR TEENS

One of the best ways to improve your Web site is to take a look at what librarians are already doing. Browsing great library Web sites for teens may inspire you to do something new and exciting with your own site. There are so many amazing public and school library Web sites for teens, it was difficult to choose just a few, and I know I've left out many excellent sites. However, I've compiled a list of a dozen sites that can serve as good examples of what libraries can achieve. For each site, I briefly describe some of the best or most innovative features.

Six Great Public Library Web Sites for Teens

Central Rappahannock Regional Library, Virginia
Available at: www.teenspoint.org
This Web site emphasizes teen creativity, with teen reviews of not just
books but also music, movies, and Web sites. It also boasts photo
scrapbooks of teen events, poetry, prose, and short fiction by teens,
and a teen art gallery. With so much content produced by young
adults, the site feels as though it's bursting at the seams with creative
energy. The home page is colorful and covered with book covers and

**Figure 1-1   The Central Rappahannock Regional Library's
TeensPoint**

photographs, drawing users in. Books take center stage, with tons of reviews and lists for every interest. A weekly poll and a Web site of the day keep the home page fresh. An online library card application and plenty of forms for submitting reviews, suggesting titles, and asking for book recommendations provides opportunities for interaction. This site also has a teen advisory group, called "Web Surfers."

Denver Public Library, Denver, Colorado
Available at: http://teens.denverlibrary.org
This Web site offers a unique, easy-to-navigate design and attractive artwork. Teens can submit reviews as well as poetry and art for display in online galleries. The site offers an e-newsletter and online registration for library cards. It also has many good links, especially to local agencies and information about sexuality, teen rights, college and careers, and other life issues.

Hennepin County Library, Minneapolis, Minnesota
Available at: www.hclib.org/teens/
This site has many innovative features, and covers all of the basics, too. The graphics are young, fun, and attention grabbing but not too distracting. There's a blog, podcasts of teen reviews, quick polls, and forms teens can use to submit their book reviews. The site offers links to 24-hour chat reference, interactive tutorials on using library

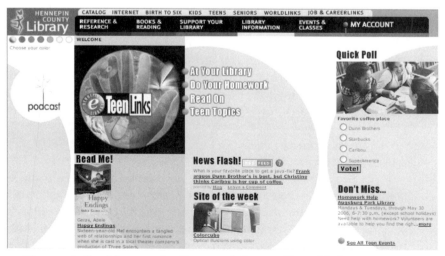

Figure 1-2   Hennepin County Library TeenLinks

resources, and an online application for a library card. The Web site also features particularly good readers' advisory resources, with reviews of new materials that link to the catalog for easy reserving. It also provides RSS feeds for the blog and new teen fiction titles. Perhaps best of all, the library system runs a teen advisory group just for the Web site, so teen participation is a vital part of this site's existence—and it shows.

New York Public Library, New York
Available at: http://teenlink.nypl.org
This colorful, very professional-looking site keeps the focus on books and authors. It emphasizes connections with the authors of books for teens, with author photographs and featured events. Teens can also read transcripts of online chats with authors. The site also has strong booklists and lists of links on topics from health to homework help. Teen poetry and writing is published in their Wordsmiths area, and the site also offers downloadable samples of teen audio books.

Phoenix Public Library, Phoenix, Arizona
Available at: www.phoenixteencentral.org
This site has a very pleasing layout, with bright colors on a black background. The pages use frames to fit nicely on the viewer's computer screen. The site has good information about the library's physical spaces for teens, with an interactive map and photos of the teen area at the main library. The site links to Web sites for most of the teen council groups at the branches. Another highlight is plentiful booklists, with a 1- to 5-star rating system that allows site visitors to weigh in and add comments about each title. The site also has an impressive events calendar, which allows users to save a list of their favorite events, get e-mail reminders, and even e-mail information about the event to a friend.

Southeastern Massachusetts Library System
Available at: www.myowncafe.org
This is an example of a library Web site for teens that truly creates a community. The site's message boards are front and center on its home page. The site offers contests, polls, and free music downloads to entice teens. The library services are part of the page, in an "Info Center" and in the form of a teen events listing, but the voices of the teens themselves take center stage. Teens are also active in volunteering

to help out with the site. A December 2005 VOYA article describes the creation of the site; read it at http://pdfs.voya.com/VO/YA2/ VOYA200512TagTeamTech.pdf.

Six Great School Library Web Sites for Teens

East Side Middle School Library, Anderson, Indiana
Available at: www.esmslibrary.com
This site has a very clean look and many links to resources for students. A blog features new titles that the librarian recommends. Students and staff can also post to the blog by e-mailing the librarian. A "Library Information Center" also features information on library programs, events, and statistics. Pathfinders relate to specific assignments, and there are also many resources for teachers.

Galileo Academy of Science and Technology, San Francisco, California
Available at: www.galileoweb.org/galileoLibrary (see Figure 1-3)
This very unique high school Web site is built around blogs—the school librarian's, but also those of teachers, staff, and students. The latest library news is available in the form of a blog. Students use a review blog to post their book suggestions. Students have online workspaces, and school clubs share their news and upcoming events as blogs. Online forms make it easy to contact the librarian or submit a suggestion. School Library Journal featured the site in its August 2005 issue; read the article at www.schoollibraryjournal.com/index.asp? layout=articlePrint&articleid=CA632382.

Greece Athena Media Center, Rochester, New York
Available at: www.greece.k12.ny.us/ath/library
This site bursts with life and color. Fun, funky graphics and photos make it especially appealing. Lots of booklists and literacy links put the emphasis on reading. Students can use a form to submit book reviews, or read reviews written by their peers. The site features plenty of original content, including a research guide. Links to teacher projects, tons of subject links, and a form for submitting reference questions make the site both accessible and useful. It also features plenty of professional links for librarians, including information on WebQuests and library Web site design.

New Trier High School, Illinois
Available at: http://nths.newtrier.k12.il.us/library/default.htm

Figure 1-3   Galileo Academy of Science and Technology Li-Blog-ary

This attractive site makes good use of graphics to guide users to their area of interest. It has a nice selection of readers' advisory tools, including book reviews submitted by students, links to local author events, bestseller and award lists, and information on the school library's newest books. Students should particularly appreciate the assignment links, which are listed under the teachers' names and provide resources for specific assignments. An online school history archive is also an interesting addition.

San Benito High School Library, Hollister, California
Available at: www.sbhsd.k12.ca.us/sbhslib/library.htm
This site includes plenty of links, but also contributions from students—book reviews, artwork, and more. The home page includes a "What's New in the Library" feature, with links for a selected topic. Plenty of booklists, a research handbook, and professional resources for

librarians are all examples of the site's original content. The video segments are especially interesting, since users can watch as students talk about their favorite books, or a teacher reads a poem aloud. The site also offers resources in Spanish.

Springfield Township High School, Springfield, Pennsylvania
Available at: http://mciu.org/~spjvweb
This site is so packed with information and resources that it might be overwhelming if it weren't organized visually, using wonderful artwork that serves as an image map to the site. The main graphic also makes the home page friendly and welcoming. The resources include not just links, but also much original content—tons of tools for students and teachers. From research guides to pathfinders to many reading lists, students will find almost anything they're looking for here. The site is also a destination for school librarians because of all of its professional resources. Innovations include an information literacy blog, a faculty wiki and another wiki for teacher-librarians.

Figure 1-4   Springfield Township High School Virtual Library

Interview

Kathy Lussier
Assistant Administrator for Technology
SouthEastern Massachusetts Library System
www.myowncafe.org

How Is My Own Café Funded?

We started the site with a $50,000 LSTA grant, all of which has gone to-wards the development of the site. The funds to publicize the site, maintain the site, and to continue developing the site are coming out of the budget for the Southeastern Massachusetts Library System. We are now investigating other sources of funding for the site.

How Is It Related to the Southeastern Massachusetts Regional Library System?

The Web site is a service to the members of the Southeastern Massachu-setts Regional Library System, a multi-type regional library system with 390 members. Cindy Roach, SEMLS Regional Administrator, and Kathy Lussier, SEMLS Asst. Administrator for Technology, came up with the idea for the Web site as a way to help our member libraries reach out to teens. We wanted to let them know about the great resources available to them at the library and to make those resources easily accessible. It made the most sense to meet the teens where they were at—online.

Despite the fact that teens probably make up our heaviest online users, we found that only a handful of public libraries in our region had a teen Web site. And those libraries that had a teen Web site found it hard to compete with the design and content available on commercial sites.

At this time, the region is fully funding the maintenance and continued growth of the site, and any library that is a member of the region is wel-come to participate in the project by customizing the site for their library and adding local information to the site. Even if a member library is not yet participating in the project, either due to lack of time or interest, we set the site up from the beginning to recognize the barcodes from all of our li-braries that use barcodes. We didn't want any teens who heard about the site from a friend in a neighboring community to be turned away during the registration process just because the staff at their libraries hadn't jumped on board yet.

Who Is Involved in Creating and Maintaining the Site?

When we received the grant, we hired Linda Braun as the Project Man-ager, and she did the lion's share of the work in getting the project going. We pulled together a Teen Advisory Group comprising librarians and teens from around the region to provide input into the site's development. After an RFP process, we selected Pixel Bridge, Inc. (www.pixelbridge.com) to develop the site. From the beginning, our goal was to allow the teens to set the direction for the site. However, we had a hard time getting teen involvement during those early months when there wasn't a site they could see. There were a couple of teens from one library who stayed on the project from beginning to end, and we pulled in teens from other parts of the region at different times to participate in online chat discussions, take part in focus groups, and fill out surveys.

Now that the site is up and running, the staff at the SEMLS office is doing the day-to-day maintenance of the site. The region's Youth Services Consultant, Vickie Beene-Beavers, and I are offering monthly classes to librarians to train them on customizing the site for their communities. Vickie joined the project mid-stream and has hit the ground running. She has done a lot of the outreach to librarians, teens and community as well as publicity for the site. I have mostly been doing site updates and working with Pixel Bridge, who continue to maintain a contract with us to maintain the site and to add new features.

Libraries are responsible for maintaining their own local content, but we also have a process in place so that teens can assist them with this responsibility. Several libraries are using teen admins to add local events to the calendar. As the job listings feature and scholarship database fully develop, teens can also assist in adding this content as well. Librarians who are particularly active in the project have also taken some responsibility for the site's maintenance. One librarian has taken responsibility for working with the music reviewers, who will review music submitted to the site and select which pieces should be made available for download. We also no longer have trouble finding teens to provide input on the future direction the site should take. All of the moderators and teen admins have access to a Teen Admin message board where they can submit ideas for improving the site and provide feedback on ideas we have.

How Long Has the Site Existed?

Our official launch party was February 11, 2006, but we were operating in pilot mode beforehand. We received the grant in October 2004 and introduced the site to two pilot libraries in October 2005. Teens from the two pilot libraries used the site for a couple of months while we worked out the kinks.

We started training other librarians in the region in November and December of 2005. Once they were trained and felt comfortable with their customization of the site, they slowly rolled out the site to their teens, even though it hadn't officially launched yet. This gave us the opportunity to work out even more bugs that hadn't shown up when the site was getting light use.

How Many Users Do You Have?

We have nearly 170 registered users under the age of twenty.

What Are the Goals of the Site?

Before we submitted the grant application, we read countless studies that highlighted the waning use of public libraries by teenagers and the negative perceptions teenagers had about libraries. At the same time, these studies were showing the soaring use of the Internet among people in this age group. Our own focus groups with teens showed that many were unaware of the online resources available through their libraries, and, those who were aware of them, talked of frustrating experiences they had with these resources.

One goal of the project was just to make it easier to get to these online resources. We require teenagers to use a library barcode when they register for an account, but once their account is set up, they don't need to enter the barcode again to access our online databases. They just need to login in with their user name and password. Most teens are much more comfortable with this type of login since they are already doing it on the other sites they use.

However, we were also thinking about the bigger picture and how this site can help improve the overall perception of libraries and how they fit into the digital future. These teens will be voters and taxpayers in our communities in a few short years. If we want teens to continue to use and support libraries throughout their adulthood, they need to view libraries as welcoming and as an essential service in an online world. Our goal is that this Web site is just one of many ways we can create that perception among young people.

Another goal that came up in the planning stages of the project was to create an online community for these teens. The one thing that distinguishes this site from the myriad of other Web sites targeting teens is that is contains local events, local jobs, and local scholarships. Even the music is coming from local bands. The message boards allow teens to meet people from different towns, but still to be close enough so that they could easily meet each other in person at "My Own Cafe" sponsored events.

What Are Your Favorite Parts of the Site, Or the Features That Are Most Used by Teens?

The feature used most by the teens is the message boards. Most of the volunteer requests we get are from teens that want to help moderate the message boards. I can sometimes get lost in reading the conversations they have there. They are exploring a variety of topics, from the South Dakota ban on abortion to pre-marital sex to their favorite video games.

From the regional perspective, I love the easy access to the library's online resources. I would love to totally Google-ize our online databases by adding a federated search tool to the site so that the teens can search them all at once. In the meantime, we have made it as easy as possible to access these resources by including a search box that searches the InfoTrac PowerSearch collection. As long as they are logged into My Own Cafe, the teens do not need to enter any more information to get into the databases. I know the teens don't care much about this part of the Web site, but if they just know it's available and easy to use for the times they need it, I'm happy.

How Do You Get the Word Out about the Site?

Our big kickoff for the Web site was held at an area mall in February. One of the My Own Cafe bands, the Stephen Chaplin Quartet, played a couple of sets, and some teen volunteers, wearing My Own Cafe t-shirts, handed out pens and parent letters explaining what the site is all about. We also had prize giveaways for teens who had library cards.

We recently had an iPod giveaway for registered users of the site who answered ten trivia questions using resources in the My Own Cafe info center. We received thirty-six new registrations through the giveaway. We have three more iPods to give away and are now thinking of promotions where we can use them.

We also have a librarians' resources section on the site available to the Library Admins where they can download posters, flyers, and sample press releases to promote the site in their communities.

Interview

Sandra Payne
Coordinator of Young Adult Services
The New York Public Library
New York, New York

How Long Has the New York Public Library Offered the TeenLink Web Site?

The New York Public Library launched TeenLink during March 1996.

Who Updates the Site? Approximately How Much Staff Time Does It Take to Maintain It?

TeenLink is maintained by the Office of Young Adult Services. A committee of young adult librarians is responsible for developing discrete sections of the site.

About How Many Hits Do You Get? Are Most Users from New York?

In 2005, TeenLink had 278,342 visitors. Though we don't know how many visitors are from the NYC area, approximately 20.58 percent of the 2005 visitors were international. 78.93 percent were from the USA.

What Are Some of the Features You Are Especially Proud Of?

1. The rolling calendar features of dynamic events at neighborhood libraries.
2. WordSmiths, an online magazine of poetry, stories and essays receives submissions by teens from New York City and beyond.
3. The annotated booklists introduce recent books for teens.
4. Meet-the-Author highlights visits by notable poets and writers
5. ListenUp! features short excerpts from audio books recorded on CD and available in branch library collections.
6. TeenLink has a direct link to the recently launched homeworkNYC.org, a collaborative project with Brooklyn Public Library, Queens Library and the New York City Department of Education. homeworkNYC.org is made possible with the generous support of The Wallace Foundation.
7. Online author chats and the transcripts of those chats give evidence of wonderful conversations with some of today's most esteemed young adult writers.

How Do You Select the Web Sites You Link To?

Sites are suggested by NYPL young adult librarians and others on staff.

Are Teens Involved in the Web Site, and Do They Participate in Design, Selection of Links, and So On?

At this time, teens are not involved in the design or the development of TeenLink. As we move forward, we do hope to involve teens as advisory board members. Teen suggestions will guide us in the areas of both content and design.

Why Do You Think It Is Important for Libraries to Develop High-quality Web Sites for Teens?

In many ways, a Web presence is the public face of the institution. To young people, the institutional face can appear somewhat unapproachable. We hope that public library Web sites can be those places in the Web universe with style, appeal, and hard information that young people will find accurate, useful, and fun.

Interview

Doug Achterman
Library Media Specialist
San Benito High School, Hollister, California

What Are the Most Important Factors to Consider in Creating a Web Site for a School Library?

First and foremost, a school library Web page is a resource for the entire school community; its design should arise from that community's needs. What that means is that each school library should have its own Web page, not just a link to district-wide resources. The library media specialist should be responsive to those needs and capable of responding to them at a moment's notice. If a resource needs to be added for a class just walking in the door, or for a teacher calling from a class, the LMS should be able to accommodate that need. The same is true for filtered content. It is the LMS who has training and expertise in information sources; it is the LMS who should have ultimate control over content filters. These are no small matters in many districts, but it is our job to help others understand why control of filters and ability to change school Web pages are fundamental in our ability to provide the best possible services to our school communities.

What Are Some of the Basic Features Librarians Should Try to Include on Their Sites?

- Resources to support specific research assignments.
- "Helps" such as how to cite sources, study tips, searching strategies, Web evaluation, research guides, homework helpers, readers' advisory, helpful forms (note-taking, citations, web evaluation guides, etc.). Administrative information: library hours, policies; links to online databases.
- Teacher resources.
- Communications to parents (i.e., summer reading lists, advice about how to manage their childrens' use of the Internet, etc.).
- Samples of student work.

What Are Some of the Pitfalls or Mistakes Librarians Should Try to Avoid?

A common pitfall is to create pages with exhaustive numbers of links for students to use for projects. Often just a few key resources are far more effective. In addition to leading students to good sources, we're also trying to help them cope with information overload by actually reducing the quantity of information to choose from.

What Other Suggestions or Advice Do You Have for School Librarians Who Want to Improve Their Web Sites?

Think about ways to make the site as interactive as possible. A blog might work well for a readers' advisory, book club discussion, or whole grade or school book discussion. A wiki is a great tool for collaboratively creating re-source lists. Make sure you provide an e-mail address so you can be contacted for suggestions and feedback. The digital library is like other libraries in that it is a dynamic, growing, changing entity. Plan for that change.

Chapter 2

Building a Basic Web Site

OVERVIEW

If you're starting your Web site from scratch, there are several elements you'll almost certainly want to include. Ten of these are described in this chapter. Once you have these some or all of these features on your site, you'll be ready to add the elements that will make your site unique—perhaps using ideas from the chapters that follow, or perhaps using your own ideas drawn from the needs of the teens you serve.

Before you begin, you'll probably want to sit down and sketch out a rough structure for your site. Things to think about include:

- What features must be accessible from the main page? Which might be better linked from secondary pages?
- How will you unify the many pages that make up your site, using graphics, colors, icons, and layout? Users should always know by the look of your pages that they are still on your site.
- How will users navigate through your site? How will they return to the home page?
- How will you give your site a look that appeals to teens, but is still professional and not too "busy"?

There are many excellent books on the philosophy and practicalities of good Web site design, so I won't go into too much detail here. There are several main ideas to keep in mind. Try to make your site:

- Easily identifiable by its audience. Teens should recognize instantly that the site is meant for them, and the design should appeal to their tastes. However, that doesn't necessarily just mean throwing up some splashy neon colors and graphics, or adding (often irritating) sound and animation. The best teen sites distinguish themselves from more staid adult sites using unique designs, artwork, and layouts.

Graphics that are professional and modern looking will win more approval than pages that are simply bright or overloaded with "stuff." Take a look at magazines and advertising aimed at teens for some hints. Also, think about the designs on the most popular book covers. Photographic images of attractive, diverse teens are usually appealing, as are patterns and textures, if not overused. Avoid using too much "teen lingo" in titling the different areas of your site, as slang is easily dated and likely simply to make teens wince at your failed effort to be "hip."

- Easy to navigate. Your site should have a consistent, unified look so that users always know when they have left it. They should always be able to find their way back easily to your home page; icons or links in the same place on every page of your site will assist them. Users should never feel "lost."

- Clear and concise. No one wants to wade through tons of text to find what they want, especially teens. Also, try to avoid creating pages where users must scroll far down on the page to find what they are looking for. Many users will look only at what fits on their screen.

- Useful. Your pages should offer real information and, whenever possible, original content. There is nothing more frustrating than sites that are just collections of un-annotated links that lead to more links and on and on forever.

- Accessible. Learn about how to make your site more welcoming and user-friendly for people with disabilities. Consider accessibility testing to make sure that people with a range of disabilities can navigate and understand your site, and that it works with assistive technologies. Learn more at the Web Accessibility Initiative site, available at: www.w3 .org/WAI.

If you've had a chance to browse some of the public and school library Web sites listed in Chapter 1, you may have some ideas about what you like and dislike about other sites. You'll want to use these feelings as you design your own site. Be sure to also use what you know about teens in your community—their interests, tastes, and the ways they use technology—as you design your site.

Remember, also, that while you want your site to be attractive, content is more important. A Web site that offers little more than sleek graphics and links to other sites will probably not be heavily used. Your basic site is just a starting point in the process—you'll want to continue adding content and features as you go along, and as technologies change and develop.

One good resource for absolute beginners who are creating a library Web page from scratch is HomeMaker for Libraries, a free Web-based service that allows you to modify basic information to create a simple Web site. Users do not need to know HTML to use the site. It is available at www.kn.att.com/wired/libmkr/. Even if you want to create a more complex Web site, with graphics and a custom design, the HomeMaker site gives good examples of the kinds of basic information you'll probably want to include. It's geared toward public libraries, but school librarians will also find it useful.

When it's time to start designing your site, you will want to pick a good software tool for creating Web sites. Microsoft FrontPage and Macromedia Dreamweaver are the most commonly used, but there are others. You can also download free Web design software, such as Evrsoft's FirstPage (available at http://www.evrsoft.com). This software is used for creating, editing, organizing, and maintaining Web sites. In the chart below, I briefly describe some of the pros and cons on FrontPage, Dreamweaver, and Evrsoft.

	Microsoft Front Page	Macromedia Dreamweaver	EvrSoft FirstPage
Pros	—For users of other Microsoft applications (Word, Excel, etc.), will have a familiar look and feel —May be easier for beginners to learn and navigate	—Often preferred by experienced Web designers —Said to generate cleaner code —Doesn't favor Microsoft's Internet Explorer browser —Allows for more flexibility and control	—Free!
Cons	—Less flexibility for experienced designers —Some users complain about "bloated" code —Favors Microsoft's Internet Explorer browser	—Steeper learning curve; may be harder for beginners to master	—Less documentation and support. For beginners especially, lack of manuals and books will be a drawback

Once you have a basic design for your site and have started to create Web pages, you'll need access to a Web server. If your library or school already has one, you may need to negotiate with the Webmaster. Find out if you will be able to make changes to your library Web pages yourself, or if every correction and addition will have to pass through someone else. Ideally, the librarian or librarians creating the pages will also have the power to access the server. Otherwise, every update and correction will be delayed while the new pages go through the proper channels. A good relationship with your school or library Webmaster is crucial.

If you do not have access to a Web server, it is possible to "rent" space from a commercial Web hosting provider. There are free hosting services, but these generally come with advertising or serious restrictions on how much server space you can use. Most Web hosting services start at around $10 month for a basic site and progress upwards depending on how much space you need and how much Web site traffic you expect. Web hosting services generally provide tools for managing your site, checking your statistics, backing up your Web pages, installing discussion forums or chat rooms, and more. You will need to learn how to upload files to the server. Tools for creating Web pages—such as FrontPage and Dreamweaver—can make this process easier.

Once you've created the first version of your site, engage in some testing. Try out your site on different computers, using different browsers. Microsoft Internet Explorer and Mozilla Firefox are currently the most popular browsers, with Explorer by far the most dominant, so those are the most important to check. Apple Safari is the browser that comes with the Mac operating system. Test out your site on computer screens of different sizes as well.

Next, ask potential users to try the site and give you feedback on such factors as ease of navigation, clarity, and visual presentation. For more on user testing, try the following article:

All Things Web
User Testing Techniques—A Reader-Friendliness Checklist
Available at: www.pantos.org/atw/35317.html

Also, make sure you avoid the most common Web design errors. If you use the Web regularly, you probably already have a sense of what those errors are. They're the design mistakes that make you recoil in horror and want to leave a site quickly, everything from animations popping up all over the place to text that scrolls across the screen, music that plays automatically, and graphics-loaded pages with painfully slow download times. For more on what to avoid, see the sites below:

All Things Web
Ten Things to Avoid in Authoring a Web Page
Available at: www.pantos.org/atw/35248.html

Ten More Things to Avoid in Authoring a Web Page
Available at: www.pantos.org/atw/35270.html

Jakob Nielsen's Alertbox
Top Ten Mistakes in Web Design
Available at: www.useit.com/alertbox/9605.html
This list is updated every few years. The latest list is from 2004, and you can
    see previous articles by clicking on the links at the bottom of the page.

Interview

Will Haines
School Librarian
Greece Athena Middle School
Rochester, New York

Will Haines' PowerPoint Presentations on Creating School Library Web Sites
    Available at: www.greece.k12.ny.us/ath/library/Webworkshop/default.htm

Why Should Libraries Have Web Sites for Teens?
- I think it is a way to "personalize" the Web for one's patrons. It gives them a springboard to the Internet that is their own.
- As the librarian, you can also select resources in the Internet just as one selects print resources for one's own library.
- It works as a great agent for collaboration with classroom teachers. When students come into our library with a teacher to work on a class research project, they have a Web page that is personalized for their needs. The teacher pages include specific directions on the task, rubrics, scaffolding, and resources.
- We have a great opportunity to provide an alternative Web portal to teens that is noncommercial, curriculum based, and complements the information needs that they have for school.

What Makes a Good Library Web Site, for Both Schools and Public Libraries?
- Ease of navigation is key—a site should tell the user up front what the options are, what's available, and the purpose of the site. Things need to be clear, concise, helpful and of value.

- A good library Web site will have resources that are unique to its community. It should not try to catalog the Internet; that's been done elsewhere. Our site caters to our classroom teachers within the school. It also provides a smooth link to our subscription databases. With one password, using what's called referring URL authentication, students can log into our database page that's a springboard to all our subscription databases.

What Do You Look at When You Evaluate a School Library Web Site?

Personally, I've always tuned in to the navigation structure and how well the library site communicates this to students and staff.

Are There Any Features That Every School Library Web Site Should Have?

Bibliography and research guides, access to school and local public library online catalogs, links to the library's online database subscriptions, a virtual reading room of some kind with reading lists, contact information for library staff, and a teacher projects section.

What Are Some of the Problems You Sometimes See with School Library Web Sites in General?

- It is evident on some sites that the content has not been updated in quite some time. It could be that the librarian does not have access to editing the site, or the district's Internet policy prevents librarians from doing so. The best sites seem to be updated frequently, whenever the need arises.
- There is nothing worse than links that no longer work, which take away from the credibility of the site.

What Advice Do You Have for Librarians Who Are Just Learning How to Create a Web Site?

- Take advantage of software that creates HTML and manages a site. Gone are the days of writing the HTML code from scratch.
- See what's already out there, but don't be afraid to be original and come up with your own design. When I was in library school, we had a class where we surfed the net and evaluated library sites. The ideas for Athena's site were gathered from my personal survey.
- Don't be intimidated of the idea of creating your own site. Rome wasn't built in a day. Start small. Spend your initial time coming up with a navigation plan.

IDEA #1: CREATE A LIBRARY LOGO/GRAPHIC

Most Web sites have some kind of graphic element, such as a logo, that immediately identifies the site. If your teen site will be part of an existing library Web site, you'll probably want to use the same logo as the rest of the site, or use the same one but modify it just enough to signal teens that they've entered "their" area. If your site is for a school library media center, you may have a school or district logo you want to incorporate or modify.

You might choose to build a navigational menu into your logo or graphic, and then include that on all of your pages. It's also a good idea to choose one design, font and color scheme that you modify only slightly throughout all the pages on your site. This kind of consistency allows users to find their way with less confusion, and also gives them visual clues so that they know if they click on an outside link and leave your site.

Your logo can be a simple graphic or it can incorporate drawings, photographs, or other elements. If you can afford professional graphic designers, make sure they have some understanding of what attracts teens. As mentioned above, teen magazines and advertising aimed at teenagers are good sources of inspiration. After all, advertisers spend millions to figure out what will draw teens in. Better yet, ask your teen advisory group for their input and let them help choose the final design.

If you're creating a do-it-yourself Web site, you'll probably want to design your graphics in a program such as Photoshop, but if you need a simpler method, a free site called Cool Text—at http://cooltext.com—can be helpful. Simply type in the text (the name of your library, for example) and choose the style, size, and color. When you click the "Render Logo Design" button, the site will automatically generate a graphic for you.

Many library Web sites for teens begin with a logo at the top or to one side of the home page and then add links, as in the next example.

Multnomah County Library
Available at: www.multcolib.org/teens (see Figure 2-1)

Another popular approach is to use an image map as your home page. To do this, you create one or several graphics to serve as the site's main page. Users click on certain areas of the graphic depending on what interests them. They may click on pictures, text that is part of the graphic, or both. One site that uses an image map is shown below.

Greece Athena Media Center (see Figure 2-2)
Available at: www.greece.k12.ny.us/ath/library

On a clickable image map, each part of the graphic is a "hotspot" that

Teens

Blogs and journals
Read some new thoughts and express some of your own about music, fashion, sports and more.

Books
Find stuff to read. Discover special lists, reviews, new comics and graphic novels, and book groups.

College planning
Resources and then some for choosing a college, applying to schools, getting financial aid, and studying abroad.

Entertainment and sports
The scene for teens. Clubs, dancing, music, movies, cycling, and parks and recreation.

Games, email, wifi and more
Get an e-mail account, make a Web site, find wireless access, or play games.

Health, sex and your body
Whether you need advice or information, get honest, accurate feedback from reliable sources.

Help and advice
It's not easy being a teen. Here are some great resources to help you cope.

Homework Center
Get free homework help from qualified tutors or explore homework topics on your own.

Para los jóvenes
Informacón relevante e interesante en español.

Spirituality
A collection of Web sites to help you explore different faiths or deepen your own.

Suggest a Web site
What's new and interesting online? Let everyone know what's out there.

Teen Lounges
A place to hang out with friends, surf the Internet, play games, eat, listen to music, and get your homework done.

Work
What's out there for teens? Find opportunities to volunteer, get a job, or start a career.

Your reviews
Love it or hate it, say what you think about movies, books, and games. Read reviews, too.

Come to one of the library's teen lounges.
Hang out with friends, surf the Internet, play games, eat, listen to music, and get your homework done.

Figure 2-1   Multonomah County Library Teen Page

links to a different area of your Web site. You will decide where each hotspot is located when you design the image map. Image maps can be created in Photoshop, Dreamweaver, Microsoft FrontPage, and other software programs.

IDEA #2: PROVIDE YOUR LOCATION, HOURS, AND CONTACT INFORMATION

There are a few pieces of information you'll want to include on your site, ideally on the main page. These include the library's location, hours, and contact information. Users will likely be frustrated if they have to search hard for this basic data.

You might choose to incorporate the library's address or the name of the school into the logo or main graphic, or list it at the bottom of the main page. A phone number and/or e-mail address should also be easy to find. A comment form that automatically sends queries to the best e-mail address is also a plus.

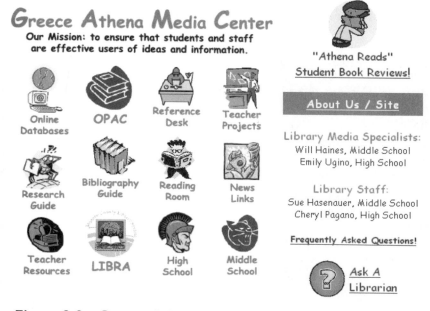

Figure 2-2   Greece Athena Media Center Home Page

Remember that Internet users will be accessing your page from all over the world, so if your town or school has a common name, it can't hurt to add the city and state somewhere on your main page. That way, users can be sure they've located the correct "Washington High School" or "Fairview Public Library."

For teen pages that are part of larger public library sites, location information and hours might be more specific than what is on the library system's main page. For example, which branches have special teen collections? Is there a homework or college center, and where is it? Do any of the teen services or areas have their own unique hours, different from those of the rest of the library?

You may also want to add some options for when the library is closed, including links to 24/7 online reference services.

IDEA #3: LINK TO YOUR CATALOG

This is perhaps the most obvious of the features you'll want to include—the library catalog, so that teens can start their searches. You might include a link to your OPAC—Online Public Access Catalog—or better yet, a search box that allows users to type their search terms directly into your Web site's main page. Even for teen sites at public libraries, a link to the library catalog is a good addition, even if it's just a text link at the bottom of the page.

IDEA #4: PROMOTE YOUR DATABASES

As above, this is an essential link. You may decide to feature the databases on the main page, with short descriptions, or link to all of them and describe them further on the secondary page. School library sites will likely feature the databases more prominently, but most public library teen sites also include a link somewhere.

Some libraries include the links to databases in their Homework Help or subject guide area. On their own, teens might not think to search an Opposing Viewpoints database. However, if they go to your subject guide as part of their research on the death penalty, and see the database listed under their topic, they are more likely to use it.

One library that does an excellent job of linking to databases from their teen page is Seattle Public Library. The links include brief descriptions that focus on how the databases will be helpful to teens. For example, instead of simply linking to downloadable e-books, the site points out that Cliffs Notes are available there. They mix the database links in with Web sites, and differentiate them using a special icon.

Seattle Public Library, Seattle, Washington
Available at: www.spl.org/default.asp?pageID=audience_teens_db (see Figure 2-3)

IDEA #5: ASSEMBLE SUBJECT GUIDES

Most library Web sites for teens link to some kind of subject guide or homework help information. This feature gives students guidance as they venture out into the wild, woolly Web, and will, one hopes, prove more help than a Google search. This is also an opportunity to feature sites with more credibility and authority than what teens might find on their own.

However, beware of making subject guides the focus of your site. Historically, as librarians began creating Web sites, they tried to recreate the physical library online. This resulted in tons of links to great sites, but it also meant that the library Web site sometimes became just another subject directory, and the librarian spent all of his or her time trying to "catalog" the Web.

Before you spend hours attempting to organize the vast online world for your

Figure 2-3   Seattle Public Library Databases and Web Sites for Teens

teens, consider whether someone else has already done so, and done it better. Think about linking instead to a reliable source that will do this huge task for you. Librarian's Internet Index (http://lii.org) is one such site; the Internet Public Library's teen division (www.ipl.org/div/teen/) is another. Also, before you pour time and energy into creating an exhaustive list of links, consider whether you really have the time and energy to maintain them. Will you be able to weed out the dead links and the pages that have not been updated? On these sites, someone else keeps the links up to date so that you don't have to.

The major exception, of course, should be for assignments your teens seem to get year in and year out. If the sophomores at your school or in your community do an in-depth yearly project on the Industrial Revolution, then creating a page of annotated links on the subject will probably be well worth your time. So, instead of tackling the entirety of the Web, think about focusing your efforts more narrowly, on subjects you can be sure will be useful to your particular community.

Multnomah County Library, in Oregon, has a great example of a virtual homework center, with guides for many subjects. It is available at www .multcolib.org/homework/.

IDEA #6: OFFER WEB SEARCHING HELP

Most teens can type keywords into Google, but often that is the extent of their Web-searching skills. Your Web site can provide additional help and guidance, not only directing users to various search engines and directories—and explaining the difference—but guiding them toward the best strategies for their search.

For example, your site might highlight the difference between subscription databases and a search of the free sites on the Internet. You might also describe some basic search strategies (such as enclosing phrases in quotation marks), tips on searching blogs, how to locate images, and how to search for scholarly journals or search the text of books.

What you don't want to do is simply offer links to search engines with no explanation. Most teens can already name a few, but they may not understand which ones work best for which purposes, or how to use them effectively.

Chico High School, in Chico, California, has an excellent example of a page that offers Web searching help. The annotations help students determine which search engine or directory is right for their needs.

Chico High School, Chico, California
Available at: http://melvil.chicousd.org/search.html (see Figure 2-4)

Public library teen sites can offer this information, too. Boston Public Library offers a list of search engines in its Teen Lounge area at www.bpl .org/Teens/SearchEngines.htm.

IDEA #7: DESCRIBE YOUR LIBRARY SERVICES

Somewhere on your Web site, you will probably want to include a list and description of the services the library offers. For public library Web sites, these services could include:

- Library tours for school classes
- Teen booktalks for classes and groups
- A teen advisory group
- A teen summer reading program

Chico High School Library, 901 The Esplanade, Chico, CA 95926 530-891-3036

Here are some "Quick Jump" links: See full descriptions below.
All the Web | Alta Vista | Ask Jeeves | Beaucoup | Buscar en Espanol | CompletePlanet
Dogpile | Excite | Google | Hotbot | Infoseek | IxQuick
Lycos | Mamma | ProFusion | Savvy Search | Search.Com | SearchEdu.Com
WebCrawler | Yahoo | Search Engine Reviews

Selected Web Searchers

Image Focused Web Searchers

All the Web
A new, FAST, and powerful search engine. Includes special areas and features for music, multimedia and FTP sites.

AltaVista
Alta Vista is one of the most powerful Internet searchers available. Includes many special options and features.

Beaucoup
Allows you to search for search engines, indices and directories which specialize in the type of information that you are seeking.

Buscar en Espanol
Un mecanismo de busqueda en el Internet y World Wide Web, en Espanol.

Google
An efficient search engine that is also quite fast! Advertising is minimal or absent.

ProFusion
Searches and puts you in touch with some of the Web information sources that normal search engines are unable to cover.

Lycos Search Engine and Web Directory
Has a reputation for its large, extensive coverage of the Web.

Mamma
The "Mother of all search engines." One option allows you to search through newspapers.

MetaCrawler/GoTo
Searches a number of search engines, organizes the results, and displays those that it feels are the most useful.

AltaVista Image Finder
This searcher offers access to a large collection of photos and graphics.

Picsearch
A search engine especially designed to find pictures and images.

Lycos Pictures and Sounds
Images, video and audio files are available here. Family friendly filters are built-in!

AllTheWeb
Images, video and audio files are available here.

Google Image Searcher
Special area of Google that just searches for images and graphics.

American Memory Photos/Images and
American Memory Films/Motion Pictures
Displays various collections that may be downloaded and used in presentations.

Image Search
From this page you can search several different major Web image sources.

Lycos Image Gallery
Search this image, music, movie trailer and sound collection by keyword.

Ditto.Com
A powerful search engine for locating images and graphics.

Ask Jeeves Search Engine and Small Web Directory
Ask Jeeves searches through other search engines and comes up with answers to your questions. Allows you to easliy modify your search.

Figure 2-4 Web Searching from the Chico High School Library

If you list your special services, Web site users will be able to see at a glance new ways they may be able to use the library. Add phone numbers and e-mail addresses so that users can get in touch. Even better, you might want to offer an online form for teens, their parents, or teachers to fill out requesting your services. Or, if you're using an instant messaging service while at work, make your screen name available so that the public will be able to reach you quickly.

The same goes for school libraries. Add a page to your Web site that describes the services you can offer to teachers or students. These might include:

- How teachers can sign up to bring a class to the library (even better, let them sign themselves up, by using calendar software or an online calendar Web site)
- Ideas for lessons you'd like to collaborate on with teachers
- Book clubs or advisory groups students can join
- Special library materials of which the school community may not be aware

IDEA #8: LIST YOUR LIBRARY EVENTS

Many users may visit your Web site just to find out about library events for teens. If you plan regular events, you'll want to have an event listing or calendar. This could be as simple as a blog where you post upcoming events as they are scheduled, or as complex as an online calendar where users can sort events by type, date, and branch. Some library systems even allow users to sign up for e-mail event reminders.

At Coshocton Public Library in Coshocton, Ohio, teens can register online for young adult programs, and also see immediately how many spaces are still available. Their calendar is at www.libraryevents.org/bycat.aspx?ID=3&lib=3.

The New York Public Library's TeenLink site has an attractive events page, with featured events in the center of the page and more upcoming programs listed on the side. Teens can click on the name of the event for more information.

The New York Public Library, New York, New York
Available at: http://teenlink.nypl.org/index.html (see Figure 2-5)

IDEA #9: USE YOUR EXISTING CONTENT

As you work to build a basic library Web site, it may seem overwhelming to think about creating so much original content, from booklists and pathfinders to lessons on searching the Web, evaluating information, and citing sources. Don't forget, though, that you probably already have many great resources all around you—they just aren't on the Web yet. Most libraries already offer printed booklists, for example. You probably also have plenty of paper forms for getting library cards, requesting information, submitting suggestions, and so on.

Figure 2-5   New York Public Library TeenLink

All of that existing content can easily be added to your Web site. Ideally, of course, all of the books on your booklists will be linked to the library catalog, so that teens can reserve them online with a couple of clicks. Your forms will ideally be Web forms that can be filled out online and submitted instantly. But that may not be realistic at first; so consider adding content as simple text files or PDF Word documents.

If you have text files, there are several options for getting them online quickly and easily. First, you can cut and paste the text into Web design software such as FrontPage or Dreamweaver. Most Web design software has a WYSIWYG feature—WYSIWYG stands for "What You See Is What You Get"—so that you don't have to add the HTML tags by hand. You simply highlight the text and change size, font, etc. in the same way you would a word processed document.

You can also convert documents to PDF, or Portable Document Format. These are documents that open in Adobe Acrobat, and look just like the document you originally created. To make PDF files, you can buy software from Adobe Acrobat or other companies. You can also download free conversion software from the Web, or use a site that converts documents for free and e-mails the results to you. One such site is PDF Online, at www.pdfonline .com.

Once you have a PDF file of your document, you can upload that file to your Web server, then link to it from a Web page. Users click on the link to open the document. This is an especially good way to make your forms and worksheets available, since PDF files print out just the way you intended them to look.

Don't forget that you can also add PowerPoint presentations to your Web site by simply uploading the PowerPoint file and then linking to it from a Web site. Once you've done that, your presentation is available to anyone who wants to view it, at any time. If you have digital video, audio, or photographs, you might want to add those to your site as well.

IDEA #10: DISPLAY SOME BOOKS

What's a library without books? Remind your Web site users that, while your library has exciting technology, fun programs, and appealing items like movies, music, and magazines, in the end, books do matter.

You might do this by featuring one book a month on your site's home page, with cover art and a blurb or review. Or put an author's face front and center. Links to your booklists are also a good choice, maybe with a book cover or two as the lead in to the lists.

Any way you choose to do it, making books a central part of your Web site will remind teens that you offer them readers' advisory services and that, as a librarian, hip and cutting-edge, you still truly care about books and reading.

Chapter 3

Learning and Honing Technology Skills

OVERVIEW

Many of the ideas in this book spring from the same basic technologies, such as blogging, message boards, or podcasting. Instead of explaining each concept multiple times, I cover many of the basic technologies in this chapter. As I mention the technologies again later in the book, a text box will refer you back to Chapter 3.

I have tried to define each concept in simple terms, describe some of its potential applications, and also address some of the concerns you may have. I also try to raise issues you should think about before beginning—such as teen privacy, or how you can discourage users from making inappropriate comments—when applicable.

This chapter also includes some "how to" information, but because the Internet is constantly changing, with certain sites gaining or losing popularity and new technologies evolving, once you choose your Web site features you will probably want to search out further, more in-depth sources to guide you through the technical details.

Some of the ideas discussed in this chapter will already be familiar. If you've been using the Web for awhile, you probably know about discussion boards and online forms. Other ideas are newer—social networking, folksonomies, and wikis, for example.

As the Web grows and evolves, it's inevitable that it will come to be used in new ways. The term "Web 2.0" encompasses some of these changes. What is Web 2.0? It's the idea that the Web is entering a new phase, distinct from the first wave of innovation and the business models that, at least for some start-ups and investors, ended in disaster. In reality, Web 2.0 is still being defined, and it remains to be seen whether the results will live up to the hype. However, there are currently several basic components.

First, there is the idea that the next trend is to offer more Web-based applications. Web sites will become more interactive and more responsive to user needs. Google is making heavy use of this idea; Google Maps is one example. As users zoom in and out, the map instantly changes to accommodate their actions. There is no delay and no software to download to your PC. Flickr, the photo site, is another good example. These sites use Ajax (Asynchronous JavaScript and XML), a Web development technique which increases the speed at which Web sites respond to users' needs. Web 2.0 is also used to refer to sites that allow users to do tasks online when they previously would have used software such as Microsoft Excel or Word. For instance, Google Spreadsheets (available at http://spreadsheets.google.com) is an online spreadsheet program, while sites such as Zohowriter (available at http://www.zohowriter.com) provide online word processors that allow users to create, edit, and share documents on the Web.

A second aspect of Web 2.0 is the idea that the Web is becoming more of a democracy. Rather than a collection of sites created and overseen by Webmasters, proponents of this theory say that users prefer sites where there is no central authority. Instead, users want to interact to create and edit content. They want tools that allow them to participate. Wikipedia is a good example of this type of site. Flickr, where users add and categorize their own photos, is another.

One intriguing aspect of the ever-evolving Web that I want to mention is online gaming. While this activity may not immediately seem relevant to libraries, it is so much a part of many teens' lives that we can't afford to ignore it. For example, huge numbers of teens are playing MMORPGs—Massively Multiplayer Online Role Playing Games. Players in these virtual worlds take on roles, often in a fantasy setting that continues to change and evolve, and interact with thousands of other players. They engage in combat, go on quests, buy and sell virtual items, form relationships, and even get "married" online. At my branch library, our young patrons usually play an online game called Runescape, but there are many, many others that are popular.

How will gaming affect the way libraries offer their services online in the future? One possibility is that patrons who grow up with role playing games will be very comfortable in a virtual environment where they interact with avatars—graphical representations of other users or players—and librarians will want to adopt some of these ideas. Eventually, we may all be helping our patrons in a virtual online library. To get a glimpse of what that might be like, take a look at the Second Life Library 2.0 blog (available at http://

secondlifelibrary.blogspot.com/). Second Life is a 3-D virtual world created mostly by its residents; the library is hoping to offer book discussions, training sessions, and other services.

As you can see, libraries are adopting some of the Web 2.0 ideas. You may have already noticed the terms "Library 2.0" and "School Library 2.0" in journal articles and blog posts. In general, advocates are suggesting that not only should library adopt new technologies that increase user participation and interaction, but they should also reevaluate their rules and services to become more accessibly and user friendly in their physical spaces.

Whether we are really at the start of another Web revolution remains to be seen. However, it's hard to go wrong with the idea that libraries should be more responsive to user needs, that our Web sites should be more useful and interactive, and that we need to get teens more involved and engaged in library services.

IDEA #11: START A DISCUSSION

"Discussion board" is a general term for an online space where users can leave messages that other users then respond to. Discussion boards might also be called Web forums, message boards, discussion forums, discussion groups, or bulletin boards. A discussion board keeps a running record of what users have posted, so anyone joining can read the entire discussion from the beginning. Some boards allow anonymous posting, while others require registration. Usually groups have a moderator, who is able to edit or delete inappropriate messages.

Advantages of Discussion Boards

- Easy to use—require no additional software beyond a Web browser and Internet access.
- Fast—a librarian could post information about the next teen advisory board meeting in just a few minutes.
- Interactive—teens can get involved, have discussions, and debate issues online.

Disadvantages of Discussion Boards

- Teens must visit the Web site regularly to view and respond to new posts.
- Open to all to read, which raises privacy concerns if teens don't know better than to post personal information.

- Should be monitored for inappropriate posts. The moderator can usually limit use of the forum to only certain participants, however, to cut down on problems. Still, spam and security may be concerns.

Getting Started with Discussion Boards

To add a discussion board to your Web site, you have several choices:

- Set up a discussion on a Web-based message board service such as Yahoo! or Google Groups, which will include ads and has a not-terribly-attractive format.
- For a nicer look, use a free or inexpensive message board service such as ezboard.com, Xorbit.com, or quicktopic.com. Usually, the free version includes advertising.
- Install message board software on your library's server. Many discussion forum software packages are available, though if you're a novice you may need your Webmaster's help to install and maintain them.

One great example of a library Web site with discussion board is MyOwn-Cafe.org, from the Southeastern Massachusetts Regional Library System. The message boards and latest posts are right in the middle of the site's home page, so users can see exactly what their peers are discussing.

Southeastern Massachusetts Regional Library System.
http://myowncafe.org (see Figure 3-1)

Interview

Kathy Lussier
Assistant Administrator for Technology
SouthEastern Massachusetts Library System
http://www.myowncafe.org/entertainmentcenter/messageboards/tabid/62/
Default.aspx

Why Did You Decide to Include Message Boards on Your Site?

From the beginning, we knew we wanted some interactivity on the website, mainly because for this age group the Web is all about interaction. In our initial Teen Advisory Group meeting, when we brainstormed ideas for the site, we talked about having private instant messaging, a book blog, and chat. The team from Pixel Bridge ultimately recommended that we go with message boards. They are a little more interactive than blogs, and also provide a greater comfort level for the librarians involved than real-time

Figure 3-1   My Own Café Home Page

technologies like IM and chat. We may move into using some of these other communication tools someday, but message boards were a good starting point.

Who Can Post to the Board? What Is Required to Register?

Only registered users can post to the boards. We require users to be thirteen years or older to register and to have a library card from a participating library.

What Are the Rules? What Areas Do Your Terms of Agreement Cover?

Our terms of agreement are posted at http://www.myowncafe.org/Default .aspx?tabid=82. In terms of conduct, we include a brief paragraph that says "My Own Café expects that you will treat each other with mutual respect. Although we may not always agree with each other's comments, My Own Café expects that you will treat others as you want to be treated. My Own Café expects that you will not post anything that is or could be perceived as being threatening, harassing, obscene, hateful or discriminatory. Keep on topic. Do not post comments that have nothing to do with the topic of the message board and are of no real interest to this message board's community."

We asked the teen moderators to develop more specific guidelines for the message boards. Since it is their community, it made sense that they develop the rules by which everyone lives. We gave them sample guidelines from other sites, but I'm not sure how closely they looked at them. They mostly came up with their own guidelines using their own language. The guidelines are as follows:

—Be respectful. Never call anyone an idiot, moron, stupid or any other insulting or demeaning name. If you mess up, apologize. People are going to disagree, that's what makes us so interesting. Never make it personal.

—QUALITY, not QUANTITY. The content of posts is more important than sheer number. Make sure your posts are relevant, sufficiently detailed and interesting.

—Posts should be in comprehensible English. Spelling and grammar aren't the main thing, but your spelling and grammar should be able to get your point across. Type as you would speak.

—Try to avoid conversations between only two users.

—Show respect for race, ethnicity, gender, and sexual preference.

—Avoid using vulgar or abusive language.

—Please try to stay as anonymous as possible. It's okay to say just a little about yourself, such as your age, your town, and maybe your first name.

Don't say your phone number, exact address, or full name. NEVER plan to meet someone outside of My Own Café (unless you know that person in real life). Also, make sure you do not share any personal information about people you know.

Do You Monitor the Posts? Have You Had Any Problems with Inappropriate Content?

For the most part, we depend on the teen moderators to monitor the posts. They all have the ability to edit and delete posts in any of the message boards, not just the ones for which they are designated moderators. They have taken their responsibility seriously.

They have tactfully stepped in when users start getting mean-spirited towards each other and have quickly edited posts where they deemed that the language was inappropriate. At the same time, those of us in the SEMLS office check in on the boards on most days. It's hard not to read what's going on because the discussions are so interesting. All of the library administrators (the librarians who have the ability to customize their own site) also have the ability to edit and delete posts. We see it as a community responsibility to keep the forums a friendly and respectful place.

Overall, we have not really had problems with inappropriate content. There have been a couple of occasions where moderators felt that language used on the site was inappropriate and they quickly edited the words with asterisks. There has never been a problem with gratuitous swearing, just a stray word here and there. We are now having discussions with the moderators about whether the occasional use of these words really should be edited, but we haven't come to a consensus yet. Our only other problem arose over a weekend when a couple of users were flooding the boards with posts that really didn't contribute to the discussion and also included some name-calling. Our moderators handled the situation beautifully and several community guidelines were added to our list as a result of the experience.

How Many Different Boards Are There, and on What Topics?

Our list of boards is available at http://www.myowncafe.org/entertainment center/messageboards/tabid/62/Default.aspx. I think this will be the standing list for a while. We have added several new topics, like school, sports, and anime, since the site was launched, and have also let go of one.

Who Are the Forum Moderators? How Are They Chosen?

The forum moderators are teen volunteers from libraries throughout the region. When a teen volunteers to moderate the board, we usually run the name by the youth services librarian in their community to make sure he/she is someone to whom they feel comfortable giving some responsibility. Until now, we have accepted anyone who has volunteered to moderate a board. However, now that the community is more firmly established, we are talking with the current moderators about some guidelines for future moderators. For example, we may want to require that they have a minimum of twenty posts before they can moderate a board.

What Kind of Responses Have You Had from Your Community? Any Feedback—Positive or Negative—from Teens?

For the most part, we have received positive feedback from the community. We have had various articles published in local publications, and we occasionally come across a blog posting from someone who says how much they love the site. We recently had a group of My Own Café teens speak at our annual Legislative Breakfast, and one of the teens referred to My Own Café as "the best Web site" she has used. I look at repeat visitors as a way to determine if the teens like the site or not. We have some teens who faithfully drop in every day, and some who come visit the site once and never come back. We also have some who visit faithfully for a while, but then stop coming to the site. I'm interested in hearing what they have to say about the site.

How Do You Publicize This Part of Your Web Site?

To be honest, the message boards don't need much publicizing. The home page lists the most recent posts as well as the most popular posts, which is an enticement into the message boards area. We also highlight the top poster for the week as a way to encourage teens to post to the boards. However, we don't do much publicity for the boards beyond this since they really are the big draw on the site. The teens just gravitate to this area. In May 2006, the message boards area received more than four times the number of requests any other page on the site received.

How Much Time Is Required for Monitoring and Maintaining the Message Boards? Who Is Responsible for Those Tasks?

Most of the time we spend on the message boards area is devoted to managing the volunteer requests we receive and working with the moderators on our Teen Admin message board. This takes a couple of hours per week. I am managing the volunteer requests, although I will be sharing this responsibility soon, and Vickie, Cindy and I talk to the moderators on the message boards. Of course, we all spend time reading the posts on the site, but I find I'm doing it more because I find the conversations more interesting than simply monitoring the boards. The teen moderators have taken the responsibility of monitoring the boards seriously and have adequately handled any situations that have arisen.

What Advice Would You Give to Other Librarians Who Want to Set Up a Similar Service on Their Library Web Site?

Don't be afraid to allow teens to post live to the site. When we first talked about using message boards, some of us were somewhat nervous about the idea of allowing live posts and we considered the possibility of having all posts go through a moderator for approval before they appeared on the site. In fact, I was just re-reading a chat transcript today from one of our planning meetings in which one of the teens was the most vocal advocate in support of sending all messages to a moderator for approval. However, we believed that a lag time in seeing their messages appear would be a real turnoff for the teens. Instead, we opted for an open environment with the idea that if the posts became a problem, we could then become more restrictive.

This approach has worked wonderfully thus far. When a lot of teens are on the site at once, they often have great discussions that mimic live chat in their immediacy. They couldn't have these types of discussions if their posts first went through a moderator. The teen moderators are very concerned about making the forums a place where people can feel comfortable sharing their opinions without being ridiculed and can read posts without worrying they will come across something that is highly offensive. Because it is their community, the teens are vigilant about making sure it is an interesting and enjoyable place to be.

Interview

Margo Schiller
Reference Librarian
Kamloops Library
Thompson-Nicola Regional District Library System, British Columbia, Canada
http://www.websitetoolbox.com/tool/mb/tnrdteenzone

How Do Teens Register before Posting? About How Many Teens Do You Have Registered?

Teens need to fill out an online form to register. There are eighty-one members of the message board.

What Are the Rules of Conduct for the Message Board?

Teens are not allowed to post personal information. If they do, the information will be deleted before the post goes live.

Rule of Conduct: Using profane, obscene, threatening, or injurious language or gestures directed at another patron or a staff member is prohibited.

If teens do not follow this rule they may be banned from using the message board.

What Discussion Categories Do You Use? What Topics Seem to Get the Most Posts?

A variety of categories including books, movies, music, suggestions for purchase, Web sites, computers. So far, the category "books" is the most popular.

How Many Postings a Week/Month Do You Usually Get?

About two or three per month.

How Do You Let Teens Know about the Message Board?

The message board was advertised throughout our thirteen libraries and Bookmobile when it was first launched. I have begun to visit some high school classes, and I tell them about it then.

Do You Screen Comments or Otherwise Monitor the Board?

All messages are moderated and do not go live until they are approved by the moderator.

Have You Had Any Problems or Challenges So Far?

The message board is really easy to use and set up. The biggest challenge is getting the word out that the library has a message board for teens.

IDEA #12: MAKE USE OF FORMS

Forms are an excellent way to get online feedback. While providing an e-mail address is nice, it requires users to open their e-mail account, cut and paste the address, then write out a message. With a form, they can simply fill it out right there on your site and then click "submit" or "send."

Notice that there are several choices for input on a Web form. You can use various elements to design your forms, such as:

- Fields for text, such as "Your Name" or "Comments";
- Checkboxes allow users to choose more than one answer. (For example, you might want to have teens check off the different types of music they like.) They can also be used to toggle a choice on or off.
- Radio buttons are best used when you have a list of two or more mutually exclusive options. For example, if you ask users to select their age range (13–15 or 16–18), you might use checkboxes. The user may select only one choice.
- Pull-down menus. This design might be used to select a branch, for example. The user may select only one choice. (This is not to be confused

with a drop-down jump menu, which will take the user to another Web page.)
- Submit buttons, which, when clicked, should send the form information. You can choose the text for this button, such as "Click to Send."

Be sure also to design a "Thank You" page that tells users their information has been submitted. On this page, you might also want to let users know what action you will take next—if you will be contacting them regarding their submission, for example. You can also set up an automatic e-mail response that acknowledges receipt of their information, if they include their e-mail address.

There are several things to keep in mind as you design feedback forms. First, remember that an overly complicated or lengthy form may discourage users. Simpler is better. Second, make sure it's clear what action users must take, whether it's checking a box or typing in text. Finally, limit the number of required fields, if possible. For example, requiring a library card number may discourage some users from submitting questions or suggestions, if they don't have a card or don't have it with them. Ask yourself whether you really need their card number to answer a question.

Comment forms can be designed using HTML or created on a Web page design programs such as Microsoft FrontPage or Macromedia Dreamweaver. You can set up the form to send the results to your e-mail address or to multiple addresses. You or a Webmaster will need to install a special program on your server to make this work. The program may be called FormMail.cgi or something similar.

If you don't have access to you server and can't install this program, you can use a service that routes messages to you. These services, however, generally either come with a monthly charge or show ads to your Web site users. A Google search for "free form processing" will turn up many such services; three are listed below:

Allforms
Available at: http://allforms.mailjol.net

Bravenet E-mail Forms
Available at: www.bravenet.com/webtools/emailfwd/index.php

Response-O-Matic
Available at: www.response-o-matic.com

IDEA #13: START BLOGGING

Short for "Web log," a blog is simply an online journal. Adding an item to one of these journals is called "blogging." Some blogs focus on a single topic, such as politics, while others describe an individual's personal experiences.

Characteristics of a blog:

- The author may be a single person, or it may be written by a group, with each member authorized to add items.
- Blogs sometimes consist of short entries that include links to other Web sites.
- The entries are often chatty and opinionated in tone.
- A blog may have a "comments" link where readers can add their own opinions or suggestions.
- A blog may include a "trackback" feature that allows users to see what other bloggers have to say about each entry. For more on this, see "A Beginner's Guide to TrackBack" at www.movabletype.org/trackback/beginners/.
- A blog is often created through a Web site such as Blogger.com, or using software such as Moveable Type or Typepad.

I have a blog on my Web site, www.teenlibrarian.com. I update it whenever I come across a news item or Web site that I think might be of interest to librarians who work with teens. I also sometimes post about a teen book I've just read. The Web site I use to create my blog, Blogger.com, makes it simple to update. I don't have to use HTML tags or worry about how the blog will look; I chose a design when I set up the blog, and the rest is automated. I just type a headline and body text into a box, possibly add a URL—Universal Resource Locator, also known as a "Web address"—or two, and click "update." If someone comments on an item I've added, I automatically get an e-mail message containing the text of the comment.

Blogs are changing the way news is reported. They are inexpensive (and often free) to create. The authors, often not part of the mainstream media, sometimes gain widespread influence. Blogs can also be updated quickly, with text, photos, and even video, making them a fast, efficient way to spread news of a disaster, for example. Blogs have been in the news recently, often because their creators blogged about work, their bosses found out, and they were fired.

Use of blogs has expanded dramatically in recent years, to become a favorite news source for many Internet users. Personal blogs report on private lives and opinions, or link to news articles, while corporate or organizational blogs provide a look into companies' inner workings. The blogging statistics for younger people is especially dramatic. A May 2005 Pew report found that

19 percent of online Americans ages 18–29 have created blogs, and 36 percent read them.

Blogs are not just a way of obtaining information; they also allow people to communicate ideas and opinions, and give each other feedback. In this way, blogging becomes an exchange of ideas, rather than simply a way to publish news. This interactive aspect makes it a great way to communicate with teens, though it also has its drawbacks, as teen librarians have to monitor the comments for appropriateness.

Before setting up a teen library blog, it's a good idea to think about goals and objectives, as well as set some guidelines. Questions to consider include:

1. What is the purpose of creating the blog? Will the simply be a place to notify teens, parents, teachers, and others when there is library news? Will it be used to express opinions, or will postings remain neutral? Will the blog allow for comments and discussion? If so, someone will need to monitor the comments for appropriateness. You can set up your blog to allow comments from anyone, to let you first review each comment before it's posted, or not to allow comments at all.

2. Who will be allowed to post? The teen librarian or school library media specialist only? Other library staff? The teen advisory council? Student volunteers?

3. What kind of content will be posted? Text entries are the easiest, but it's also possible to add graphics, photographs, audio, and even video. Libraries that post photos—of teen programs, for example—should have a policy that addresses whether they need permission from parents and from the teens themselves before using pictures of those under eighteen.

4. What links will you add? Most blogs include an area to one side with a list of helpful links. It's always a good idea to link back to the library's home page. Many teen library blogs also provide links to book lists, useful sites on college and careers, and homework help sites.

5. How often will new posts appear? If they are too infrequent, the audience may lose interest and stop checking the blog (also see the next idea, on feeds, to deal with this problem).

6. Does the library hosting the blog have a policy on blogging? How will the blogger make sure that posts are appropriate and error-free? More and more corporations are developing guidelines for employees with blogs, and libraries may want to come up with a list of their own rules to avoid embarrassment or misunderstandings.

The major advantage of using a blog, rather than a traditional Web site, is that blogs take advantage of software that makes it quick and easy to add items. Some blogs allow users to e-mail photos to their blog, and those photos are posted automatically. Some blogs even allow "audio blogging," where bloggers call a special phone number and leave a voice message that is posted immediately. Mobile phone blogs, or "moblogs," allow users to add photos and video taken with their mobile phone, often from a distance, without even logging onto a computer.

Bloggers usually don't need to know much HTML—Hypertext Markup Language—unless they want to tinker with the design of their site. It can also be very simple to get started. Librarians without much of a background in Web design might want to use one of the free or inexpensive online blogging services, which allow users to set up a blog and start publishing items within minutes. Those who want more flexibility and control should think about using software such as WordPress or TypePad.

Choose the Right Blog Tools

You have two basic options when creating a blog. You can:

A. Use a free Web-based service such as Blogger.com or LiveJournal.com. Your blog will be hosted by the Web site, not on the school or library's own server. While this means that you won't have as much control over the blog, it is the easiest option for beginners. You can also get more features by upgrading to paid accounts.

B. Use software such as WordPress or Movable Type, installed on your own servers. This will give you far more control over the look and feel of your blog, and also many more features, such as TrackBack and the ability to organize your posts by topic or category.

If you choose option A, the next step is to decide which site should host your blog. There are many free blogging sites. Most provide upgraded blogs with more features and no advertising if you are willing to a pay a monthly fee. All allow photos and graphics as part of your blog, though some have limits and you may have to host the graphics on another free site. Popular free blogging services include:

• Google's Blogger.com. Sign up for a free account, choose a style and layout for the blog, then type up the first post and click "publish." This service is very simple to use, but doesn't offer much in the way of customization. Users can choose to let Blogger.com host the blog or, by entering server information and passwords, to transfer their blog onto their own server. Blogger also allows users to moderate comments, handy if you want to review responses to your blog before letting the rest of the world see them. Of the free services, Blogger generally gets the best rating in reviews. However, it lacks some features, such as Track-Back, a service used to notify other bloggers when you comment on what they have posted.

- LiveJournal.com. Another free service that is simple to use, LiveJournal puts an emphasis on community, with "friends" lists and profiles. It has more of a social networking feel than Blogger. However, users' ability to change the look and feel of their free blog is very limited.
- Xanga.com. Xanga began as a place to share book and music reviews, but is now a full-scale blog site. It offers "blogrings" for users with shared interests. Xanga is very popular with teens. However, it does display ads on free blogs.
- MySpace. MySpace lets users create a blog as part of their profile page. The main advantage of using this blog would be to reach teen users who are already spending much of their time on MySpace. The site displays lots of advertising, however, and is somewhat controversial.

To choose a blogging service, think about which sites your teens use most, and which features are most important to you. Try creating blogs at more than one Web site—signing up and posting your first item should only take a few minutes—to see which one seems easiest to use. Some of the things to consider include:

Does the blog display ads, and is that acceptable to you?

How much do you need or want to customize the look of your blog?

Does the blog allow multiple authors to post, so that several librarians can all contribute to one blog?

Is the blog part of a community that teens already use? Sites like Xanga and MySpace have their drawbacks, but they are also very popular with teens, and being part of their communities might increase your readership.

Do you need a "TrackBack" feature that allows better communication with other bloggers? Do you want to sort your posts by category? Consider using a paid version or blogging software.

Do you need to review comments before they are posted? All blog sites allow you to turn comments on and off, and to block certain users, but not all of them allow for screening.

The chart below provides an overview of the most basic free service at four popular blog Web sites.

If you want to get more serious about blogging, consider option B—downloading software and hosting it yourself. For librarians with access to their own server—or a cooperative Webmaster—blogging software offers

	Blogger.com	LiveJournal.com	Xanga.com	MySpace.com
Can you customize look of blog?	Yes	Limited	Yes	Limited
Displays ads in free version?	No	No	Yes	Yes
Allows more than one author?	Yes	No	No	No
TrackBack feature?	No	No	No	No
Allows for sort posts by category?	No	No	No	No
RSS or Atom feed generated automatically?	Yes	Yes	Yes	Yes
Can host blog on your own server?	Yes	No, not easily	No	No
Can review comments before they are posted?	Yes	Yes	No	No
Strong community and social networking features?	No	Yes	Yes	Yes
Popularity of the community with teens	Low	Medium	High	Highest

much more flexibility. Experienced bloggers, especially those with corporate or commercial blogs that need a professional look and feel, generally skip the free blogging sites.

Software such as Movable Type (available at www.sixapart.com/movabletype, pricing varies) and WordPress (http://wordpress.org, free) allows for more customization and more control over the blog. For example, you can organize your posts by category, which most of the free sites don't allow.

Both Movable Type and WordPress allow for categories, TrackBacks, feeds, search, multiple authors, and moderated comments. If these are all features you want, but you prefer not to host your own blog, consider using a paid service such as Typepad. TypePad, at www.typepad.com, uses the Movable Type platform but is aimed at less experienced users and offers blog hosting. You can try it out for free, then pay a monthly fee.

For a comparison of blogging software, see the excellent chart created by the USC Annenberg Online Journalism Review, available at www.ojr.org/ojr/images/blog_software_comparison.cfm. The chart compares two hosted services: Blogger and TypePad's three types of paid service (Basic, Plus, and Pro). It also compares four types of blogging software: Moveable Type, WorldPress, Blogware, and Expression Engine. As you will see, there are many features to consider.

You will have to decide which features are important to you. Do you need to add content with your cell phone? Then choose an option that permits moblogging. Do you want to create photo galleries? Do you want to create more than one blog, perhaps one for book reviews and one for upcoming events? These are all issues to consider.

In my opinion, the most important features for library blogs are:

- No ads—they make the blog look unprofessional, and the library may appear to be promoting the advertisers;
- Ability to recognize more than one author, so that multiple librarians can post to the blog under their own names or nicknames;
- Ability to screen comments and approve them for posting, or at least e-mail notification when new comments are posted;
- Ability to customize the blog, at least with the library's logo, so that it's clear that users are still on a library-sponsored Web site.

However, your criteria may be different. For a librarian who is the only one posting to the library's blog, multiple authors won't be a high priority. Others might decide that being part of a community such as MySpace or Xanga outweighs the disadvantages of the advertisements that come with the sites. As you decide on your best blog tools, keep the needs of your community and your teens in mind.

Find Other Library Blogs for Teens

It's always helpful to see what other librarians are doing. An excellent source for links to public and school libraries with blogs is, surprise, another blog!

Blog Without a Library
Available at: www.blogwithoutalibrary.net
Click on the "Blogging Libraries" link on the top right side of the page for the list.

Open Directories
Available at: http://dmoz.org/Reference/Libraries/Library_and_Information_ Science/Weblogs

Publicize Your Blog

Once you have a blog, how do you get teens actually to read it? One way is to create a feed to which teens, teachers, and others can subscribe. Feeds are covered later in this chapter.

If e-mail seems easier and less confusing, there are services that automatically e-mail each new post to anyone who has signed up for a subscription. Feedblitz—www.feedblitz.com—is one of them. Bloggers sign up, then point their readers toward the site to sign up, too. In this way, your blog doubles as an e-mail newsletter, one where readers can subscribe and unsubscribe as they please.

Blogs are so popular and easy to use that some libraries are even replacing their more traditional Web sites with blogs. At Galileo Academy of Science and Technology, a public high school in San Francisco, California, their school library Web site is the "Li-Blog-ary" (available at www.galileoWeb .org/galileoLibrary). Teachers, staff, and students at the school use linked blogs to communicate and learn.

IDEA #14: LEARN ABOUT VLOGS AND MOBLOGS

A video blog or "vlog" is a blog that uses digital video rather than text. Vlogs are also called "video podcasts." Coupled with a feed, a vlog can provide users with a subscription to the site. The growing popularity of video iPods will likely fuel this trend; users can already download videos from the iTunes store. For example, they might buy an episode of a favorite TV show and watch it on a video iPod or other portable video device, including some cell phones.

One of the most popular video blogs is Rocketboom, which provides daily news and commentary at www.rocketboom.com/vlog/.

Any librarian with a blog can record video clips using a digital camera or video camera. You'll then need to find server space to store them, then link to them on your blog. A good tutorial for beginning vloggers is available at Freevlog.org.

A "moblog" is a mobile phone blog. The blog is set up to accept information sent through a cell phone or portable digital device. Contributors generally post photographs or video clips taken with their cell phones, or call in audio content. Moblogs are especially useful during emergencies or during major events, where timeliness and the ability to post quickly come in handy.

Moblogs might be a way to let students or teen patrons contribute to a library Web site. Say your school is going on a field trip, and you want students to post photos of the sights they see. Or maybe you're a teen librarian going to a conference, where you meet young adult authors, see new titles you'd like to share with your patrons, or just want to stay in touch while away. With a mobile phone that takes photos, you can easily set up your own moblog. TextAmerica is one site that offers free moblogs at http://textamerica.com/.

Google's Blogger.com also supports mobile blogging. For more information, see their Frequently Asked Questions on Blogger Mobile at http://help.blogger.com/bin/answer.py?answer=1137.

You can also "call" your blog from any phone. This is useful when you're on the go, maybe traveling or attending an event you want to share with your audience. Your voice mail message is then added to the blog for anyone to listen to. To add audio to your Blogger blog, see the FAQ at www.audioblogger.com/faq.html.

IDEA #15: GET TO KNOW FEEDS

If you aren't using feeds already, it may be difficult to grasp exactly what they are and what they're good for. Talk of RSS, Atom, XML, Feedburner, and news aggregators will probably be enough to make your eyes glaze over. Keep reading, though, and I promise that you'll start to see why feeds are so important. Here are some of the things you can do with feeds:

- You can look at all the headlines for the fifty different blogs you read, all at once, on one convenient Web page.
- You can subscribe to audio and video content, also known as podcasts and vodcasts.
- You can use feeds to track all of your eBay auctions on one page.
- Some libraries let you subscribe to a feed to see when they get a new book on your favorite subject, or when your reserved books are ready to pick up.

- You can add entertainment news headlines to your library's teen Web site and have the headlines update automatically, twenty-four hours a day.

I use feeds primarily to keep up with library blogs and technology news. Over the past few years, I've found many favorite blogs about librarianship, teen books, and technology. If I checked each one every single day, I'd never get any work done. I would also be wasting a lot of time, since not every blog gets updated daily. In fact, some go weeks without new items.

Luckily, I discovered feeds. Feeds are also referred to as "syndication," RSS feeds, Web feeds, and so on. Feeds work for blogs and also for any Web resource where new information is added regularly. By adding an RSS—Real Simple Syndication—or Atom feed to a site, Web designers allow users to "subscribe" to their site.

You probably already use many Web sites that offer feeds. For example, go to the *New York Times* Web site at www.nytimes.com and scroll down to the bottom of the page. You'll see two orange buttons. One says "XML," another "RSS." If you click on either button, you go to the NYTimes.com RSS feeds page. Scroll down to see the many categories of feeds you can choose from, including movie reviews, soccer news, and job listings by type or location.

To organize my feeds, I use a Yahoo! service called MyYahoo!. The figure below will give you a snapshot of some of my feeds on a particular day.

Of course, users have many choices—they don't need to use MyYahoo!. Some users download a desktop application such as FeedReader or SharpReader. More often, they use an online service such as MyYahoo!, Bloglines, or NewsGator. Because desktop news aggregators are software loaded on a particular computer, they are best for users who use only one computer to access their information. For those who move around to several different computers during the day—perhaps one at home and another at work or school—a Web-based online service such as MyYahoo! or Bloglines is probably a better choice. Using an online service means that you can read your feeds on any computer with Internet access.

There are several ways to subscribe to feeds. For MyYahoo! users, it may be as simple as clicking on the button offered on a Web site that features a blue plus sign and the words "My Yahoo!." Other sites may have a link or button that says "RSS 1.0" or "RSS 2.0," or an orange button that says "XML."

As feeds become more widespread, it will probably become easier to subscribe to them. Currently, users sometimes need to click on the link for the feed, then cut and paste the URL into their news reader.

It's fairly simple to subscribe to feeds, and getting easier all the time. You can get updates on information from:

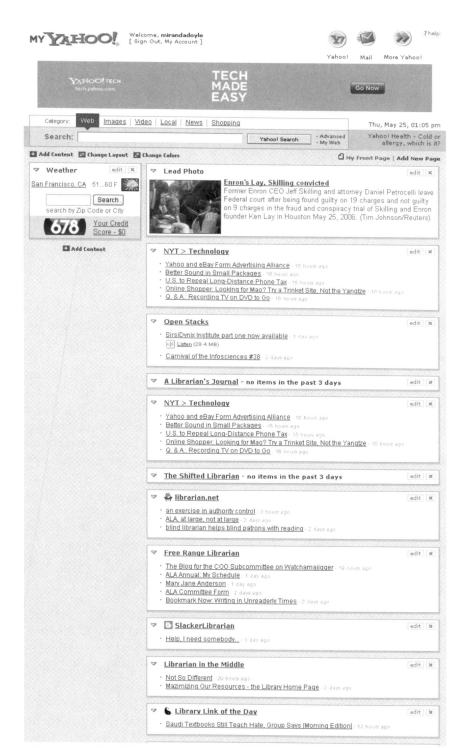

Figure 3-2   Author's MyYahoo! Page

- Blogs
- Online magazines and newspapers
- TV stations
- Radio stations
- Services such as Technorati (available at www.technorati.com) that allow you to search blogs, and also automatically locate keywords online and let you know when something new appears. For example, you can subscribe to a search for your own name, so that you know immediately if anyone on the Web mentions you!
- Library information—for example, Seattle Public Library has added RSS to their circulation and catalog system. This allows users to get automatic updates when new titles are added on topics of interest, get alerts through their news reader when their books are due, or get notified when a hold comes in for them.

How can you use feeds to enhance your library Web site for teens? First, if you have a blog, you will want to add a feed to that so that teens can subscribe. Second, you may want to add feeds to your library Web site, so that the site automatically updates with new content.

Adding a feed to your blog is important because it gives teens another way to read it. Let's say you have a blog on your school or public library Web site. Teens check it regularly and enjoy the items you post. But what if you're on vacation, out sick, or just too busy to post? Users may have the discouraging experience of checking the blog multiple times without finding new information. If their visits to the library's blog are unsatisfying, they may stop coming back.

If you add a feed (and if you use a service like Blogger.com, you already have one—you just have to locate it and create a link), then a hypothetical teen can see your new posts on her news aggregator. She may even access her feeds through her cell phone or PDA. When you go to your blog and add an item about a teen author scheduled to visit the library, this teen will see the headline and know about the event right away.

Feeds are also a useful way to show brand-new information on your Web site automatically, without any effort on your part. For example, you can set up a feed to display the latest news or entertainment headlines right on your library Web site. You could also add your blog's latest headlines to your teen homepage, so that teens can see what you've just posted before going to the blog.

Set Up Your Feed

At this point, the easiest way to add a feed to a blog is to use Blogger.com or a similar service. Blogger generates a feed automatically. Web designers simply need to "find" the address of their feed and then provide a button or link on their home page. Blogger's help page explains about syndication and how to use it. In the "Settings" area, users can activate their feeds and find out where they are located. Full details are provided at http://help.blogger.com/bin/answer.py?answer=698&topic=36.

Blogger uses Atom, a publishing standard that is a competitor of RSS. Many news readers can make use of either Atom or RSS, but since not all of them can, it's a good idea to run Blogger feed through FeedBurner or a similar free service. Feedburner—at www.feedburner.com—allows users to create a new feed that all news readers can use.

Once a feed is set up, there is no need to maintain or update it daily. Any new posts to a blog automatically generate new headlines in the news readers of anyone who has subscribed. This ensures that subscribers see new posts in a timely fashion.

IDEA #16: EMBRACE INSTANT MESSAGING

If you ask me, instant messaging—also called "IM"—is one of the greatest procrastination tools ever invented. I use Yahoo! Messenger with Voice, a piece of software I downloaded to my desktop for free. When I start up my home computer, my family and friends who use the same software can see that I'm online. They can then send me text messages, which pop up on my screen, or call me using the free voice service.

Because it's in real time, we communicate directly, rather than exchanging time-delayed e-mails. The drawback is that if I'm working on something that absorbs my attention, the instant messages feel like an interruption. So I often sign in as "invisible to everyone" so that no one can tell I'm online.

As annoying as I sometimes find instant messaging, however, teens can't live without it. So if I want to communicate with teenagers, I'm going to have to learn to love it, too. A July 2005 Pew study found that:

- "Instant messaging has become the digital communication backbone of teens' daily lives."
- 75 percent of online teens—or about two-thirds of all teenagers—use Instant messaging.
- 48 percent of teens who use IM services say they use them every day.
- Many teens IM for more than an hour a day.

In addition, research has found the instant messaging has far surpassed chat rooms as the preferred method of communication for teens. Also, teens will often exchange IMs with several people at once—conducting three or more conversations at any one time.

So, if you were trying to reach someone like me with information about the library, you'd probably use e-mail. But you're not—you're trying to reach teens. So it makes sense to use the tools they prefer. Instant messaging is a great way for librarians to make themselves easily available to the teens they serve. For example, instant messaging can be used to:

- Answer quick reference questions from teens who are at home, in a classroom, or in the school's computer lab (more on this in Chapter 8);
- Stay in touch with members of the library's teen advisory group;
- Send out program reminders to teens who signed up for an event;
- Notify individual teens about a new book they might like.

Many libraries are already using instant messaging to answer reference questions. The Library Success wiki offers a good list at www.libsuccess.org/index.php?title=Online_Reference#Libraries_Using_IM_Reference.

Before you decide to use instant messaging, consider the advantages and disadvantages.

Advantages of Instant Messaging

- Because IM is so popular with teens, you may be able to reach them quickly and efficiently this way.
- Using IM will make you look cool, since it's so popular with younger people.
- Teens will appreciate the fact that you're using one of their preferred means of communication.
- You can also send files and photos this way, useful if you need to transmit documents to a teen council member, for example. You can send music and videos, Web pages and more.

Disadvantages of Instant Messaging

- Generally, you contact one person at a time, rather than sending a message to everyone on a list, as you might with e-mail. It is possible to set up "conferences," however.
- Usually, you must use the same software teens uses, since IMs currently depend on a specific service such as AOL or Yahoo! Instant Messenger. For now, you'll probably have to download software from multiple services.
- You will have to be tolerant of interruptions if you sign in as visible to other users.
- Instant messaging comes with a language of its own, which can be baffling for new users. I can figure out XOXO (hugs and kisses) and even

ROTFL (rolling on the floor laughing), but BB4N? YSYD? RUUP4IT? For the record, that's "Bye bye for now," "Yeah, sure you do" and "Are you up for it?" Bone up at NetLingo.com—www.netlingo.com/e-mailsh .cfm—if necessary.

Getting Started with Instant Messaging

To get started with instant messaging, you'll most likely need to download software. The first step is to find out which services teens in your community use. If your teen patrons use multiple services for instant messaging, you may need to download software from more than one service, as many teens do.

Messaging services allow you to send messages only to those using the same service, unless you use an aggregator like Trillian or Gaim. Google is working on open communications standards that would allow users of different services to talk to each other via instant messenger. For example, you could download the Google tool but talk to someone who uses Yahoo!. Also, Microsoft and AOL recently signed an agreement that will allow communication between their services, so that AIM users can chat directly with Windows Live Messenger users.

New Web-based IM services such as Meebo—available at www.meebo .com/—may also make it easier to juggle multiple accounts and communicate with all users. There are also instant message "aggregators," such as:

- Gaim
     Available at: http://sourceforge.net/projects/gaim
- Trillian
     Available at: www.ceruleanstudios.com/

This type of software allows users to communicate with users on various services, including AIM, ICQ, Windows Live Messenger, Yahoo! Messenger, and IRC. You can download the basic versions for free.

Currently, the most popular services are:

- AOL (AIM)
     Available at: www.aim.com
- Google (Google Talk)
     Available at: www.google.com/talk
- WLM (Windows Live Messenger)
     Available at: www.imagine-msn.com/Messenger/Default2.aspx
- Yahoo! (Yahoo! Messenger)
     Available at: http://messenger.yahoo.com

Below is a comparison of these four services and a few of the features that might be useful to librarians. Of course, the software is constantly changing as new features are added, so check the Web sites for more up-to-date information.

	AIM	Google Talk	Yahoo! Messenger	Windows Live Messenger
Supports audio chat?	Yes	Yes	Yes	Yes
SMS (cell phone) messaging?	Yes	No	Yes	Yes
Can send files?	Yes	No	Yes	Yes
Whiteboard for sharing information?	No	No	Yes	Yes

Once you've set up your service or services, you'll have many options for contacting teens who use your library—you can send an instant message, create a chat room, use Voice Chat, set up a conference between several contacts, send text messages to cell phones, and so on.

If you want to initiate an instant message, you'll need to get each teen's contact information, usually either an IM nickname or their e-mail address. You can then add these contacts to your address book, often called a "buddy list." When you're ready to, for example, send a program reminder, you click on that person's nickname and type in your message. If they're offline, it will be delivered later, when they log on.

IDEA #17: TRY TEXT MESSAGING

Teens seem to find cell phones indispensable. According to a July 2005 Pew study on technology and teenagers:

- 45 percent of young adults have cell phones.
- 33 percent use them to send text messages.

In the world outside libraries, text messaging is becoming a common way to connect with teenagers. For instance, in San Francisco, anyone can get information on safe sex from the Department of Public Health by sending the message "sexinfo" to a phone number set up by Public Health. Users choose from several options to get brief information, written in text message lingo, and phone numbers to call for more help. The department is hoping that the privacy and immediacy of this service will appeal to teens.

A few libraries are also beginning to take advantage of this technology. University libraries, in particular, are offering live reference services that allow users to exchange text messages with a librarian.

Sims Memorial Library at Southeastern Louisiana University, for example, has a "Text A Librarian" service at http://www2.selu.edu/Library/Services Dept/referenc/textalibrarian.html.

A few libraries are also offering alerts by text message when new reserves come in for patrons. This is a technology that libraries are just beginning to explore, but because teens use cell phones so heavily, and love text messaging, it's a great option for teen librarians.

You may even be able to send graphics or sound files to your patrons' cell phones, depending on what kind of service they have. There are two basic types:

SMS (short message service)—allows users to send and receive up to 160 characters per message.

MMS (multimedia message service)—allows users to transmit graphics, video clips, sound files and text messages.

To get started, you'll want to download instant messaging software to your computer. See the previous section for a list of options. Once you've downloaded the software:

- Collect teens' cell phone numbers, with their permission;
- Be sure that they are aware of any school or library rules limiting the use of cell phones that you might be encouraging teens to break;
- Check to make sure teens aren't charged by their wireless provider for each text message they receive—these fees can be steep, and if you send frequent messages, cell phone users might end up with a big bill;
- Add the numbers to your instant messenger address book or "buddy list;"
- Click on the numbers and type your message. You may be limited to 160 characters, if the phone uses SMS, so keep messages brief.

IDEA #18: ADD SOME AUDIO

When I think about the basic elements of a Web site, I think of text and graphics. As librarians, we are sometimes very focused on print resources. Library Web sites tend to be heavy on text. However, many teens are auditory learners, and prefer listening to reading. This is the theory behind offering audio books, after all.

Moving beyond books, audio is an excellent way to reach library users. Many people, myself included, own iPods or MP3 players. I use mine to download radio programs from National Public Radio, listen to audio books, and catch up on professional and technology issues by listening to podcasts. When I ride public transportation to work, it seems as if half of my fellow commuters are wearing white ear buds attached to iPods. Libraries can also use audio to capitalize on teens' interest in music, by offering downloadable songs performed by teens or local bands.

According to a February 2005 Pew study:

- Almost one in five (19 percent) of those under age thirty have iPods/ MP3 players.
- Those who use the Internet are four times as likely as non-Internet users to have iPods/MP3 players.
- 16 percent of parents living with children under eighteen in their home have iPods/MP3 players, compared to 9 percent of those who don't have children living at home.

Many teens regularly download and listen to music on their MP3 players; others plug headphones into computers and listen to music while online. Why not have them do the same with library news and information?

Podcasting is addressed later in this chapter. But any type of podcasting begins with audio files. In fact, it isn't really necessary to provide a "podcast" at all—you might choose simply to post audio files on your Web site for downloading at any time. Teens, parents, and teachers can access and listen to these files at their convenience.

Getting Started with Audio

Creating basic audio files is fairly simple, and requires little in the way of special equipment. Aside from a computer, you will need:

- A computer headset with a microphone, available for as little as $10 at any electronics store. Do you use a Mac rather than a PC? Macs come with built-in microphones. An alternative, if you will need more mobility and want to record on the go, is a portable digital voice recorder. These can be found at office and electronics stores—be sure to get one that allows you to download audio files to a PC—and start around $70. Portable MP3 players can also serve this same function; iPod users can buy a voice recorder attachment, while many podcasters like iRiver players with built-in microphones. Of course, professional recording equipment is another option, but recordings made with an inexpensive headset and microphone can sound surprisingly clear.

- Editing software. Most audio files will require some editing to remove background noise, amplify sound, and delete errors and silences. One popular program is Audacity, available for free at http://audacity.source forge.net/. You will also need to download an additional file, called "LAME MP3 encoder," in order to export your files in the MP3 format. That file is available through the same site. If you have more complex needs, you might choose to purchase sound editing software such as Garageband (for Macs) or Adobe Audition (for PCs).

To record an audio file, plug the headset into your computer, open your editing software, click the "record" button, and start talking. Next, edit your file, deleting any mistakes or long silences. You may also want to "clean up" your file by getting rid of background noise and amplifying the sound.

When you finish, you'll need to save the file—probably as an MP3, but there are other options. You will then want to upload this file to your server, and place it in a folder accessible to the public. If you already upload files— for example, pages on your Web site—to a server, you are familiar with this process. If not, you'll need to confer with your Webmaster or the person in your organization who manages the Web server.

Next, you will link to the audio file from your Web site. By linking to the file from your Web site, you allow Internet users to download or play the file. It is also possible to record phone conversations and save them as audio files, in the case of a long-distance interview with an author.

Advantages of Audio Files

- High appeal to teens who like to listen to information rather than read it;
- A great way to "time shift" programming, speeches or lectures, since users can choose a time and place to listen;
- Useful for offering music clips, songs, "Battle of the Band" programs, and more;
- Sound files are portable. Once they download the files, teens can listen anywhere and any time.

Disadvantages of Audio Files

- Audio takes up much more memory than text or even graphics. Spoken audio can be saved at a much lower bit rate than music files and still sound good, but most files are still quite large. If you have limited server space, this is something to consider.

- Creating audio files can prove very time consuming. If you're a perfectionist, you may find yourself editing out every stumble or misspoken word. Adding music takes additional time.

IDEA #19: CONSIDER PODCASTING

"Podcast" is a term that combines "pod"—from iPod, the most popular type of portable MP3 player—and "broadcast."

Podcasting simply takes audio files one step further, by allowing listeners to subscribe to audio content. Instead of frequently checking your site to see if you've added new files, listeners simply sign up for your podcast, using software such as iTunes. Then, whenever you add a new audio file, your subscribers' software automatically downloads it to their computer or to a portable device such as an iPod.

The first podcast I listened to was "Open Stacks," librarian Greg Schwartz's excellent program about public library issues. I went on to record my own podcasts for my Web site, interviewing other librarians, authors, and editors. What's so exciting about this new technology is that anyone can produce a podcast with very little equipment. You're simply putting together audio files and then allowing people to subscribe to them. Audio files have long been available on the Internet. The ability to subscribe—using feeds, which are described in Idea #15—is really what's new about podcasting.

"Podcast" is a somewhat misleading term, since you don't need an iPod to listen to a podcast, nor do you receive them over the public airwaves as you do a broadcast. You actually have several options:

- Listen online by clicking on the sound file on the creator's Web site;
- Manually download the sound file to your MP3 player and listen on your player;
- Or, to make it a true podcast, use software such as iTunes or iPodder to subscribe. Then, when you check for new sound files, they will be downloaded for you automatically.

Some portable players can also display images and video, so users are already subscribing to video podcasts.

Podcasting is best for audio programs that appear on a regular basis, such as weekly or monthly. One-time audio files might as well appear as links on a Web site, since there is no point in subscribing.

If many of your teen users have iPods or other portable media players, consider producing a weekly or monthly library podcast. A library podcast might include:

- A full-scale radio-type show produced by teens or by the librarian
- "Read alouds" from a new teen book
- A booktalk on a new teen book or books
- Information on new library databases of interest to teens
- Creative content produced by teens—poetry, music, and so on
- Booktalks by and for teens
- Interviews with young adult authors
- News about upcoming teen books—publication dates for popular sequels, for example
- Announcements from the last Teen Advisory Council meeting

In other words, a podcast can include anything a librarian might put on a flyer, in an e-mail message, or as an item on a blog. Remember that listeners will often be tuning in while they're on the go, so any content that requires note-taking or sustained concentration may not make sense for that part of your audience.

Also, instead of being the sole "voice of the library," why not have teens take over the production of the podcasts? This is a perfect activity for a teen advisory council. The librarians might contribute parts of the podcast or step aside and let the teens produce the whole thing.

Getting Started with Podcasting

The first step is to produce the audio file. See the section on audio, also in this chapter.

Once the audio file is completed, you will upload it to your server and create a link to it. In order to create a podcast, the page where you post it must have an RSS or Atom feed. The easiest way to do this is if you already have a blog on Blogger.com or a similar service. You simply add an item announcing your new podcast and include a link to the audio file.

The feed is what podcast listeners will actually subscribe to. Then, as you post each new audio file, their software will download it automatically and allow them to sync it to their portable media player.

For more technical information on how to create a podcast using Blogger.com and a site called Feeburner.com, try the following site: www.podcastingnews.com/articles/Make_Podcast_Blogger.html.

IDEA #20: DISCOVER VIDEO AND VODCASTING

Online video is taking off, with many television stations now offering episodes of TV shows for free or for a few dollars each. Many teens watch music videos online already. The video iPod and similar devices makes downloading video even more enticing, since users can watch on small, very portable screens.

Libraries are also getting into the act. Denver Public Library has an eFlicks service where users can download videos—mostly educational titles and classic movies—for free. They can watch these videos on their computers or on mobile devices such as Pocket PCs or certain cell phones. This is a service that promises to be wildly popular as more and more people own these devices.

The rise of online video involves more than just downloading movies and episodes of favorite TV shows. More people are also making their own videos, using camcorders, Webcams, digital still cameras and cell phones. They may upload this video to the Web or send it to each other using e-mail or cell phones. New Web sites also make it easy to edit homegrown video clips without buying software. Instead of using software downloaded or installed to your PC, you can now easily edit video, make a soundtrack, add titles, and create special effects using Web sites like Jumpcut, Eyespot, Grouper and VideoEgg. The sites also allow for collaborative editing, making them perfect for class assignments or teen advisory group projects.

One recent trend in online video is called "viral video." This term refers to the way in which video clips—sometimes ads or clips from TV shows, sometimes amateur video, often amusing—spread online through e-mail. One person sees the clip, thinks it's funny, and sends it to all of his or her friends, who send it to their friends. Companies have attempted to use this trend as a marketing strategy, but more commonly it is not an organized effort. Some clips start out by showing an ad, while others are just the clips themselves. To view some examples, try the ifilm Web site—www.ifilm.com—and click on "Viral Video." Other popular sites for sharing homemade videos include YouTube, at www.youtube.com, and Veoh, at www.veoh.com.

Offering video clips on your library Web site has advantages and disadvantages similar to those of audio files.

Advantages of Video Files

- High appeal to teens who like to watch and listen to information rather than reading it;
- Appeal to teens who want to produce or star in your video clips;
- You're providing more sensory input than text, audio, photos, or a combination of all three can provide.
- Video files may be portable, if teens have video iPods or other devices. Once they download the files, teens can watch and listen anywhere and any time.
- Users can view your videos at their convenience.

Disadvantages of Video Files

- Video files are very large. If you have limited server space, this is a consideration.
- High-speed Internet access is crucial. If your patrons have mostly dial-up access, they might not be able to view your video files, or they will take so long to download that users will give up.
- You'll need equipment such as a digital video camera, which may be beyond your library budget. You may be able to use a regular digital camera to make short clips, or even cell phones that record video. However, make sure the quality of the video is high enough that users won't be frustrated.
- Editing video is time consuming, especially if you're a perfectionist.
- You'll need to be especially aware of privacy issues, more so than with audio because you're including images along with sound.

If you do decide to offer video, the technical details are much the same as with sound. You'll be uploading video files to your server and storing them there. Next, you'll want to offer a link to the file from somewhere on your Web site.

The next step is a "video podcast"—also called "vlogs" (short for "video blogs") or "videocasts" or "vodcasts"—basically, allowing users to subscribe to new video clips, if you plan to update your site regularly. The iTunes software will automatically download video as well as audio files for users.

Another great tool for your Web site is screencasting, which just means making a video of what you do on your computer screen. Screencasts allow you to create a movie demonstrating a new software program, a feature on your library Web site, how to use a particular database, and much more. For more on making and using screencasts, see Idea #69.

IDEA #21: EXPERIMENT WITH WIKIS

A wiki is a collaborative Web site where every user is an editor. "Wiki" is short for "wikiwiki," which is Hawaiian for "quick." (The first wiki was created in Hawaii in 1995.)

Users of wikis can change, add, edit, or delete content. The best known wiki is probably Wikipedia, an online encyclopedia project where amateur editors contribute to the articles. Of course, wikis can fall prey to "vandals" who insert inappropriate content. They are also controversial because of the lack of authority—anyone can be an editor. But they are also an exciting way to share ideas and work together.

For example, you might use a wiki to have your students or teen patrons collaborate to create booklists. Invite teens to make a list of the fifty best manga titles, or the ten best nonfiction books they've read. Opinions will differ as everyone contributes to the list, of course, but that's what makes a wiki so much fun. Librarians can watch the list grow and change, tracking the edits along the way.

Most wiki software allows creators to set up passwords and administer user privileges, so you can take control of some aspects of your wiki. If you don't allow anonymous users, for example, you'll be able to track changes and catch vandals. For this reason, a wiki would probably work best for a smaller group—a teen advisory council, for instance, rather than the general public. A classroom or school setting is also an ideal place to try a wiki, since the users will be identifiable and accountable for the changes they make.

To find out more about wikis, and try your hand as an editor, try the Library Success Wiki at www.libsuccess.org/. For example, here's the Library Success entry under "Programs for Young Adults:" www.libsuccess.org/index.php?title=Programs_for_Young_Adults#Great_Ideas_for_Young_Adult_Programming.

If you want to set up your own wiki, you can use a free (usually ad-supported) site or one that charges a small fee. Some sites to try include:

- EditMe
  Available at: http://editme.com
- Jotspot
  Available at: www.jot.com
- PBwiki
  Available at: http://pbwiki.com
- SeedWiki
  Available at: http://seedwiki.com
- Wikispaces
  Available at: www.wikispaces.com

You can also download and install wiki software on your server. Most wiki software is currently free. Popular software includes:

- MediaWiki
  Available at: www.mediawiki.org/wiki/MediaWiki
- MoinMoin
  Available at: http://moinmoin.wikiwikiWeb.de
- PmWiki
  Available at: www.pmwiki.org
- TWiki
  Available at: www.twiki.org
- UseModWiki
  Available at: www.usemod.com/cgi-bin/wiki.pl

Since wikis are relatively new, librarians and others are still exploring their applications. So far, it seems that any kind of collaborative project works well as a wiki. Everyone involved can contribute what they know, and work together to create something greater than what each could come up with alone. For example, you could offer teens a chance to work together to create booklists. Participants would add their favorite titles, add their comments to those of others, and perhaps remove titles they feel don't quite fit on a particular list. They could also use a wiki to brainstorm a mission statement for a teen advisory council, with each member taking a turn with the editing.

Wikis aren't really appropriate, however, for presenting information that doesn't (or shouldn't) change. Your library's address and phone number should probably appear as a regular, static Web page, not as part of a library wiki. The library's location isn't really a matter of opinion or a good topic for debate.

Still, wikis depend on cooperation and good behavior, so it's no wonder that many people are proceeding with caution. It might be a good idea to start with a wiki that allows the administrator to set up a password, then give that password to a selected few. This way, you limit the number of people involved.

Wikis are also useful to librarians as internal documents that allow them to collaborate with colleagues. Schools are also finding wikis helpful. For example, School Library Journal reported in February 2006 that the Bering Strait School District in Alaska had launched a wiki so that their teachers, who are spread across thousands of square miles, can collaborate on curriculum.

IDEA #22: FIND YOUR VOICE WITH VOIP

If you're interacting with teens online, actually talking to them may make communication much easier. Typing—as in e-mail, instant messaging, chat or text messaging—can be too slow.

VOIP, or Voice Over Internet Protocol, is one way really to talk to teens while you're interacting online. Skype—www.skype.com—is probably the best known service. You can download the free software, sign up for a screen name, and talk for free (using a headset and microphone that plugs into your PC, or the microphone built into your Mac) to any other Skype users. For a small fee, you can also use Skype to call regular phone numbers. Skype can be used for person-to-person conversations or for conference calls open to all Skype users.

Many instant messaging services also offer free voice communications now, including Yahoo! Messenger, AOL Instant Messenger and Windows Live Messenger. On Yahoo!, you download their voice messenger software, plug in headphones with a microphone, and call other Yahoo! users. You can leave voice mail messages if they are not logged on when you call. The quality is similar to calling on a regular telephone.

Consider adding your Skype user name to your library Web site so that other users can contact you at your work computer. Also, if you are currently using instant messaging software without a voice option, think about upgrading your free software to one that allows voice contact.

IDEA #23: EXPAND YOUR SOCIAL NETWORK

Social networking sites are Internet sites that focus on developing and expanding friendships, connecting with people who share similar interests, and interacting with a large group of friends. MySpace and Friendster are probably the best known, but Facebook, Tribe.net, Xanga, and others are also popular. On these sites, users usually post their profiles, photos, videos, and other personal information. They may then link to friends who also have profiles, and to friends of friends. They may also have their blogs on these sites, or participate in discussion groups and forums.

Most of these sites also allow for interaction through Instant Messaging and other means. A broad definition of social networking sites would also include online dating sites and blog networks such as LiveJournal.com. Sites such as MySpace are controversial because of the perceived danger that teens might post or give out identifying information, leaving them vulnerable to pedophiles. In addition, such sites can also give rise to gossip and lead to hurt feelings among peers. For this reason, some schools have banned the use of social networking sites.

Still, as a librarian, it's good to know what teens are using on the Web, and to think about what draws them to these sites. While these trends may not find their way onto your Web site just yet, you should be aware of them and begin to think about how library Web sites might take advantage of the trends. Obviously, teens like to share photos and personal information. They like to create networks of friends online, and communicate with these friends, usually through instant messaging. If your library Web site for teens can recreate some of these elements, in a safe way that protects teen privacy, your site will have far more power to draw users in.

If you're willing to be adventurous, think about creating a profile for your library on a social networking site. It pays to be where the teens are—they can then link to your site, communicate with you through it, and start thinking of the library as part of their network.

A few libraries have already created their own MySpace sites. View a growing list—or add your own library—at the Library Success wiki, available at: http://libsuccess.org/index.php?title=MySpace_%26_Teens.

Hennepin County Library, Minnesota
Available at: www.myspace.com/hennepincountylibrary (see Figure 3-3)

Thomas Ford Memorial Library, in Illinois, also a site at http://myspace .com/thomasford. The library has a photo, a listing of hours, contact information, and a blog about teen events.

Some young adult authors also have MySpace profiles. For some examples, check out the site for Not Your Mother's Book Club, a teen book group in San Francisco, California, at www.myspace.com/notyourmothers. If you look at the group's list of "friends," you'll see familiar names, from Rachel Cohn to Blake Nelson to David Levithan. Some authors include blogs or post excerpts from their upcoming books. Others have links to their Web sites.

There are also discussion groups or forums on MySpace. One that focuses on teen books has almost 500 members. You'll find it at http://groups.my space.com/teenlit.

As you can see from these examples, MySpace has much potential to be a place for book lovers to gather. The next step is for libraries to determine how best to harness and participate in this virtual space. For more on how libraries can harness social networking sites and use them to promote themselves, see the following blog posts:

Libraries in Social Networking Software
Meredith Farkas
Available at: http://meredith.wolfwater.com/wordpress/index.php/2006/
    05/10/libraries-in-social-networking-software/

Social Software for the Rest of Us (or Librarian 2.0)
Michael Stephens
Available at: www.techsource.ala.org/blog/2005/11/social-software-for-
    the-rest-of-us-or-librarian-20.html

Another important aspect of social networking is the display, organization, and exchange of photographs. With digital cameras and cell phones that take snapshots, photos are now easy and inexpensive to take and upload to Web sites. Users of sites such as Yahoo! Photos can store their photos online and share them with friends and family. Teens are more likely to use a site such as Photobucket—at http://photobucket.com—which works well with social networking sites such as MySpace. Flickr—www.flickr.com—is another photo site worth looking at. It allows users to "tag" photos and organize them using keywords, and also to comment on photos posted by others.

Cell phone users are also embracing social networking through text messaging. For example, a service called Dodgeball (available at www.dodgeball .com) allows you to "invite" friends and add them to your network, much in

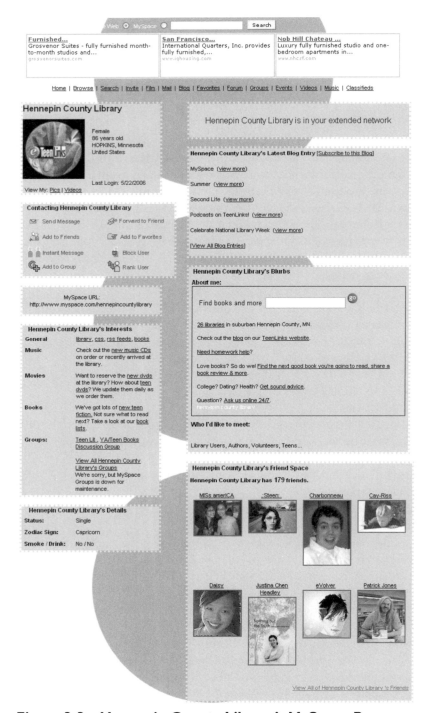

Figure 3-3   Hennepin County Library's MySpace Page

the way sites like MySpace and Friendster do. You then send out a text message with your current location—for example, a favorite park or club—and a note goes out to all of your friends, letting them know where you are and that you'd like to meet up. The service will also send out messages to any friends of your friends who happen to be within ten blocks of your location. In addition, you can specify a list of "crushes," who will be notified when you're nearby. Sites such as MySpace, Yahoo!, Google, and Facebook are all looking at how they can get into the mobile social networking business as well.

IDEA #24: DISCOVER FOLKSONOMIES, TAGGING, AND BOOKMARK SHARING

Combining "folk" and "taxonomy," "folksonomy" describes the way much information is now being organized on the Web. Users are encouraged to choose keywords to describe their information, whether it's a list of Web bookmarks, a collection of photographs, the subject of their blog entries, or their interests as part of a social networking site profile. Instead of a central-ized cataloging system with rigid subject headings, this is an informal way to group and organize information. The keywords assigned by individual users are called "tags." Of course, because no two people will choose exactly the same keywords, or use words in the same way, organization of a folksonomy is more chaotic than a formal, centralized system.

Tagging is a method used to identify pieces of information in an online environment. Users assign tags, which can then be used to organize or group information. In other words, tagging is an informal way to "catalog" online information. For example, a user might look at a photo of an adorable cat and assign tags like "cat," "kitten," "cute," "orange," and so on. Users of the site can click on one of the tags to see all of the other photos tagged with the word "kitten" or one of the other tags. Teens—and other Internet users—love to share their interests online using tags as one method of organization. One very popular site is del.icio.us, a social bookmarking site (available at http://del.icio.us). Another good site for organizing and sharing bookmarks is Furl, at www.furl.net/.

On del.icio.us, you can upload your list of favorite Web sites, then add comments and subject tags. This allows other users to see what sites you visit. It also allows you to find others who share your interests, and then look at their list of favorite sites. You can do the same with lists of favorite books, music, and more.

At first, it seems strange to want to share your bookmarks with others. Why would they even be interested? But if you give the site a try, you'll find that by clicking on other, similar tags, you locate people who have bookmarked the same sites as you. Their lists may give you new ideas and new sites to visit. You can also see which sites are most popular with other users. It's similar to using a site like Amazon.com for book suggestions. When you look up a title on Amazon, you can also see what other readers who bought your title also bought, and their lists of suggestions for other books you might like. Using a bookmark sharing site, you can get suggestions for new sites you might like based on your interests.

Bookmark-sharing sites could be used by librarians to create quick pathfinders for students. The sites allow users to annotate their bookmarks by adding comments. You could easily create a list of bookmarks and then share them with users. You might also want to have students contribute their own links and comments to share with their classmates in a collaborative project.

Tagging and folksonomies definitely have other applications for libraries, though it will likely take a while to figure out the best use of this idea. As Internet users grow more used to organizing and sharing information, they will likely demand more interactive library catalogs and Web sites. While user-based tagging might not replace formal cataloging systems, it offers an interesting alternative method.

It's a good idea for librarians to be aware that the teens they work with are probably already creating tags for their bookmarks, photos, and so on, which will in turn shape the way they think about your library catalog and the way it is organized.

Part II.
Communication

Chapter 4

Getting the Word Out

OVERVIEW

Teen librarians with programs to publicize once had limited choices. They could distribute information on paper, in person, or by telephone. They could post flyers around the library, or send them by mail to teens and groups. They could also visit classrooms to speak directly with students and teachers.

Anyone who has laboriously folded flyers and stuffed envelopes know that it's not the most exciting task. I have volunteers who prepare my program flyers, but it's still a chore. I would much rather send e-mails with the click of a "send" button—and have the recipients respond with questions, comments, or a promise to attend.

Of course, e-mail is only the beginning. For example, teen librarians can also post events and reviews on their Web sites. They can create a blog—an easily updated online journal. They can create a podcast—an audio file that is automatically updated—that teens download and listen to on their iPods.

Choosing a Medium

The key to reaching teens is to know exactly how they prefer to receive information. Personally, I like getting e-mail. It's waiting in my inbox when I have a chance to read it, but I can also ignore it when I'm busy.

But I'm definitely behind the times. Many teens prefer more instant gratification. They want to stay constantly connected to their social network. They stay online all the time, and love getting instant messages on their computers or text messages on their cell phones. They welcome what is, to me, an interruption. Others like to stay in touch using social networking Web sites such as MySpace or Friendster.

The first step, then, is to find out how the teens in your community prefer to get their information. If they rarely check e-mail, e-mail messages will go unread. If they read blogs obsessively, a library blog makes a great deal of sense. You might want to start by surveying or simply observing the teens in your community. Notice:

- What Web sites do they constantly use?
- Do they check and send e-mail?
- Are they chatting online? Using instant messaging software?
- Are they creating profiles on MySpace or other sites?
- Are they reading blogs?
- If so, do they use sites like MyYahoo! or Bloglines and add their own feeds?
- Do they carry cell phones? If so, do they send text messages? Do they take and send photos? Do they listen to music or watch video on their phones?
- Do they walk around with iPods or other MP3 players surgically attached?
- Do they have PDAs—Personal Digital Assistants—such as a BlackBerry or Palm?
- Do they have portable devices, like the new video iPod, that let them watch video on the go?

You might also want to ask teens in the library, or on your teen advisory board, how they would prefer to get information about the library. Once you know that, you can design your publicity campaigns accordingly. You'll also want to stay flexible, observing teens as their choice of technology changes, so that you can update your own methods.

Librarians who work with teens are already using many options to get the word out and market their libraries. In searching out the ideas in this section, I was tremendously impressed by what libraries are already doing, and teen librarians' willingness to take risks and try something new.

IDEA #25: BUILD A BLOG FOR LIBRARY NEWS

For more on blogs, and how to set one up, see Chapter 3

BLTeens Blog

The Bryant Library -- for children, for teens, for adults -- for the community of Roslyn. Stay current with the latest teen happenings, workshops, events, websites, etc. We're all about sharing information.

May 2006
S M T W T F S
- 1 2 3 4 5 6
7 8 9 10 11 12 13
14 15 16 17 18 19 20
21 22 23 24 25 26 27
28 29 30 31 - - -

2:10:11 PM

Free Blog Content

Wednesday, May 24, 2006

For Want of a Music Education

Speaking as someone who is admittedly not music savvy, I've been having fun playing with a great new toy. One of our library teens (thanks, Erica!) told me about a fantastic website called Pandora. Pandora is an idea that grew out of the Music Genome Project. This project began 6 years ago by people with a vision -- these musicians and technicians developed a way of dissecting individual songs into "genes" and in this way created the ability to find songs that are similar in characteristics to one another. How it works is this: after registering for a free account, you enter a song or artist that you enjoy. Pandora plays that song for you, then continues to play songs that have similar characteristics. As the songs play, you "teach" it by telling it if you like or dislike each piece. It builds what it calls a radio station based on your music preferences. They have tens of thousands of songs in every genre -- including club and garage bands! This is a great way to learn about new music!

Back to my "bookish" self, I have to tell you that there is already a way to do this for books. Novelist is one of our Electronic Databases. Once you enter your library card number, you can put in a favorite title or author and it generates a list of subjects. Once you select the subjects that are interesting to you, Novelist returns a list of recommending reading! Now I've given you two new toys to play with -- enjoy!

posted by Michele @ 6:22 PM | 0 comments links to this post

Tuesday, May 23, 2006

American Idol vs. Bryant Library

I must admit that "reality" shows are not really my style. I know that there are some households whose weekly schedule revolves around the American Idol lineup -- we don't fall into this category. We tend to watch the last 15 minutes or so, just so we don't look like idiots the next day. For the most part, I think these shows are harmless fun. But, I was shocked when they announced last week on the show that they had gotten around 50 million votes!! Last week, we were stressing over getting enough people out to vote in the library/school budget election, and American Idol pulled in that many votes -- I couldn't believe it!! Where are our priorities?

What does American Idol offer that we don't? American Idol offers entertainment, music, videos, ringtones, interactivity in terms of the web... Here is what the Bryant Library offers:

- Music (cds and cassettes)
- Videos (dvds and videos)
- Books (paperbacks, hardcovers, books on tape, books on cd, downloadable audio books)
- Computers (including computer training, laptop area, wi-fi hotspot, etc.)

Figure 4-1   Bryant Library's BLTeens Blog

A library blog is a powerful way to reach teens. It's also easy to set up and simple to update regularly. So, what do librarians who work with teens include in their blogs? I give five examples below. You can also see that each blog has its own unique look and character.

Bryant Library—BLTeens Blog
Available at: www.nassaulibrary.org/bryant/blteens/blog.html (see Figure 4-1)
This blog from Bryant Library in Roslyn, New York, includes photos from teen programs, descriptions of upcoming events, and book reviews. In addition, the librarian adds reflections on events in her life, stories in the news, funny Web sites she's discovered, and other items that give this blog a more personal slant.

Coshocton Public Library
Available at: http://yablog.coshoctonpl.org/teens/default.aspx (see Figure 4-2)
This outstanding blog for Coshocton Public Library in Coshocton, Ohio, includes book reviews, author birthdays, programs and events for teens, news about the Teen Advisory Board's activities, contest winners, Web sites of interest, and more.

Framingham Public Library Teen Blog
Available at: http://fplya.blogspot.com/ (see Figure 4-3)
This blog for the Framingham Public Library in Framingham, Massachusetts, announces library events for teens, book reviews, useful Web sites, new magazine subscriptions, and general commentary from the young adult librarian.

The Reading Room: NMH Library Blog
Available at: http://nmhlibrary.typepad.com (see Figure 4-4)
This blog from Northfield Mount Hermon School in Northfield, Massachusetts, includes photos of students, announcements of events, blurbs on the history of the school, reviews of new books and videos, database trials, and more.

Whippany Park High School—Library News
Available at: http://whippanylibrarynews.blogspot.com (see Figure 4-5)
This school library blog from Whippany Park High School in Whippany, New Jersey, reports on school events, news, and contests. It also offers items on new databases and Web sites that might be of interest to students and teachers.

Thursday, May 25, 2006

Da Vinci Code Read-Alikes
If you loved *The Da Vinci Code*, you might like these titles:

Baldacci, David. *Absolute Power*
Berry, Steve. *The Templar Legacy*
Crichton, Michael. *Jurassic Park*
Cussler, Clive. *Treasure*
DeMille, Nelson. *The Charm School*
Finder, Joseph. *Paranoia*
Khoury, Raymond. *The Last Templar*
Mosse, Kate. *Labyrinth*
Preston, Douglas and Child, Lincoln. *Riptide*
Reilly, Matthew. *Seven Deadly Wonders*
Rollins James. *Map of Bones*

from Booklist May 1, 2006
9:02 AM |

No Sew T-Shirts
Click here for couple of fun t-shirts you can make without sewing!

T-shirt do-it-yourself guru Megan Nicolay shows you how to turn ordinary T-shirts into bold fashion statements.

Check out her book and try the 106 more ideas!
Generation T : 108 Ways to Transform a T-Shirt by Megan Nicolay

8:34 AM |

Thursday, May 18, 2006

New Slide Show

Our techie found a neat new program for showing photos.... check out the Teen Program Photos!

Thanks, Kevin!

11:16 AM |

Wednesday, May 17, 2006

YAToday Online

YAToday, Library News for Teens is now available online! Click here for the Summer Edition.

4:50 PM |

Tuesday, May 16, 2006

New Book Lists by Email

You can sign up to receive emails of the new fiction and nonfiction books in the YA room.

Go to Newsletter Sign Up and choose the lists you want to receive.

Links to the catalog for each title in the lists makes it easy to place holds on the titles.

10:53 AM |

Monday, May 15, 2006

Creature Feature Summer Reading Events for Teens

Check out the CPL teen page for all the events just for teens this summer. Sign up now and mark your calendars!

10:47 AM |

Search

Go

Archives
Show postings from:
This Month
Last Month
Two Months Ago

Links
Back to the CPL Teen Page
Back to See YA Around
Online Registration for teen Events
Teen Advisory Board
YAToday Newsletter
Teen Program Photos

Figure 4-2   Coshocton Public Library's Teen News Blog

I would love to know when this blog is used in a presentation. Please inform me!

You have entered the Framingham Public Library Young Adult Blog! - the place for reading tips, book chats, library events, groovy websites, news, and more - all put together by your friendly neighborhood YA librarian!

defining "blog"

archives

good book box - recommend a good book!

talk to me!

bookends

Link It!

fpl teen page
minlib teen links
framingham hs
walsh ms
fuller ms
cameron ms
charter school
biblionix

webcomics
teenreads
teen lit
teen ink
teen central
teen angst books
spark notes
snopes urban legends
schoolwork - ugh!

Tuesday, May 23, 2006

STOREWARS
Have you ever wondered what the cast of Star Wars would be like if they all became produce -- Tofu D2, Chewbacca...? A short flick featuring organic foods is today's web pick. StoreWars.

The library will be closed this weekend for the Memorial Day holiday -- Sat, Sun, & Mon!
~emily - 9:31 AM~
0 comments

Monday, May 22, 2006

IT'S A BIRTHDAY
I've always been a fan of detectives, mystery stories and such. So with wonder I discovered that today is **Sir Arthur Conan Doyle's birthday!** -- the author of all those wonderful Sherlock Holmes stories. To get the lowdown on Doyle and how to celebrate a birthday such as his, check these Google listings. For books he's written that you can find at the library, click here. I think I'll have to dash home and read one of those "short" mysteries I have. Woohoo! I love birthdays!
~emily - 3:21 PM~
0 comments

Friday, May 19, 2006

BOOKENDS
So one of the things I did while I was away in Brazil was read summer reading books -- two of the titles below are from the Framingham Middle Schools list. The other was my own pleasure reading. See if you can guess which is which....

California Blue by David Klass
John has always felt out of place in his family of stubborn and tough football players, auto mechanics, and loggers -- he's a runner and a student, excelling particularly in science. When John discovers a new butterfly while running in the forest, he finds that his interest for science threatens not only the community in which he lives, but also the tenuous relationship he has with his family -- particularly his father, who has just been diagnosed with leukemia.
A different kind of sports story, a different kind of family story, a different kind of science story. Klass is able to blend all three aspects of this book into an interesting plot that hashes friends, family, and community members against themselves, each other, and other communities. It's a short book, but well done -- it made me want to study butterflies again and look into environmental protection groups!
YPB K

Figure 4-3   Framingham Public Library's Teen Blogmatic

the NMH Library

Reading Room

"I can hear the library humming in the night ..." - Billy Collins, from his poem, "Books"

Library Links

.Citing Sources

.Find Books, CDs, Films in the Library Catalog

.Find Encyclopedias & Dictionaries

.Find Magazine & Newspaper Articles

Course Research Guides

InterLibrary Loan

Library Hours

Official NMH Library Webpage

Teachers! Schedule a research instructional session for your students

Our Workjob Crew 05-06

 We work at the Library's circulation desk, in the Media Center, in the Information Commons and in the Archives. Click on our pics to find out more about us...

Hoggers Visit the Library

 On a recent day, we followed a group of Hoggers as they utilized the NMH Library for research, leisure reading, relaxation and study...

Library Lounge Lizard of the Week

Asheley Storrow '07

"Be cool, and stay in school."

May 22, 2006 in **Lounge Lizard Archives** | **Permalink** | Comments (0) | TrackBack (0)

Read Me

Comments on Comments

Email Me

Categories

Acoustic Fridays

Bookmark of the Month

Breaking News

Free trial!

Lounge Lizard Archives

New Films + Music

New & Recommended Books

Poetry Contest

Smarter Searching: Tips!

Special Events @ NMH

Staff Website Picks

This Week in NMH History

Recent Posts

Library Lounge Lizard of the Week

Be Afraid

Library Lounge Lizard of the Week

NEW Thicker Than Oil: America's Uneasy Partnership with Saudi Arabia

NEW Let Me Play: The Story of Title IX

NEW Women's Letters:

Figure 4-4   Northfield Mount Herman School Library's Reading Room Blog

---

Interview

Gretchen S. Ipock
YA Librarian, Sellers Library
Upper Darby, PA
Available at: http://sellerslibraryteens.blogspot.com

Why Did You Decide to Start a Blog?

Our library Web site is not a great source of information for our community. In trying to think of a way to have a Web presence for teen programs and issues, I thought about blogging. At the time, blogging was getting a lot of attention because of the 2004 Presidential race.

WHIPPANY PARK HIGH SCHOOL
165 Whippany Road, Whippany, NJ 07981   973.887.3004 Phone   973.887.0451 Fax

Home | General | Academics | Athletics | Guidance | Health Office | Performing Arts | Library | District

▷ Article Databases
▷ Periodical Holdings
▷ Library Catalogs
▷ Recommended Reads
▷ Other Libraries
▷ Local & World News
▷ Teacher Resources
▷ Library News
▷ Works Cited Tips
▷ Tech Tips
▷ Ask a Librarian
▷ Why Libraries?

Home of the
WILDCATS

Whippany Park Library News
Contact Ms. Kowalsky if you have additional news or ideas for this page.

Friday, April 28, 2006

Essay Contest - Social Impact of Computing

The Schubmehl-Prein Prize for best analysis of the social impact of a particular aspect of computing technology will be awarded to a student who is a high school junior in academic year 2005-2006. The first-place award is $1,000, the second-place award is $500, and the third-place award is $250. Also, last year's winning entries were published in the Association for Computing Machinery's Computers and Society online magazine, which can be found at:
http://www.computersandsociety.org/sigcas_ofthefuture2/sigcas/index.cfm

Topic for the 2006 Competition. The topic for the 2006 competition is: Is the Computing Technology for Electronic Voting Secure and Reliable Enough for National Use?

Eligibility. Students who are in their junior year of high school in the 2005-2006 academic year and in the top one-fifth of their class are eligible to enter. A letter from the school principal or corresponding administrator certifying the junior standing and academic rank should be submitted with the essay.

Entry Guidelines. An essay should be organized as a title page, main body, and list of references. The maximum length of length of the main body of an essay should be limited to 2,500 words in length. A figure or table taking one page should be counted as 250 words. The essay must be the original work the entrant. All sources and quotations must be appropriately documented. The language for the competition is English.

Judging. The essays will be judged for accuracy of technical concepts, quality and clarity of expression, logic of argument, originality of ideas, and conformance to the entry guidelines. The decision of the judges is final.

Timeline. Essays should be submitted by midnight, Eastern Standard Time, 31 May 2006. More information is available at http://www.cse.nd.edu/EssayContest/

Thursday, April 13, 2006

Win a Trip to the Baseball Hall of Fame

Step Up to the Plate @ Your Library -- Step Up to the Plate @ Your Library encourages people of all ages to visit their library and use its resources to look up the answers to a series of baseball trivia questions designed for their age group (10 and under, 11-13, 14-17 and 18 and over). Through answering the questions, people can improve their literacy skills, which today include not only reading but also how find, use and evaluate sources of information in various formats.

One grand-prize winner will win a trip to the Hall of Fame's World Series Game One Gala event in Cooperstown, N.Y., in October, and a behind-the-scenes tour of the Museum. The grand prize also includes an Ozzie Smith autographed baseball.

Twenty first-place prize packages also will be awarded, including a commemorative hardbound copy of the Hall of Fame Yearbook, Hall of Fame t-shirt, commemorative set of 20 Hall of Fame baseball card and more.

Download the questions and entry forms at: http://www.ala.org/baseball.

Figure 4-5   Whippany Park High School's Library News Blog

sellers library teens

WELCOME TO OUR GROUP BLOG BY THE TEENS AND LIBRARIANS AT SELLERS LIBRARY (76 S. STATE RD. IN UPPER DARBY, 610-789-4440). WE BLOG ABOUT ANYTHING RELATED TO OUR LIBRARY: EVENTS, IDEAS FOR FUTURE EVENTS, MATERIALS WE HAVE, MATERIALS WE THINK WE SHOULD HAVE, OR WHATEVER. PLEASE READ AND COMMENT ON THE POSTS OF OTHERS. ALSO, EMAIL GRETCHEN AT GRRLLIBRARIAN@YAHOO.COM IF YOU WOULD LIKE TO BE A CONTRIBUTOR. GET YOUR VOICE HEARD AT THE LIBRARY!

5.25.2006

Unshelved + Gregor

Last Sunday's Unshelved book club cartoon featured Gregor the Overlander as its subject. This is a great underground adventure story that reminds me of *The City of Ember*. Plus, it features giant rats, spiders, and cockroaches! You can find it in our J section at the library.

// posted by Gretchen @ 2:20 PM 0 comments

5.24.2006

Girl Pirates Are Cool!

Look what I noticed in *Publisher's Weekly* this week...

"Atypical Entertainment and ASR Productions have optioned the film rights to L.A. Meyer's novel *Bloody Jack* (Harcourt, 2002). AnnaSophia Robb (from *Because of Winn-Dixie* and *Charlie and the Chocolate Factory*) is attached to play the title role of Jacky Faber."

How cool is that!?

// posted by Gretchen @ 7:03 PM 0 comments

5.23.2006

Teen Nonfiction Craziness

I saw today that the teen nonfiction section has grown beyond one shelf! That's amazing because the section isn't even a year old yet. Here are the newest titles:

- **Gunstories: Life-Changing Experiences with Guns** by S. Beth Atkin
- **Mirrormask** by Neil Gaiman and Dave McKean
- **Where We Are, What We See: Poems, Stories, Essays, and Art from the Best Young Writers and Artists in America** by David Levithan
- **Fortune's Bones: The Manumission Requiem** by Marilyn Nelson
- **Big Book Unplugged: A Young Person's Guide to Alcoholics Anonymous** by John R.
- **Open the Unusual Door: True Life Stories of Challenge, Adventure, and Success by Black Americans** by Barbara Summer
- **A Teen's Guide to Living Drug Free** by Bettie B. Youngs, Jennifer Leigh Youngs, and Tina Moreno

These books cover everything from art to self-help, from history to guns. Teen nonfic has something for everyone!

// posted by Gretchen @ 4:45 PM 0 comments

contributors

Gretchen
Freya
WhiteMystik
Megan G.
Purple Lover
Kara
katie
viOleta*
marissa

links

Local

Sellers Library
Delaware County Library System Homepage
Upper Darby School District Homepage

Online Reference Help

Ask An Expert
Black History from the Encyclopaedia Britannica
Internet Public Library Teen Space
Librarians' Index to the Internet
Library Spot
Spark Notes
Teens Health

What to Read???

Best Books for Young Adults
FlamingNet Teen Book Reviews
Guys Read
No Flying No Tights (Graphic Novels)
Reading Rants!
SimonSays Teen
Teen Genreflecting
Teens @ Random
Teenreads
Teens' Top Ten

Authors

YA Authors Cafe (live chat with authors on Tuesdays)
Laurie Halse Anderson
Clive Barker
Holly Black
Meg Cabot
Rachel Cohn
Kate Constable

Figure 4-6 Sellers Library Teen Blog

This is how it happened: I was talking about starting a blog with the children's librarian before a preschool storytime. During her 45-minute storytime, I found Blogger (http://blogger.com), set up a blog, and put up a few posts! Then we went to our wonderful, flexible library director and said, "Can we keep it?"

How Long Have You Been Blogging?

I started my blog in June of 2004, a few months after I started working at our library. It began as a summer experiment, but we decided to keep it going because the teens really liked it.

How Do You Promote It to Teens?

I basically harass them with flyers at every event. Teens need to be reminded of stuff often! I also post pictures from events on the blog, so they can go there and view them afterwards. We do not identify teens in photographs by name. (Side note: we started adding photos without permission forms, but are now moving toward that.) Finally, when I do school visits, I show the blog as a part of my presentation. Some libraries print up pencils, keychains, or other small items with their blog address to pass out to patrons. We don't have a huge budget, and the flyers seem to work fine for us so far.

What Kind of Comments or Reaction Have You Gotten from Teens?

They seem to like having the blog as a place to read or talk about the library, books, or other news. Even if they don't post or comment, they mention things to me that they could have only found out from the blog. So I know they are reading it! Incidentally, I decided not to put a counter on the blog. Counters are notoriously inaccurate measures of Web site traffic. Some people really like them, but I prefer to rely on commentary from the teens to find out how the blog is working.

Why Do You Think a Blog Is a Good Way to Reach Teens?

They are all totally addicted to the Internet, so it is a good place to connect with them. Since new items appear at the top of the blog, there is always something to grab teens' attention as soon as they load the page. Also, the immediacy of it is great for me. I can update it from any computer, any time, and with a minimum of fuss. Currently, our library Web site has to be copied to a disk and sent to the county office to be updated to the Web site. It is not worth putting time-sensitive information on the teen portion of the Web site. The blog is a much better way to appeal to teens' last-minute timing!

What Kinds of Information Do You Post?

I post anything and everything that I think will get our library teens' attention. Of course, most of my posts are related to the library and books. I routinely post lists of new books, book reviews, thematic book lists, Teen Advisory Board activities, event announcements and reminders, and photos of events. But I also post links to Web sites, my opinions about movies or pop culture stuff, quizzes, and other random musings.

The teens who contribute write about a variety of items. Recently, they have added posts about the PA teacher of the year (from our high school!), a school that fought censorship, the Lennon musical closing on Broadway, an uprising among YA book group members, and French class. They also comment on the posts of others.

How Often Do You Post to the Blog?

I try to post to the blog at least five times per week. Sometimes I do it every day. Other times, I let something sit at the top, hoping to develop some interest in it. It only takes ten or fifteen minutes a day to update the blog. When I have time, I might write several entries at once, but only post one. The others, like book reviews or Web sites, I save to post later. That way, I can use them on a day when I don't have much time to work on the blog.

Who Are the Teen Contributors?

The teen contributors are almost all members of my Teen Advisory Board. A few other "regulars" asked to join. On Blogger, the administrator (me) has to send contributors an electronic invitation. The teen contributors have privileges beyond those who just comment, but I am the only administrator.

How Did You Recruit Them?

I specifically asked the TAB members if they wanted to join. For a while, I had a flyer on the counter for people to fill out if they wanted to join the blog. I sent invitations to everyone who expressed an interest, and most of them were acted on.

Why Do You Think Teen Participation Is Important?

Our library is small for the size of the community that we serve. Our teen collection space is not much bigger than a closet. Seriously. I feel that it is important for the teens to have something that is "theirs," and it certainly isn't going to be a real space any time soon. So this virtual space can help bring them together and give them a way to express themselves that they wouldn't have otherwise. If the blog were just about me talking at them, it would get old really fast.

How Do You Encourage Them to Contribute to the Blog?

I give them blog flyers at almost every event we do. I figure if they find it in a pocket later, maybe they'll actually visit the blog and make a comment or two. Also, any time a teen wants to rant and rave about something, I ask them to post it on the blog! I put the blog in my conversation a lot, as well. I say things like, "Did you see the list of new books on the blog?" or "What do you think about what Kayla said on the blog? Oh, you didn't see it? Why don't you read it now!" Sometimes I post info on the blog and tell teens they have to read it if they want to know what I am talking about. I also periodically devote part of a Teen Advisory Board meeting to the blog. Finally, I am in the process of planning a teen program centered on blogging.

Do You Find Blogger Easy to Use? Would You Suggest It to Others?

I like Blogger, and find it very user-friendly. They have excellent help files. Also, there are recent books specifically geared to Blogger users. I would recommend it, with one caveat. That is, you should use the blogging site that the teens in your community are using. That way, it's one fewer username/password combination they have to remember and it's more convenient for them. In my community, I started the blog before the teens really got into blogging. Even now, there is not one site that everyone uses. I have teens who use MySpace, LiveJournal, Xanga, and Blogger. So that's a bit of a drawback. Each site has its own unique functionality, which is another consideration.

Do You Allow Comments, and Have You Had Any Problems with Inappropriate Comments or Posts?

I do allow comments, and the number is increasing. I have never had a problem with inappropriate posts from anyone, library teen or not. I do, as the blog administrator, get an e-mail every time someone comments on a post. I always check them out, just to be sure! Blog administrators can set up the comment section in several ways. Ours is at a medium level of security, where you must have a Blogger ID, but you don't necessarily have to be a library teen to comment on our blog. I could limit comments to only Sellers Library Teen contributors or leave it open to anyone, even if they weren't a Blogger member. Some blogging sites, like LiveJournal, offer you the opportunity to make your blog completely closed to anyone but those you consider "friends."

The only problem I have had with Blogger is two episodes of comment spam, where a spammer leaves a bizarre comment and a link to a commercial Web site. In both cases, I went back to the post in question and hid the comment section so these posts wouldn't be viewable. I have since activated Blogger's new verification process to eliminate comment spam.

What Advice Would You Give to Other Teen Librarians Who Want to Start Blogging?

I would say, "Go for it!" It might take a while to develop a readership, but it is a great way to keep in touch with teens. Library Web sites are usually somewhat formal, with static lists of books, events, and links. Library Weblogs are a much more dynamic and interactive environment. Teens thrive on what's new and novel, and the flexibility of the blog format is very appealing.

One other word of advice for library bloggers is this: keep it professional. The focus of the blog is about the library, even if it does cover topics other than library books and programs. A post now and then about pop culture, a contest or quiz, a topical list of links, or a teen-oriented news article are all appropriate for a library teen blog. It keeps them interested and may spark discussion that a list of new books would not. A lot of personal commentary about your life and interests is not really appropriate, unless it relates directly to them. For example, if you presenting a teen library program at a conference, it makes sense to post that. If you want to rant and rave about the state of politics in America, you should probably start another blog!

Interview

Jessy Griffith
Young Adult Librarian
Alexandrian Public Library
Mount Vernon, IN
Available at: www.apl.lib.in.us/yablog.html

Why Did You Decide to Start a Blog?

The reference department has one, and I wanted an online space for new materials and events.

How Do You Promote It to Teens?

I made 1/4 sheet flyers that I give out at every class visit and put in a lot of the new books. This past summer, there was a trivia contest and all the questions were on the blog. I'm working on having the URL on our calendar, as well.

Have You Had Any Comments or Reaction from Teens? Do You Think It's a Good Way to Reach Them?

I seem to get a lot of hits from all over, but I'm not really sure how many of my kids use the blog. I do think it's good to be a part of the online teen reader community, however, no matter where those teens live.

What Kinds of Things Do You Post?

I put all the new fiction, the non-homeworky nonfiction, some of the new DVDs and CDs, complete with publisher's info, a picture of the cover, and, if I can find it easily, a link to the author's Web site. I also post any programs we're having, and add a link on the right side of the page to that event's posting.

How Often Do You Post to the Blog?

Whenever I get new stuff or have an event to talk about. Due to the way I order and we process materials, this can be as many as twenty in one day, or as little as once a month.

Do You Find Blogger Easy to Use? Would You Suggest It to Others?

I really like Blogger, and it seems to be getting easier and easier with every new thing they add.

Do You Allow Comments, and Have You Had Any Problems with Inappropriate Comments?

No inappropriate comments yet (knock wood). There have been a couple that give away books' endings, but I just edited the post and added a spoiler warning.

What Advice Would You Give to Other Teen Librarians Who Want to Start Blogging?

Decide before you start what you want to do with it, but leave room to wing it as well.

Interview

Vicki Builta
Library Media Specialist
Anderson High School, Anderson, Indiana
Available at: www.esmslibrary.com/blog/

When Did You Start the Blog?

The blog was added to the East Side Middle School Web site in the fall of 2005.

Why Did You Start It?

The purpose of the blog is to promote discussion and interaction about reading material. Primarily, we are seeking student book reviews in order to have a better understanding of the types of books that our students choose to read (not just those assigned to meet classroom requirements). Also, we wanted to encourage students to share their favorite books with others.

What Kind of information Do You Post to the Blog?

The blog is mainly student and staff book reviews. Additional information is posted about the various reading groups that we have at our school (Sci-Fi Fans, Sleuth, Got Books?, East Side Reads) and about other events that are sponsored by the library, especially our Library@Lunch program. Other library news is included as well.

How Did You Decide Whether or Not to Allow Comments or Posting Directly from Students?

Having worked with middle school students for a few years, I feel that I know their foibles well. I decided that all postings must be sent through my e-mail first, before they are posted to the blog. Not all sixth, seventh and eighth graders are mature enough to handle free expression in an open forum. I want to avoid unneeded distractions from the focus of the blog and also to avoid the possibility of interaction that is not positive or constructive.

How Many E-mails Do You Get with Reviews, Etc. for the Blog?

When I remind my various book groups about the blog, they remember to send me information. They may just tell me about the book and tell me that I can post it to the blog, too. If the students have just read a book that they found to be totally awesome, they will pass on their reviews. A fair amount of the time, I have to give students gentle reminders about the existence of the blog because it is a new feature of our Web site.

How Did You Publicize the Blog?

Announcements were made at school daily when the blog first went on line. E-mails were sent to English faculty members so that they could post to the blog and mention it to students. Mini-posters were posted throughout the school. Student and staff newsletters are published each month; information about the blog is included there as well.

Have You Had Any Feedback on It from Students, Teachers, or Others?

Students have been forthcoming with positive comments about the blog. They think it is "cool" that our library site has this feature. Staff, too, have mentioned that they think it is a good idea.

What Advice Would You Give to Other Librarians, Especially School Librarians, Who Want to Add a Blog to Their Web Site?

Students (at least at my middle school) seem to think that this is a pretty good thing for a school library Web site to have. To do it right, this is something that you should plan to devote a fair amount of time to. To get a blog started, time must be spent in promoting it heavily. Since I am also reading all of the entries for the blog before they are posted, some time is involved with that.

teens @ apl

wednesday, may 24, 2006

DragonBall Z 26

by Akira Toriyama:
Goodbye, Dragon World
The world's greatest heroes have fallen, absorbed by the ever more powerful Boo, who has slaughtered everyone on the planet. Only Goku remains alive to fight...but even his strength will not be enough, unless he uses the Fusion Earrings to permanently merge with another warrior! Who will he choose...and when the dust has cleared, who or what will he become? On earth, among the stars, and in Boo's body, the last battle rages!
The final volume of Akira Toriyama's martial arts masterpiece Dragon Ball Z!

posted by apl young adult department at 6:39 pm | 0 comments

Rurouni Kenshin 27

by Nobuhiro Watsuki:
Kenshin and his comrades have finally discovered the location of Enishi's island compound, but to free Kaoru from captivity, a good deal of fighting will be necessary. Woo Heishin, Enishi's mysterious second-in-command, meets them on the beach and brings his deadly bodyguards, the Su-shin or the "Four Stars," to serve as a welcoming committee. Yahiko, Sanosuke, Saitô and Aoshi dive into combat with Woo Heishin's warriors as Kenshin prepares himself for his fateful, climactic duel with Enishi. Each of them a ferocious fighter, the Su-shin are set on stopping Kenshin's friends dead in their tracks.

posted by apl young adult department at 6:38 pm | 0 comments

yell at a librarian
IM a Librarian!

be the library's friend
APL's MySpace Page

teens @ apl events
Make Stuff @ Your Library!
Anime Club!
Board Game Night

www.flickr.com

what is this?

links
APL's Main Homepage
Free Comic Book Day
Guys Read Website
Reading Rants!
Smooch Books
Teen Reads--reviews, author info, and new books
Teen Ink: Written By Teens
Other Writing Links
N2Arts--exclusively for teen artists
No Name-Calling Week
No Flying, No Tights--tons of comics info, all in one handy place

funniest. lines. ever.
"In other words, if Pamela Brown remembers anything about me, it's that I drink girl soda."
--Jack Grammar, *24 Girls in 7 Days* by Alex Bradley

"That is all. Fly to your perches, my little magpies of learning."
--Mr. Pewsey, principal, *Kissing Vanessa* by Simon Cheshire

"*Art*--Read the article on Van Gogh. Sketch something interesting you find in your room. There's that piece of pizza that fell behind my dresser last month."
--Scott Hudson, *Sleeping Freshmen Never Lie* by David Lubar

previous posts
DragonBall Z 26
Rurouni Kenshin 27
School's Out--Forever (Maximum Ride 2)
King Dork
Ultimate Spider-Man 15: Silver Sable
Lulu Dark and the Summer of the Fox
LBD: Friends Forever
Things You Either Hate Or Love

Figure 4-7 Alexandrian Public Library's Teens @ apl Blog

East Side Middle School Library

Choose a different page: ▾

This new feature gives our students and staff a forum for book discussion, book reviews, and other comments relating to the library. Tell us what you've read and enjoyed lately!

Students and teachers, send your blog entries to Mrs. Builta at **vicki@esmslibrary.com** with the subject heading "Blog entry."

Saturday, January 28

Builta's Best

Everyone knows that Mrs. Builta loves to read and talk about books. So in this column (hopefully updated often), she will tell you about some of her favorites.

Red Kayak by Priscilla Cummings is a book with so many components....adventure, heroics, suspense and loyalty...that it compells you to keep reading it and enjoying it all the way to its powerful conclusion. How close are you to your friends? Do you really know what they are like? How much do you trust them and vice versa?

Defiance by Valerie Hobbs features a boy named Toby. He is on vacation with his mother (while his dad continues to work in the city) and wants to do fun,exciting things that can help him escape the reality of his life as a cancer patient. He meets Pearl, a 94 year old poet, and her special cow, Blossom, and begins to learn about true courage.

Flush by Carl Hiaasen finds Noah visiting his father, in jail for trying to sink a gambling boat near the family's home in Florida. Noah's father is certain that the owner of the boat is flushing the boat's toilets directly into the water instead of having the contents hauled to a sewage treatment plant. There is no immediate proof against the owner. Noah and his sister Abbey vow to prove that their father is right. Many dangerous adventures and family surprises develop in this exciting book by the author of *Hoot*.

The Penderwicks was recently awarded the National Book Award for young adults. It is a great story about a family of four daughters , who, along with their father, take a very special vacation one summer. They meet incredible people and become ever closer as they each deal with the death of the girls' mother. The book is the first written by its author, Jeanne Birdsall.

Links

◈ ESMSLibrary.com
◈ Pathfinders
◈ Library Blog
◈ Library Information Center

Previous Posts

◈ Builta's Best
◈ And Here Is What They Have to Say....
◈ Builta Bunch
◈ What's New
◈ Library@Lunch

Weekly Archives

◈ December 11, 2005
◈ December 18, 2005
◈ January 22, 2006

Figure 4-8   East Side Middle School Library's Blog

Interview

Patrick Delaney
Librarian
Galileo Academy of Science and Technology, San Francisco, California
Available at: www.galileoweb.org/galileoLibrary/

Why Did You Decide to Adopt a Blog Format for Your Library Web Site and for Your School?

Well, it's a bit more than a blog format. What we have is a content management system with a Weblog face, giving the domain manager the ability to create multiple, thematically similar and universally navigated Weblogs. So in some ways, a Galileo "blog" is just a very easy to use Web site that can be edited by more than one person from any computer with Internet access, both inside and outside the school's intranet [internal network], and linked within the community's universal navigation system.

Advanced users have the ability to dive into an aggregation of RSS feeds, page-within-page insertions, commenting and discussing, podcasting and vidcasting. Not many of the teachers do that kind of thing yet.

Our aim was pretty simple. We wanted to use the Web for five purposes:

To provide school information and news to groups within our community;
To guide community members to resources;
To provide online work spaces for students' works-in-progress;
To publish exemplary teacher and student work;
To explore and evaluate new technologies for teaching and learning.

A school's best resource for achieving those purposes is its human population: teachers, administrators, support staff, students, parents, and community members. A Weblog-based content management system has the potential to let all those stakeholders become an online community. The library was a natural place, real and virtual, from which to start that effort. Folks came into the library for research lessons and projects and I used a Weblog to demo how easy Weblogging is. A few early adopters jumped right in. They brought a few others along. The administration noticed the value of the public relations aspect to what we were doing. By the third year, all teachers were required to have a Weblog within the community.

How Long Has the Li-Blog-ary Been Around?

My first "liblogary" blog was started in 2000 at Dr. Martin Luther King Academic M.S. That work was sponsored by UC Berkeley's Bay Area Writing Project, where I work as a part-time Associate Director for Technology. I took the concept and hosting set-up with me when I moved to Galileo Academy of Science and Technology in August 2003.

How Do You Arrange and Link the School Blogs? Who Contributes to Them?

galileoWeb.org is a community of thematically and hierarchically linked Weblogs (easily updated Web sites) initiated and supported by our 'Li-Blog-ary', and maintained by our teachers, staff and students. By using the "drop down" navigation bar at the top of pages within the community, you can click through sites representing student clubs, parent organizations and services, individual teachers, curricular departments, and our rich library of online research tools. Each site has its own editorial managers. There is no bottleneck to posting, no waiting for the "webmaster" to get around to posting important or timely content. There is an agreed-upon etiquette, of course. All student-edited blogs are viewed regularly for appropriateness of content. Some teacher-edited blogs for groups of students are run behind password protection.

How Does Using Blogs Help Make the Library Central to the School Community?

First, the library's online research links are available from the universal navigation on all pages of all Weblogs within the community. That drop-down menu item labeled "Research" includes links to databases purchased by Galileo and San Francisco Unified School District, San Francisco Public Library databases, and other useful links.

Second, the library is the place to go to learn how to make maximum use of the content-management system for teaching. The tech department keeps the hardware and network running. If a teacher wants to know how to use the Web, they come to the librarian. Gradually, this makes the library office a sort of den of digital wannabes. Folks hang out and talk to each other and share tips and tools and lessons.

In the best of all possible worlds, that sharing will slowly move out and into department meetings and other collaborative groupings. It's already got quite a few teachers here using Instant Messenger efficiently during and after the work day.

Third, teachers are encouraged to use the CMS [content management system] Weblogs to request materials and then to visit the librarian to negotiate budget allocations for print and non-print resources in the context of what is already digitally available.

What Kinds of Reactions Have You Had from Students, Staff, and Parents?

There are early-adopter teachers who love it. Those are the ones keeping up multiple Weblogs, some for student postings, with Bloglines and Net-NewsWire used to aggregate feeds. They are very, very few, even after three years. For others, the gradual deployment allowed them some time to get ready for something new. In the third year, the principal required Weblogs of all teachers but then made sure to provide staff development time (about two hours) for workshops.

Students get the idea of it for clubs but there is no concerted effort to train student coaches yet, so the pickup in that area has been a bit low. For example, there simply has not been time to get the newspaper working with the content management system, an obvious possibility for school Weblogging, if there ever was one.

Parents, especially our incoming parents from middle school, seem to appreciate the handy information sharing. We have about 125 individual Weblogs now, but the range of use and quality of content varies.

What Are Some of the Challenges You've Faced in Implementing This Project?

The biggest problem is hosting . . . [T]he fact is that we have got to find a way of getting this kind of powerful, flexible, and affordable web-based content management system hosted locally. Most school districts' IT [Information Technology] departments are not focused on providing tools for use in libraries and classrooms. There are reasons for that disconnect. I really am not sure about the future. There has to be a way to start a conversation about solving this major problem. It should include schools, IT departments within districts, and the wider community of education-focused groups in our area, including public libraries, county offices of education, non-profits and education advocacy groups.

What Are Some of the Ways Librarians Can Get the School Community Involved and Excited about This Kind of Project?

Start a blog. Use it in the library to teach research and promote the print collection. Target the tech-friendly teachers and seduce them with a Web-based project that they want but that the librarian puts together.

Do You Review Student Contributions or Discussions before They Are Posted? Have You Had Any Problems with Inappropriate Posts?

No problems yet with inappropriate postings on our sites. Almost all of our student work is behind password protection and focused on particular curricular aims. We don't have the capacity to give every student a Weblog. If we did, that would change things quite a bit. My focus has been getting teachers investing in a digital presence. The students are, in general, light years ahead of the staff.

Would You Recommend That Other School Librarians Give This a Try? What Advice Would You Give Them as They Get Started?

Sure. There's a learning curve; but, fact is, this digital paper is here to stay. Might as well start to climb the curve as soon as you can. Take it at your own pace. Start with a simple "new books in the library" blog. I've done workshops for several groups of librarians. I haven't seen much pickup from any of those, but certainly the number of blogging libraries and librarians is growing enormously. It might be worthwhile to look at doing something like this within a limited organizational or geographical area.

IDEA #26: OFFER FEEDS TO KEEP TEENS CURRENT

For more on feeds, and how to set them up, see Chapter 3

If you have a blog on your teen library Web site, adding an RSS feed is the next step. This will allow teens to "subscribe" to your blog—or your podcast, or your video program—or to be alerted to new teen items in your catalog.

Hennepin County Library in Minnesota offers an RSS feed for their "News Flash" blog on their main page at www.hclib.org/teens. Note the green and blue icon next to the words "News Flash!", which alerts users that they can sign up.

Edmonton Public Library in Edmonton, Canada, offers a feed for their new teen titles, as well as for general library events and for job postings, at www.epl.ca.

West Branch Public Library in West Branch, Michigan, offers a feed that allows users to subscribe to reviews of featured teen books. Their site is at www.westbranchlibrary.com/teen.htm.

IDEA #27: USE E-MAIL TO KEEP IN TOUCH

While blogs and feeds are new and exciting, plain old e-mail may sometimes be the best way to reach your audience. It's simple, it's delivered to their in-boxes, and most likely the teens at your library already know how to use it. They may consider it old-fashioned, and prefer instant messaging, but a 2001 Pew study of teens found that 92 percent do use it.

You can create an e-mail distribution list in Microsoft Outlook or another e-mail program to contact the teens you work with. You may want to use the "Bcc" (Blind Carbon Copy) field so that recipients can't see the names and e-mail addresses of everyone on the list, to protect privacy.

You can also have teens sign up for your e-mail list through a form on your Web site, or simply post an e-mail address where teens can write to subscribe to regular mailings. This may be the easiest option, especially if you expect to have just a handful of subscribers. However, you will probably have to manually add and remove addresses from your list. If someone on the list no longer wants to receive e-mail, or if they change their e-mail address, they will have to ask to be removed. For a large list, maintenance may become an issue.

For this reason, it may be easier to set up a discussion group or listserv, using a service such as Yahoo! Groups, Google Groups or Topica. A listserv is an online group that discusses a subject, usually a predefined topic, by e-mail. A message sent by one subscriber goes out to all of the subscribers. Users subscribe electronically, either on a Web site (such as Yahoo! Groups or Google Groups) or by sending an e-mail message to a computer running special software.

Listserv is another term for an e-mail discussion group. Popular lists for librarians include PUBYAC, YALSA-BK, and LM_NET. Many discussion groups also keep their archives on the Web so that they are searchable and can be read without an e-mail subscription. Again, many teens will probably consider this mode of delivering information rather outdated, so make sure it's something your audience will find relevant.

Listservs should not be confused with RSS feeds, though users "subscribe" to both. With RSS feeds, users usually set up a single Web page that displays links to newly posted articles, blog posts, and so on. Listserv users, on the other hand, send an e-mail to an automated request processor, sign up for a list, then get new posts to the list as individual e-mails (or as many e-mails compiled into one, if they subscribe in digest form). These new posts come directly to the subscriber's e-mail inbox.

Before setting up a group, be sure to find out whether teens in your community already use a particular service. If they already subscribe to several Yahoo! Groups, for example, Yahoo! might be the best one to use—teens won't have to set up another subscription or remember another login and password.

The drawback of the free, commercial services is that they include advertising. However, sites such as Topica do offer paid, ad-free versions. In addition, librarians with more technical skill may want to install a program such as Listserv or Majordomo on their own servers or ask their Webmasters to do it for them. Again, check with the teens you want to reach—they may consider e-mail-based listservs hopelessly old-fashioned, since users have to use particular commands—such as "digest" and "unsubscribe"—to communicate with the listserv software. Web-based programs, with graphics and Web forms for submitting information, are usually easier to use.

IDEA #28: PUBLISH A NEWSLETTER

If you want to start e-mailing library information to teens, the next thing to consider is what, exactly, you want to send them. What kinds of news bulletins will you create? What form should your mailings take?

An e-mail newsletter is simply an extension of an e-mail list or listserv. Many libraries do go a step further, however, by posting the newsletter on the Web as well. This way, subscribers can access it, but casual visitors to the library Web site read the newsletter too. A teen e-newsletter is also an excellent opportunity for teen participation. Teens can write and edit news items, contribute poetry or art, be in charge of updating the Web site, or submit their book reviews.

Denver Public Library's eVolver Report is a great example of the newsletter idea. The site offers an online form for signing up at http://lb.bcentral.com/ ex/manage/subscriberprefs.aspx?customerid=40766. The newsletter itself offers reviews, news, events, information on award-winning books, and more.

Denver Public Library
Available at: http://teens.denverlibrary.org/media/evolver_report.html
   (see Figure 4-9)

IDEA #29: SEND PROGRAM REMINDERS

As a teen librarian, I have too often had the experience of telling a teen about an upcoming event and getting an enthusiastic reaction. Then, to my disappointment, that teen would forget to come. Teenagers today have busy schedules, and aren't always terribly organized. (The same can be said of many adults, of course!)

This makes program reminders a great idea. Reminders could be as simple as asking for e-mail addresses when teens register in advance, then sending a brief e-mail to everyone the day before the event. Be sure to put teen e-mail addresses into the BCC—blind carbon copy—field if you don't want to share private e-mail addresses with everyone on your list.

An automated reminder system is even more easy and elegant. The truly impressive events calendar at Phoenix Public Library allows users to sign up online for e-mail reminders. Teens can decide whether they want to be notified about teen programs one week or one day in advance.

Phoenix Public Library
Available at: www.phoenixpubliclibrary.org/events.jsp (see Figure 4-10)

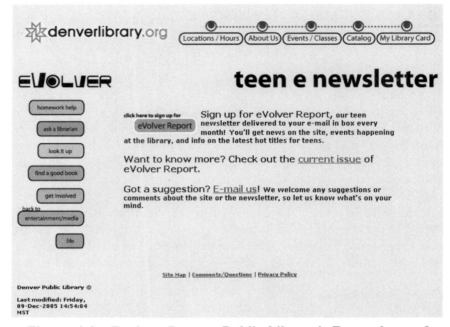

Figure 4-9   Evolver, Denver Public Library's E-newsletter for Teens

IDEA #30: ADOPT INSTANT MESSAGING

> For more on instant messaging, and how to get started, see Chapter 3

Instant messaging is so incredibly popular with teens that this may be one of the very best ways to reach your patrons. It's better for one-on-one communication than for mass distribution, so you might want to try it as a way to remind individual teens about programs, or to tell a teen that a new book has come in and you think he or she might like it, or to contact a member of your advisory council with a question.

First, you'll need to sign up for a service (or several), and download software. Once you're set up to send and receive instant messages, you'll want to start letting teens know how to contact you, and collecting instant messaging nicknames or e-mail addresses so that you can get in touch with them.

Figure 4-10   Phoenix Public Library's Event Calendar   111

IDEA #31: START TEXT MESSAGING

> For more on text messages and how to send them, see Chapter 3

Text messaging, or texting, is another great tool for reaching teenagers in your community or at your school. You can use it for the same types of communication you might use instant messaging for—program reminders, contacting your Teen Advisory Board members, answering simple reference questions, and so on. You don't have to use a phone to send text messages. Simply use instant messaging software to send text to their phones.

Before sending text messages, be sure to check to make sure your teens aren't charged by the individual message or, if they are, that they are willing to be contacted this way.

IDEA #32: LISTEN UP: AUDIO FILES

> For more on audio files, see Chapter 3

Audio files on your Web site could have many uses for "selling" the library and publicizing your services. You'll want to get creative here, and let your imagination loose as you come up with possibilities. Here are a few ideas to get you started:

- Record a "welcome message" that encourages teens to come in, use the library, and ask the librarian for help and advice. Describe your library's services, programs, and materials.
- Post a photo tour of your library, with an audio component. Teens can then see photos of the different parts of the library and hear the accompanying audio commentary on speakers or headphones. By the time teens physically enter the library, they will already have an orientation under their belts, and also perhaps know what the teen librarian looks and sounds like.
- Record audio versions of library programs for teens. For those who can't attend, listening to the audio might be a good substitute. For example, librarians could record a guest speaker or visiting author—with their permission, of course—and post the audio to the Web site. Audio files

are also a great way to capture teen talent, as with a poetry slam or battle of the bands. Participants will get a thrill out of having their voices or music on the Web, and those who missed the show will have a chance to listen in and perhaps be inspired to attend the next event.

While sound files aren't yet widely used on library Web sites, they are gaining popularity. For example, Salem Public Library, in Salem, Oregon, sometimes advertises their library concert series by providing MP3 samples of the music. By clicking on the name of the performer, users can listen to a sound clip.

Another great audio project is at the Johnson County Library in Johnson County, Kansas. The library offers their Battle of the Bands program through archived audio or as a podcast. To hear the 2005 performances, visit www .jocolibrary.org/?displaypageID=1897&textversion=false.

IDEA #33: BECOME A PODCASTER

> For more on podcasts, and how to set one up, see Chapter 3

With so many teens owning iPods and other MP3 players, it's no wonder podcasts have caught on. As librarians, we can start providing content that publicizes and promotes the library. Here are just a few ideas for what to include in podcasts:

- Recorded teen events, such as author visits, poetry readings, and more
- Information about the teen summer reading club
- Audio reviews of books, music, movies or Web sites for teens
- News about the library's teen advisory group or book discussion group
- Information about new library policies, libraries that are closing for renovation, or other library news
- New scholarship or college information
- New library databases of interest to teens
- Introduce new library staff members

While library podcasts for teens are just getting off the ground at most libraries, there are already several very exciting projects, from book reviews to news shows to audio recordings of programs and classes.

Interview

Sarah Kline Morgan
Youth Librarian
Cheshire Public Library, Cheshire, Connecticut

Cheshire Public Library offers an audio magazine for teens. On the site, it's described as "a teen-driven cultural magazine featuring teen writers, musicians, reviewers, commentators, and more." The magazine accepts "club news/local announcements, original creative writing, music, music/book/event reviews, and more" from local teens. To listen online, click on the "hear the current episode" link at www.cheshirelib.org/teens/cplpodcast.htm.

How Did You Get the Idea of Doing Library Podcasts?

I look at new technologies and ask myself: "Could we use this at the library?" I'm particularly interested in creating technology programs for kids and teens. In the past, I've done a web-browsing program for elementary kids and an e-book program for middle schoolers. I'm an avid radio fan, so podcasting grabbed my interest immediately. Cheshire boasts an active crowd of creative and tech-savvy teens looking for opportunities to share their talents, so a library podcast seemed like a good fit for the community.

Why Do You Think This Is a Good Way to Reach Teens?

New technology is always a draw for teens, but my initial recruitment drive wasn't particularly successful because podcasting was so new that it was unfamiliar. I got a lot of blank stares in the beginning. As word began to spread, however, I got an overwhelming response. Teens were curious about the technology.

Creative control is also big part of the draw, as is the knowledge that the show is available to a global audience. All our shows are produced, performed, and edited by teens, so the project fosters creative expression and the development of leadership and organizational skills. I guide the project and handle much of the logistic work, but the teens involved feel a real ownership of the final product.

What Factors Did You Consider while Developing the Idea? What Kind of Content Do the Podcasts Include?

I began my recruiting drive at Writer's Block, a club for teen writers at our local public high school. Those students continue to be our most reliable contributors. I also recruited members of the Teen Book Board (an advisory committee at the library) to provide book reviews and other commentary. Once a group of teens were committed to the project, we began to talk about expanding to include other content areas. Our focus evolved to include not only creative writing and book reviews, but music reviews, songs by local bands, announcements of local events, commentaries, and comic sketches. Podcasting technology is cutting edge, but our content is very much tied to the library's historic role as a place of books and culture. We describe ourselves as a "teen-driven cultural magazine."

The CPL Podcast works on a freelance model. Our contributors may appear once, more than once, or on every episode. For instance, we have a recurring segment featuring music reviews (The Love/Hate Musical Debate). We try to have a mix of recurring segments and new content.

The Podcast Editorial Team is involved with every episode; they meet monthly to talk about content, publicity, and recruitment. One student acts as the General Manager of the podcast; he's been around since the very beginning and has been involved in every aspect of the project.

How Have You Publicized the New Program?

The CPL Podcast got national publicity before we released our first show. I sent a press release to our local weekly newspaper, in hopes of attracting some new faces to the project, when, to my horror, the story was picked up by Google News and sent out on the "public library" news feed. This led to more stories—from *School Library Journal* online to our regional daily newspaper.

The early publicity was scary, since it put pressure on me to deliver the first episode as advertised. However, the early publicity was very exciting to the teens involved in Episode #1, and increased their enthusiasm for the project. They were motivated to start strong, since they knew they had an audience ready and waiting.

Once we delivered the first episode, our publicity targeted high school students, our primary audience. To reach this group, we advertise in the library, on the library Web site, at the school, and in the other places where teens congregate in town. A teen designed a logo for the podcast, to give us a brand identity; later, the same teen designed a poster for us in his graphic design class, which we plastered everywhere. He's also in charge of publicity at the high school, where he leaves chalk messages on classroom blackboards, reads announcements on the loudspeaker in the morning, and talks to teachers about promoting the project in their classes.

Our most successful promotion began when we released our first episode. Knowing that many people were still confused about what exactly we were doing, we burned 100 CD copies of Episode #1 and distributed them at the library and at the high school, with directions enclosed on how to subscribe to the feed online. This worked so well that we decided to continue offering CD versions of the show, for teens and other community members who have limited or no Internet access. Also, after Episode #1, we held a Podcast Open

House event at the library, where we had food, drinks, flyers, signups, and an Internet-connected computer set up to demonstrate the iTunes software and our recording procedures. This event was particularly successful in promoting the project to library staff and other adult community members.

Ongoing publicity is necessary to support our monthly release schedule. Measures of success include the number of subscribers, the number of downloads of each episode, and the "buzz" level in the teen community. The Editorial Board works with me to strategize new and better publicity.

What Special Equipment Do You Need? What Kind of Expenses Are Involved?

No special equipment is needed for a podcast project. We use an eMac loaded with GarageBand software, and record the podcasts on a microphone purchased for that purpose. The only hardware I purchased is the microphone, which cost $150. Our podcast is hosted at the Internet Archive, which is free. We use the free services at Blogger and Feedburner to create the RSS feed, and we list the podcast on the iTunes music store, which costs nothing.

Who Records the Podcasts? Who Does the Editing and Other Technical Work?

In addition to the Editorial Team, we have a Production Team that works on the technical end: recording, editing, and mixing the show.

Teens selected to appear on the podcast make appointments to record their segments, and I try to schedule a Production Team member to sit in to monitor the recording session. I'm rarely in the room. The night before the show is released, I meet with the Production Team and we work on integrating and editing the segments. The Production Team is also responsible for the music clips (created with GarageBand) that appear in the beginning and end of the show, and during transitions. I do the final editing and uploading myself.

What Kind of Feedback Have You Received about This Project?

I've received phenomenal feedback on the project, from teens, Cheshire residents, and members of the wider library community. The positive feedback really buoys the teens, and me, too, when we hit the inevitable snags in production. They like knowing that the podcast reaches a broad fan base.

What Advice Do You Have for Other Librarians Who Want to Start a Similar Project?

Podcasts are flexible. I would encourage aspiring podcasters to listen to youth radio as well as all kinds of podcasts, teen and not, to get a sense of what's possible in an audio environment. Our podcast is closest to a radio show, but other podcasts are more like journals, or sketches, or serials. We shoot for a thirty minute show, which works for us, but the most popular podcast on iTunes is the Onion Radio News, which is only sixty seconds long.

I'm the first to admit that it is hard to cede leadership to teens, but if I hadn't, this project would never have got off the ground—and we wouldn't have the momentum we've got now. In certain stressful moments I've been tempted to run our podcast with an iron hand, dictating content and mandating discipline. But our subscribers choose to listen because they hear the authentic voices of their peers. I've come to believe that teen leadership is key to success in an ambitious creative project like this.

Interview

Kelli Staley
Head of Information Technology Services
Lansing Public Library
Lansing, Illinois
Lansing Library Teen Dept Podcast
Available at: http://feeds.feedburner.com/lansinglibraryteen/podcast

How Long Have You Offered Podcasts to Your Library Patrons?

We began offering podcasts in November 2005. Our first podcast was November 19, 2005.

What Kinds of Podcasts Do You Offer?

So far we've podcast one program about science project strategies. This was a joint project between Teen, Reference, and IT (me) to cover Web sites and online databases. Actually, this was our first joint presentation for the three of us. Science projects and science fairs are huge in our town, but with staggered due dates among different schools, we didn't get quite the attendance we had hoped for. We figured making it available online for those who couldn't attend, it could reach a larger audience.

I've also podcast one of the computer classes I teach at the library for the public. Demand is great, and I found a lot of people retaking some of the more intensive classes a few months later as they forgot things. I figured these could help with patrons wanting to review sections, or since the hands-on classes are limited to six students, this could help some patrons who couldn't wait for the next scheduled class.

Here's our podcast directory.

www.lansing.lib.il.us/podcast_directory.htm

[*Note:* Since this interview, the Lansing Library has added many podcasts, including audio from their Teen Poetry Café].

What Kind of Content Have You Offered So Far, or Do You Anticipate Offering, to Teens?

The science fair podcast was targeted at junior high students (grades five through eight). Some younger students have the option of doing projects, but it usually is not required of the younger grades.

Anticipated projects include the Annual Teen Poetry Café. There's a poetry contest, then the teens are invited to read their poetry and enjoy refreshments. I expect subscribers to increase after Poetry Café.

The Teen Librarian requires book reviews as entries for the prize drawing for summer reading, and she's going to offer the teens the chance to record them.

It's also our library's 70th anniversary this year, and we're talking about our own "Library Memory Project" involving all ages reminiscing about library experiences, or good books, etc.

Other Teen podcasts have included the Teen Librarian interviewing attendees at one of our Great Games Afternoons, and National Library week short promos that were recorded by staff, reading the "radio" scripts from the ALA Web site.

Dream projects:

- I'd like to see staff get involved with book talks;
- Podcast the book discussion groups;
- More in-house developed programming (such as the science fair strategies) based on school assignments;
- More on how-to use library resources for homework projects.

Why Did You Decide to Start Offering This Service?

As I state on our Web site, "We know you're busy. It's difficult to schedule a program when everyone who is interested can attend. Podcasting offers those patrons a chance to listen to our content whenever, and wherever they want!"

Other reasons: Podcasting is inexpensive. (Well, it depends on what you buy.) We already had blogs, so adding a feed that could handle enclosures was not a big step.

Metropolitan Library System (MLS) offered a workshop on podcasting, and The Shifted Librarian [www.theshiftedlibrarian.com/] Jenny Levine presented it. We're in that system, and it seemed like a very attainable project, I left Jenny's presentation excited about the possibilities.

What Were Some of the Challenges You Faced?

People can be very self-conscious about being recorded. (Once we got going, though, everybody forgot there was a microphone there.) I'm not a radio personality, but sometimes it's just about getting the information out there!

Technology blunders: I was nervous about missing things on the science fair workshop, so we actually tried to make two separate recordings. One on the laptop, using an external microphone, a second on an iPod, using a lapel mic. We later discovered that the lapel mic was not on. If people in the audience asked a question, it wasn't picked up well by the microphone. Our meeting room is not really large, so we (as presenters) didn't use a microphone.

How Much Time Is Involved in Creating and Editing Podcasts?

These were created "on the fly" and were relatively unscripted. We had prepared the presentation we were giving, but there wasn't additional consideration to the podcast. With editing, it can depend on how 'clean' you want the finished product, or if you have to edit out undesirable content. I was shocked how many times I said "um" the first time I recorded. (I chose to edit those out).

The e-mail class was a ninety minute recording originally. I spent probably two or three hours editing, mostly because of the "dead air." On average, allow two or three times the length of the recording.

What Kinds of Expenses Are Involved?

* Microphone (as low as $10);
* Web server space to store the audio files;
* Staff time;
* We have our own server, but there are companies out there that will host the files for you for a fee.

Who Creates the Podcasts at Your Library?

Right now, our podcasts are all created by the library staff. The poetry café will be recorded by staff (me) but the teens will provide the content. It will be recorded during the regular annual event; hopefully, the teens won't get overly nervous.

What Kind of Feedback Have You Had from Listeners?

I haven't had any feedback yet. I've heard from other podcasters that this can be common. One of the main attractions of the podcast is the portability, so listeners are not in a position to provide a comment on the blog, or send an e-mail when they're listening to the podcast, if they're truly downloading it to an MP3 player.

Would You Recommend That Other Libraries Launch a Similar Project?

I think podcasts are going to become more popular, as more people learn about them. As Internet Explorer 7 is released, more people will learn what RSS is, and as a result, podcasting. Also, the TV show "One Tree Hill" on the WB network has a character who is podcasting. It's in iTunes, so the teens that watch this show are probably more aware of the technology than you may think. I think this shows how in tune with the culture the show's writers and producers are, that they're doing a weekly podcast tie-in. The character, Peyton, used to have a Webcam; now she's more into podcasting.

The time-shifting element can have great appeal to patrons who want library programming on their schedule, not necessarily when we schedule the events. Podcasting is easy to experiment with, as there is little expense to get started. Libraries of any size, and even those with limited budgets, can try podcasting. Audacity [an open-source sound editing program] is relatively easy to navigate, and you don't need huge mixing boards or lots of audio training to put together a podcast, although if you have a patron very interested in audio, you may be able to get some assistance! You may even be able to recruit teens to help with recording other library programs or doing some of the editing duties.

Podcasting is just one more way we can reach our users on their terms, in their "space."

What Advice Would You Give to Other Library Systems That Want to Offer Podcasts?

Don't start podcasting just to be cool. Have content to deliver.

I wouldn't recommend lists of upcoming events. If the listener has to grab paper to write down the dates and times, it defeats the purpose of the podcast portability.

Take a listen to the content other podcasting libraries are offering. Listen to the OPAL—www.opal-online.org—presentation by Greg Schwartz (www.opal-online.org/archivetraining.htm). Greg gives a great overview of what you need to do.

Visit the Library Success Wiki (www.libsuccess.org) to see which libraries are offering podcasts, and what kinds (www.libsuccess.org/index.php?title=Podcasting).

Don't announce that you'll be doing a weekly podcast unless you know you can keep that schedule. We only podcast when we have content or a new event to broadcast.

Patron education about the new offerings and publicity is crucial. Do your best to alert the patrons that podcasts don't need iPods.

A common intro for each of your podcasts can add unity, and when listeners hear it later on their MP3 player, the familiar introduction will identify it.

If you use Feedburner.com, you'll have some subscriber stats available, and they have tools for adding all the info you need for your feed to display in iTunes.

When you save your MP3 file, add info in the author, album, title, and genre fields. I get frustrated when I'm trying to locate a podcast on my iPod and the author didn't fill in the fields, leaving it difficult to find.

Do some Web searches to see if anyone else in your community is podcasting. I was very surprised to find one of the smaller local churches listed in iTunes. Perhaps we can get them to mention our podcasts on their broadcast as publicity!

What about Publicity?

I got some publicity around the blogosphere for my podcast info page on our Web site. We're in the iTunes and Yahoo! podcast directories. Be where your users are and they will find you! We also distribute a brochure at events we record for podcasting, encouraging patrons to share the information with a friend who could not attend [available at: www.lansing.lib.il.us/technology_guides.htm#Podcasts].

We have also recently added some podcasting books to our collection, which will increase exposure to the terms and concepts. We are also burning CDs of the longer podcasts, which will be available for checkout to serve our patrons with dial-up Internet connections. The familiar format could serve as a gentle transition to original, quality content.

We have also added a branded version of Juice, the open-source podcast aggregator. Patrons can download it, and it comes preloaded with our podcast feeds. Even if the patron deletes our feeds and continues to use Juice, our logo remains. Friends of the Library donated the funds for this project.

IDEA #34: INCLUDE VIDEO

> For more on using digital video on your site, see Chapter 3

After audio, the next step is video. Teens love watching music videos, movie previews, and other video clips on their computers. The debut of the video iPod opens up even more opportunities. Users are able to download episodes of their favorite TV show, for example. Why not make library programming available as well?

As use of portable media devices becomes more widespread, libraries may want to offer:

- Video clips of teen library programs
- Videotaped booktalks
- A library news show anchored by the young adult librarian or by teens themselves
- The work of teen filmmakers
- Teen talent shows or Battles of the Bands on video
- Visual tours of your library

One great example of teen-created video is a "commercial" for the teen summer reading program at the Public Library of Charlotte and Mecklenburg County, in North Carolina. The library system's excellent "Library Loft" teen Web site includes a link to the video, at http://www.libraryloft .org/videos/srLow.ram.

Chapter 5

Feedback Forms

OVERVIEW

A good library Web site goes beyond providing information to allowing for the exchange of ideas. The library offers content, but users need a way to respond and communicate as well. For example, teens might want to read book reviews on the library site, but they will also want to submit their own reviews. They will want to ask questions, express opinions, and interact with the site, rather than being passive readers.

A general comment form is an excellent way to allow for quick, easy input from Web site users. Forms can also be modified to provide more specific feedback. This section addresses comment forms, interest surveys, and materials suggestion forms, but the uses of forms on library Web pages are almost unlimited. They are also an excellent way to communicate with teachers and parents, as in the "assignment alert" forms addressed in Chapter 9.

Why use a Web form? Many Web sites use the "mailto" command for feedback instead. When users click on that link, an e-mail program such as Outlook automatically loads, with the contact information inserted in the "To" field. The problem with this is that users usually must be on their own computers. They must also have configured their e-mail program. If teens are using a computer at school, the public library, or a friend's house, or if their e-mail account is with Yahoo!, Google, Hotmail, or another Web-based service, they probably won't be able to send e-mail easily. The advantage of a Web form is that anyone, on any computer with Internet access, can fill in the form and send it with one click of the "submit" button. The results of that form can be sent directly to an e-mail account.

It is also possible to provide PDF forms for feedback. PDF stands for

Portable Document Format. It is used to create an electronic document that looks like a printed page, usually read using Adobe Acrobat software. For example, some libraries provide PDF versions of their library card application. Users must then print these, fill them out, and physically take them in to the library. Other forms can be filled out online but then must be printed. This is an option if you absolutely must get a hard copy of the form, but it isn't the most convenient format for the user.

Besides forms, there are other ways to get teen feedback. Polls and quizzes are extremely popular with teens, and easy to set up. Wikis are growing in popularity, and allow for exciting opportunities for collaborative work. All of these ideas are addressed in this chapter.

IDEA #35: ASK FOR COMMENTS

Forms for comments, suggestions, and questions provides an easy way for teens and others to communicate with the library. Fresno County Public Library provides several Web forms for teens, including "Ask a Young Adult Librarian," where users send in questions, and "Speak Out!," where teens submit their thoughts on the topic of the month. Recent topics include, "Have you made any New Year's Resolutions?" and "What do you look for in choosing a friend?"

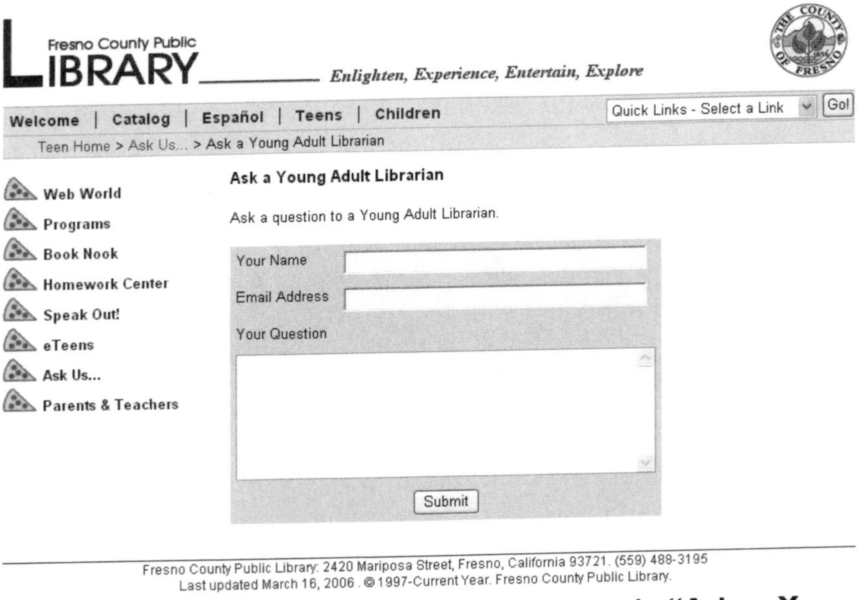

Figure 5-1   Fresno County Public Library's "Ask a Young Adult Librarian" Form

"Ask a Young Adult Librarian"
Available at: www.fresnolibrary.org/teen/asktn/ask.html

On their very appealing teen Web site, Kalamazoo Public Library in Kalamazoo, Michigan, has a "Suggestion Box" where teens can submit their comments. They use the same form for "Raves & Rants," which are teen opinions about books, movies, Web sites and CDs. The best "Raves & Rants" are posted on their Web site.

Kalazmazoo Public Library Suggestion Box
Available at: www.kpl.gov/teen/EmailForm.aspx

IDEA #36: TAKE A SURVEY

Surveys are an excellent way to gauge teen interest for collection development and programming. You can hand out paper surveys within your library, but why not put the form online and collect data that way?

The Port Washington Public Library in Port Washington, New York, uses a simple survey to collect information about favorite books, music, movies,

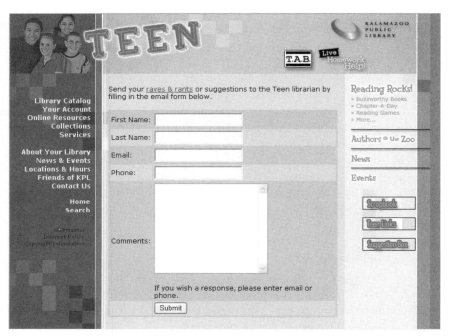

Figure 5-2 Kalamazoo Public Library's Rants & Raves Form

and program interests. The survey can be found at www.pwpl.org/teen-space/teenspaceinterestsurvey.php.

San Jose Public Library, in San Jose, California, has a very attractive Web form to survey teen interests.

San Jose Public Library, San Jose, California
Available at: www.sjlibrary.org/forms/teen_survey.htm (see Figure 5-3)

One nice aspect of both surveys mentioned above is that they ask teens whether they are interested in getting more involved with the library. This would be a good way to compile an e-mail mailing list or to recruit members for a teen advisory board.

To increase use of the form, you might offer to enter names into a raffle and give prizes to winners. Compiled results could also be displayed in the library or on the Web site so teens can see how their peers answered the questions.

IDEA #37: SUGGESTION FORM FOR MATERIALS

When teens don't find what they're looking for at the library, they need an easy way to submit requests. An online suggestion form for purchases also makes it easier for teen librarians and school library media specialists—no paper forms to keep track of! You might also consider letting teens submit suggestions for books to withdraw, if they find something outdated in the library.

Many public library systems already have an online form for submitting requests. In this case, it would be easy to add a link to that form to the teen page. If no such form exists, teen librarians can create their own. School librarians might find such a form especially helpful for receiving requests from teachers, as well as from students.

For this form, you will have to decide how much information to require. It's better to keep it simple, asking teens for author and title but making details like publisher, date of publication, and ISBN optional. Asking for too much information may discourage users. Also, name and e-mail address could be optional unless you decide to notify teens about the status of their requests.

Boston Public Library uses a form that asks for all of the relevant information and then gives patrons the option of reserving the material if it is purchased. While it's not specifically for teen requests, it provides a good example of what a materials suggestion form could look like. That form is available at www.bpl.org/BookRequestForm/request.asp.

Library Home   Library Catalog   Research   Services   About Us

TeenWeb
- Best of the Month
- Teen Reading Lists
- Teen Wild Reviews
- Homework Help
- Teen Web Links
- Teen Talent
- teensReach
- Teen Events
- Teen Book Clubs
- Teen Survey
- Summer Reading Celebration

Home > Paths to Learning > TeenWeb > Survey

Teen Library Survey

Help us improve your library! Fill out this survey and tell us what you think:

1. How often do you visit the library?

○ Every day   ○ Irregularly
○ Once a week   ○ Never visit the library
○ Once a month

2. Which library do you most often use?

[CHOOSE A LIBRARY   ▾]

3. What is your reason for using the library? (Check all that apply)

☐ Library materials for school   ☐ Visit with friends
☐ Materials for personal interest   ☐ A quiet place
☐ Homework   ☐ Help from a librarian
☐ Internet/Email   ☐ Library events & programs
Other: [_____]

4. What kinds of resources do you use in the library? (Check all that apply)

☐ Internet   ☐ Music CDs
☐ Videos/DVDs   ☐ Graphic Novels/Comics
☐ Books   ☐ Books-on-Tape
☐ Magazines/Newspapers   ☐ Online Databases

5. What is the best time for you to come to a library-sponsored event?

○ Weekday afternoons   ○ Saturday mornings
○ Weekday evenings   ○ Saturday afternoons
                         ○ Sunday afternoons

6. What kinds of library-sponsored events would you attend? (Check all that apply)

☐ Music/dance performance   ☐ Author Visit
☐ Craft projects   ☐ Contests
☐ Guest speakers   ☐ Magic
☐ Teen talent show   ☐ Field Trips
☐ Open-mike poetry reading   Other: [_____]

7. What kinds of books would you like to see in the library? (Check all that apply)

☐ Fiction   ☐ Horror
☐ Science Fiction   ☐ Sports
☐ Fantasy   ☐ Poetry
☐ Anime/Manga   ☐ Biography
☐ Romance   ☐ Video Game Strategies
☐ Mystery/Suspense

8. Name titles of books, CDs, videos, DVDs, magazines or comics that you would like to see in the library:

[   ]

9. What do you like about the library?

[   ]

10. What do you NOT like about the library?

[   ]

11. Would you like to volunteer in the library or join a teen advisory council?

○ Yes
○ No
○ Maybe - I'd like more information

If you answered 'Yes' or 'Maybe', please provide your name and a way to contact you:

[   ]

12. Do you have additional comments and/or suggestions?

[   ]

[Submit]   [Start Over]

Figure 5-3   San Jose Public Library's Teen Library Survey

127

IDEA #38: CREATE A QUIZ

Teens (and adults) love taking online quizzes. They're also quick and easy to create, with plenty of free Web sites that will help you design one in minutes. The Discovery Channel's Quiz Center, for example, at http://school.discovery.com/quizcenter/quizcenter.html, lets you sign up for a free account. You can create a customized quiz, using multiple choice, true and false, or essay questions. Users can either see corrected quizzes immediately or you can have the results e-mailed to you. Once you create the quiz, you can link to it from your Web site.

Quia is another popular site for educators that allows you to create quizzes, available at www.quia.com. After a thirty-day free trial, however, there is a charge for this service.

Other quiz creation sites include:

- All The Tests: www.allthetests.com
- Quizbox: http://quizbox.com
- Quiz Em All: http://quiz-em-all.com

If you do orientations and tours for middle or high school classes, a quiz could start the tour and give you an idea of how much students already know about the library. It could also end the tour and give you some feedback on how much of the information you presented actually sank in.

You could also use the quiz format for contests, with the top scorers awarded prizes. Questions might address author and book-related facts, for example.

MyOwnCafe.org, the teen Web site for the Southeastern Massachusetts Library System, offers many just-for-fun quizzes on its site.

MyOwnCafe
Southeastern Massachusetts Library System
Available at: http://myowncafe.org/entertainmentcenter/quizzes/tabid/64/
    Default.aspx (see Figure 5-4)

IDEA #39: POLL YOUR USERS

Online polls are another a quick, easy, fun way to get feedback. They are easy to create using free Web sites. Type "free polls" into Google and you'll find many options, such as pollhost.com and freepolls.com, (though most will include banner ads with the polls).

Bravenet.com allows you to register for free and create a customized mini poll. You then copy and paste their HTML code onto your Web site. Users

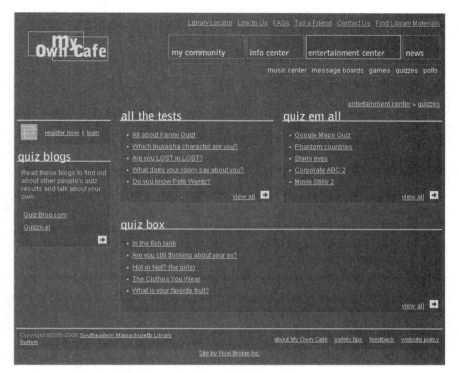

Figure 5-4   My Own Café's Quiz Page

can answer the question you pose and then click on a link to see a graph showing the poll results so far. The poll is hosted on the Bravenet site, so you can log in at any time to make changes to it. For a fee, you can get an ad-free version with additional options. You can choose whether or not to be notified by e-mail whenever someone takes the poll. You can also restrict users to answering the poll questions just once a day.

A weekly library poll might be a fun feature to keep teens coming back to your Web site. Questions could be library related (Which of these authors do you prefer? Which of these programs would you be most likely to attend?) or more general, related to pop culture or politics.

Denver Public Library's eVolver site offers a poll on their "Life" page. Recent questions include "What is the best movie out there right now?" and "What is your favorite online community?"

Denver Public Library, Denver, Colorado
Available at: http://teens.denverlibrary.org/life/index.html (see Figure 5-5)

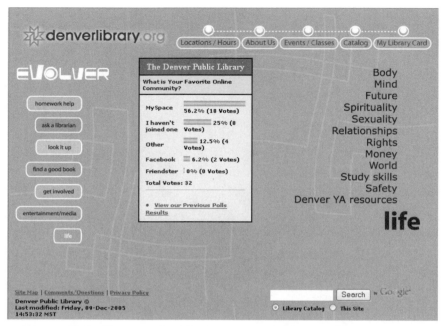

Figure 5-5　Denver Public Library's Online Poll

IDEA #40: TEST OUT A WIKI

> For more on wikis, and how to set one up, see Chapter 3

Wikis are an exciting new technology that allows for collaborative projects online. Anyone can add content, edit, or delete information from a wiki. While a wiki might work best for group projects, it could also be used to solicit feedback about the library.

Try setting up a wiki with an area that allows teens to add to a list of titles they would like to see in the library. Another page could deal with program ideas—have teens comment on which ideas they like best. You could have a part of the wiki dedicated to "compliments" and another to "suggestions."

Chapter 6

Library Operations
and Policies

OVERVIEW

With so much exciting new technology for Web sites—podcasts, video, wikis, feeds, discussion forums, instant messaging, and so on—it's important not to neglect the obvious. When most people visit a Web site, whether they're shopping, doing research, or just surfing the Web for fun, they expect to be able to find answers to their most basic questions: Whose site is this? What are the company's, school's, or organization's policies? Who can I contact for more information?

Teens will expect to find this kind of information for the library. It's also important that teachers, parents, and community members have access to the library's rules and policies. If your library doesn't have an Internet use policy, a mission statement, or a collection development policy, it's a good idea to develop one, ideally with plenty of feedback from teens.

One good way to present all of this information is through a FAQ, or Frequently Asked Questions, page that covers all the bases clearly and concisely. Berkeley Public Library uses a simple FAQ to answer questions:

Berkeley Public Library, Berkeley, California
Available at: http://berkeleypubliclibrary.org/teen/about.html

Another possible format is to cover separate aspects of your teen services on different pages—for example, have a page for staff, one for collection development policies, another for the mission statement, and so on.

Booklists
Careers
College
Berkeley High
Libraries
Magazines
More books
Programs
Reviews
Search & Chat
Sites
HOME

Berkeley Public Library Teen Services

About Teen Services

What is Teen Services?

Teen Services, a division of the Berkeley Public Library, supports the individual's right to know by providing free access to information and by developing collections and services which meet the diverse needs of our multicultural community. Designed as a point of entry for teen patrons learning to use the library independently, Teen Services provides access to the full range of Berkeley Public Library's resources.

How do we decide what links to include on our pages?

Library staff investigate the sites by checking for origins, maintenance and content. Where does the site originate? Who is responsible for maintaining it? What kinds of materials do the sites include or link to? Does the content fit the parameters of our collection policy? For more details about site evaluation, see Evaluating Internet Resources.

Teens and their parents or guardians should keep in mind that the Internet is a chaotic medium where *anyone* can post *anything*. Links will sometimes lead to unexpected destinations. We advise discretion.

The Berkeley Public Library assumes no responsibility for what you find on the Internet. We cannot, and do not attempt to, control the complex pathways of the Information Superhighway. Instead, we provide indexes, or *access points*, for guidance.

If you are concerned about the appropriateness of certain sites, see Teen Safety on the Information Highway. If you are concerned about censorship on the Internet, see Communications Decency Act Issues and learn about the Telecommunications Act of 1996.

Library staff also consult with teen advisors and actively solicit feedback from teens.

Teen Services Collection Development Policy

Scope

Teen Services maintains collections responding to the informational, recreational and educational needs of patrons aged 14 to 18.

Print Materials

Nonfiction

- The collection spans the entire subject range, including titles addressing teens' personal interests, school assignments, and those which support the professional needs of young adult librarians and educators.

Fiction

- The collection includes both hardcovers and paperbacks. Librarians select hardcover titles for popular appeal and lasting value.

Paperbacks

- The collection includes paperback fiction, romance, series books, science fiction, fantasy, horror, high demand classics and some nonfiction personal interest titles.

Periodicals

- Librarians maintain a collection of popular, circulating magazines, including comics

Nonprint materials

The collection includes popular music on cassette and books on tape. A variety of nonprint formats will be added.

Maintenance

Teen Services librarians review the collection regularly. Weeding for condition and accuracy keeps material current and allows for adequate shelf space.

Open Access

In accord with the Berkeley Public Library policy of open access, Teen Services collections are open to patrons of all ages. Based on the foundation of intellectual freedom and in accordance the the Library Bill of Rights, the collection represents diverse viewpoints.

Figure 6-1   Berkeley Public Library's "About Teen Services" Page

IDEA #41: PUT YOUR FACE ON THE WEB

It's always easier to approach a stranger with questions if you know their name and a little bit about them first. This section of your Web site could be as simple as a photo and a caption that announces your name and title and welcomes teens to the library. Or it could be a bit more detailed, with photos and biographies of everyone who works in the library, from aides to pages to volunteers.

The New York Public Library's Teen Central gives the staff page a nice twist by letting teens interview the staff and then posting the interviews on their Web site. Teens ask the librarians about their favorite music, foods, hobbies, why they like their jobs, and more.

Melissa Jenvey and Jack Martin

Interview with Melissa Jenvey By Danielle

Danielle: Hi, what is your name?

Melissa: Melissa Jenvey.

D: What is your job title at the library?

M: I'm a C.L.A.S.P. librarian.

D: What borough do you live in?

M: I live in Queens.

Interview with Jack Martin by Catey, Coretta, and Rebecca

CC&R: Why this library?

Jack: Teenagers are much more fun than adults.

CC&R: What kind of computer do you own?

J: An old Dell

CC&R: What's your favorite brand of shoes?

J: Prada (not that I own any))

CC&R: What is your favorite heavy metal band?

J: Comets on Fire

CC&R: What is your favorite book?

J: Anything by Salinger

CC&R: What do you think

Interview with Joanne Rosario by Danielle

Danielle: What is your name?

Joanne: Joanne Rosario

D: What is your job title?

J: I'm the supervising young adult librarian?

D: Where do you live?

J: I live in Jackson Heights, Queens

D: Are you married?

J: Yes

Figure 6-2   New York Public Library's Teen Central Staff Page

The New York Public Library, New York, New York
Available at: http://teenlink.nypl.org/teencentral/staff.html (see Figure 6-2)

In addition to names and titles, an introduction to library staff members might include:

- Contact information: phone, e-mail address, instant messaging service and nickname, contact form link, etc.
- What that person can do to assist teens, teachers, or parents. For example, a teen librarian might want to list services offered, such as class visits, booktalks, library tours, and so on.
- Biographical and resumé information. School librarians can use this as an opportunity to let students know that they are teachers with additional credentials.
- Favorite books, movies, Web sites, music, etc.
- An audio or video file students can click on to hear or watch an introduction or interview.

One more thing to consider when creating a staff page: Anything you make publicly accessible on the Internet is available to anyone, worldwide. If you or other staff members have privacy concerns, it might not be a good idea to post photos or biographical information. You'll need to weigh loss of privacy against the benefits of being accessible and easily contacted. If some staff members prefer that their photos not appear, you'll want to be sympathetic to their concerns. Also, before you post photos or names of students or teen volunteers, be sure to consider privacy issues.

IDEA #42: DESCRIBE YOUR RESOURCES

This Web page could describe the library's collection, as well as any special collections. It might also include information on online databases or other resources. It might also incorporate instructions on how to access the library's online resources from home or school. For a school library, this section would concentrate on all of the library's resources. For a public library, it might focus on the teen collection—including books, audio, video, magazines, and graphic novels—and also on library collections of special interest to teens, such as the college and career section. A good, clear description of resources might also include digital photos showing where to find each collection in the library. The Web page might also include graphics that show any special stickers or spine labels used on the teen collection to help with readers' advisory.

San Jose Public Library's main King Library provides a "self-guided tour" and a map of the teen collection at www.sjlibrary.org/services/youth/tour_teens_area.pdf and www.sjlibrary.org/services/youth/map_teens_collec.pdf.

The King County Library System's Bothell Regional Library, in King County, Washington, provides a brief summary of materials and services for teens and for teachers on their Web site, including custom booklists, homework help, class tours, online databases, and more.

King County Library System's Bothell Regional Library, King County, Washington
Available at: www.kcls.org/bothell/teens.cfm

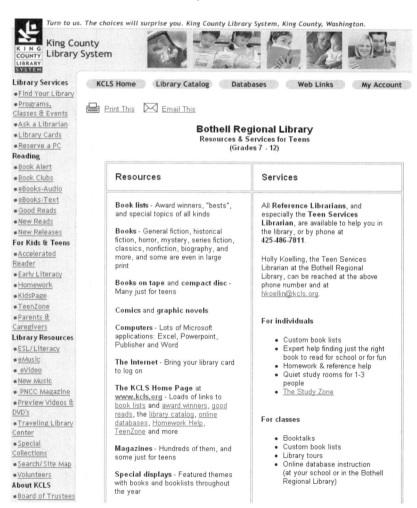

Figure 6-3   Bothell Library's Resources & Services for Teens

IDEA #43: STATE YOUR MISSION

If you have a mission statement for your school library, or for your teen services department, why not display it prominently on your Web site? Or the mission statement may apply to the teen Web site only.

The Newington High School Library Media Center, in North Newington, Connecticut, has developed a mission statement for their Web site at www .newington-schools.org/nhs/media/Mission.htm.

IDEA #44: EXPLAIN HOW TO BECOME A BORROWER

Somewhere on a library's Web page, it's a good idea to explain who can borrow from the library, what can be borrowed, how long borrowers can keep an item, how to renew items, and so on.

In public library systems, there is probably a Web page that explains library policies. Teen librarians could link to this page or design their own page that explains any special policies that apply to teenagers. For example, because many teens do not have state-issued IDs or driver's licenses, there may be alternate rules about getting a parent signature or using school IDs to obtain library cards. Some libraries waive fines for anyone under eighteen. This is the place to explain what those teen policies are.

At a school, the librarian may want to spell out borrowing policies for students, teachers, and parents. Do students need to show school IDs, or just give their name at the circulation desk? How does the library deal with overdue and lost items? Do teachers get any special privileges? Can parents borrow school library items?

If your library has an online library card application, online renewals, or other services, you might want to link to them from this page.

IDEA #45: LAY DOWN THE LAW

There are many approaches to making rules of behavior for the library. Hopefully, at public libraries, the rules for teens will be the same as for any other patron, and teenagers will be held to the same—not stricter— standards. At schools, librarians may have special rules for the library or simply expect students to follow school regulations. Some libraries have long lists of "don'ts," while others prefer a simpler statement about respecting the library facility and the rights of others.

Regardless of approach, having the rules spelled out on your Web site will help make them clear and easy to access. It may also be a good idea to spell out the consequences for breaking library rules.

Overly restrictive rules are one of the barriers teens mention when asked why they don't use the library. If we want to attract teens to the library, common sense suggests that it might be more useful to rephrase rules in more positive terms and to eliminate as many as are practical.

One way to make the library's rules more teen-friendly is to give teens a say in writing them. This is an ideal use for a wiki, a collaborative online space where anyone can add, delete, or edit content. Why not invite the teen advisory board or the whole school community to participate in co-authoring the library rules? Invite discussion on why certain rules exist and whether they are really necessary. If everyone has a say in writing the rules, they will also have more stake in following them. Another idea is to include a link to your library's comment form at the end of the list of rules, and invite suggestions for revision.

Another key element to include in your teen Web site is the library's Internet Use Policy, or a link to it.

IDEA #46: PROVIDE YOUR COLLECTION DEVELOPMENT PLAN

If you have a collection development plan, you can easily make it available on your Web site. At public libraries, this could be either the general plan for the library system or a plan developed specifically for teen materials.

You could also provide a collection development plan for your virtual library, the links you choose for your teen Web site. The Internet Public Library has a very nice plan for its teen collection in that it uses plain, relaxed language to describe the collection, and addresses teens directly.

Internet Public Library
Available at: www.ipl.org.ar/teen/teencolldevplan.html (see Figure 6-4)

This part of the site might also be a place to include information on your materials reconsideration policy. The Internet Public Library also does this well, in that it describes "the freedom to read" and provides links to the Library Bill of Rights before giving information on where to send requests for reconsideration. Find their policy at www.ipl.org.ar/about/ifpol.html.

IDEA #47: ENHANCE YOUR OPEN HOURS

Most likely, your library hours are already on your Web site. However, there are many ways to enhance a basic listing of hours. Most important, you will want to offer Web site visitors other options in case they are checking the site when the library building is closed.

 the Internet Public Library

Collection Development for the IPL Teen Division

This document is designed to help the members of the Teen Division's Advisory Board select resources for the Teen Division.

We went over the basics in Collection Development Questions and Answers. If you haven't read that yet, please do so before going any further.

WHAT DO WE COLLECT? Currently, we collect three different kinds of resources:

1. Recreational: Fun stuff. You know what recreational resources are. They're the things you end up looking at when you should be finding URLs for your term paper. We collect them because we want the Teen Division to be more than just a boring place to find stuff for school.

The thing to remember when you're looking for recreational resources is that we are always going to want sites that have broad coverage rather than narrow coverage. That means, for instance, that we don't want a Melrose Place homepage. Instead, we want an index to the homepages of all different kinds of television shows. The reason for this is that we don't want to reinvent the wheel: if someone else is already doing a great job providing an index to TV homepages, there's no reason we should be trying to duplicate that job. That's why we have a listing for the Ultimate Band List, instead of for Joe Random Surfer's Marilyn Manson page.

2. Informational: "News you can use." Relevant information about topics you need to know about. Informational resources cover issues such as cultural diversity, sexuality, violence and abuse, and health, as well as information about colleges and careers to help you plan your future.

Sometimes when you're looking for this kind of resource, you'll find a site that seems to have exactly the kind of information you want -- and then it turns out, when you look at it more closely, that the site is designed for social workers, or psychologists, or parents, not for teenagers. This is frustrating. We try to collect sites that are actually designed for teenagers. But you should feel free to use your judgment: good information is good information, no matter what the intended audience. One case where we've elected to include a site that isn't designed specifically for teenagers is the Adolescence Directory On-Line. After all, sometimes it's good to see what adults think teenagers need!

3. Educational: Information that will help you in school. Literature, math, science, politics, history, et cetera.

Educational resources are another area where the trick is to find sites that are actually useful to teenagers. There's a lot of sites that are designed for young kids, and a lot of sites that are designed for college students, but finding sites that aren't written either for 8 year olds or for college seniors isn't always easy. Use your judgment, and trust that your judgment will develop as you spend more time working with the Teen Division.

HOW DO I KNOW IF A RESOURCE IS GOOD?

Here are some things to think about, and questions to ask yourself, when you're looking at a site and evaluating it for the Teen Division:

What does it look like? Lots of images and animation, lots of text, or some of both? If it has a lot of images and animation, do they add to the information the site is trying to provide, or do they get in the way? We're definitely interested in sites that make good use of graphics and plug-ins, but we do want the use to be **good**.

Think about what the site is trying to accomplish. If you find it difficult to **tell** exactly what the site is trying to accomplish, that's an indication that we might not want it for our collection. Good sites generally will have a page that describes the site's intended purpose and provides information about the people involved in creating and maintaining it. Good sites should also include a way for you to get in touch with the creators of the project, either by email or via Web form, or both.

If the site does seem to be doing what it sets out to do, the next thing to think about is whether that thing, whatever it may be, is appropriate for the Teen Division. For instance, if the site does a super-fantastic job of covering the latest research done in high-energy theoretical physics, it is probably appropriate for **some** of the Teen Division's audience, but not for a majority of the audience. On the other hand, if the site does a super-fantastic job of presenting ideas for science projects, that probably **is** an appropriate site for the Teen Division.

(continued)

Is the information contained at the site accurate? It may not always be easy to tell, particularly if the site covers a subject you don't know much about. But there are some ways to get a sense for how accurate the information is:

- **Who Did It?** Does the information come from a source that you would trust? For instance, you might pay more attention to a site about ancient Egypt designed by an Egyptologist than to one designed by a company trying to sell Pyramids of Giza Beer. The line here is getting more and more blurry, however. Companies such as Absolut Vodka are sponsoring artists to create images and commentary that may or may not have anything **directly** to do with the products they're trying to sell. And of course, there are also many companies that are trying to sell educational products, and their sites may contain a "teaser" for all the great information you could access if you'd only buy their software, or database subscription, or whatever it is.

- **When's the Last Time Anybody Did Anything To It?** When was the site last updated? If it hasn't been updated for a long time, chances are that nobody's paying attention to it, and that the people who were in charge of it are doing other things. Sometimes, though, this isn't important. If what you've found is an online version of Mark Twain's *Life on the Mississippi*, Mark Twain isn't going to be changing it any time soon, so the date it was last updated doesn't matter that much.

- **Can You Find Your Way Around?** At any point while you are wandering around in the site, do you know how to get back to where you started from? Is it clear how the different parts of the site fit together?

I hope this gives you some idea of what to do when you're selecting resources for the Teen Division. Please feel free to ask me if you have any questions about it, or anything else related to the Teen Division or the Internet Public Library.

--Sara Ryan, Teen Division Coordinator

Figure 6-4 Internet Public Library's Teen Collection Development Plan

For school libraries, a link to local public library hours will guide students to a library that might be open late into the evening. For both school and public libraries, it's important to link to any 24/7 online references services or online homework help services available to patrons. There are now many Web sites where patrons can get reference help around the clock—see the chapter on online reference for a partial listing. Some cities also have homework help phone hotlines. A link to one of these services will redirect any teen patron who checks your library's hours to a librarian who can help them immediately, regardless of the time of day (or night).

Be sure also to point out "anytime" options such as downloading e-books or audio books. Finally, be sure to direct teens toward online resources that could be helpful, such as databases and Web sites.

Chapter 7

Library Access Online

OVERVIEW

I'm always saddened by the fact that some teenagers rarely set foot in school or public libraries. Whatever it is that keeps them away—perhaps a lack of time, interest, transportation, or just little knowledge of what the library has to offer—it's a shame to lose even one of our potential patrons.

Maybe we can reach some of those teens online, however. Especially if it is a time or transportation issue, the Internet can offer solutions. There are also many services these days for library patrons who want access from home or school. Besides access to databases, many libraries are now offering downloadable e-books, audio books, and even feature-length videos. Providing these services will allow your teen patrons multiple ways to access information, even if they can't visit a library in person.

This chapter covers some of the ways libraries can and do reach teenagers even before they step inside a library building.

IDEA #48: PUT YOUR ORIENTATION ONLINE

Teens showing up at your library for the first time may have an overwhelming array of questions. Where do they find the materials they want? How do they get a card? Where's the restroom and the drinking fountain? How do they use the catalog? How many books can they check out? Where's the teen area? What do they do if they need help?

Creating virtual tours or orientations on your Web site can help make the first library visit easier. Before they even set foot in your library, you can give teens a pretty good idea of what they will find. You can also answer all of their most basic questions, so that they know the rules and feel at ease.

For instance, a class could "visit" the library online through a school computer lab. The class might view an orientation slideshow using PowerPoint, or click their way through linked pages of photos, or view a map of the facility. By the time they arrive at the library in person, they will know their way around, or at least grasp the basic organization of the collection (and the Web site).

The Tempe Public Library in Tempe, Arizona, offers a "virtual tour" where users can actually navigate their way around the library using a fun, if somewhat dizzying, interface similar to the one used on some real estate sites. Try it at www.tempe.gov/library/360/default.htm.

River Falls Public Library, in River Falls, Wisconsin, has an online photo tour that includes the young adult area. Users can click on areas of a library map to see photographs of each section, with brief descriptions of what's offered.

River Falls Public Library, River Falls, Wisconsin
Available at: www.rfcity.org/library/tour/ya.htm

Young Adult Area
River Falls Public Library Virtual Tour

The Young Adult area features fiction, non-fiction, graphic novels (comics), and audio for teens. The Young Adult area is tucked away behind the reference desk. Lounging, hanging out, and talking with friends in not just encouraged, but required! Two computers with scanners, color printers, headphones, CD-burners, and tons of imaging software are also located in the Young Adult Area.

To see a larger photograph, click on a thumbnail below.

Read or listen to
fiction and audios

What's new in YA?

A private corner in YA

Young Adult
Computer 1

Young Adult
Computer 2

Visit another area		Lower Level	Return to Map
Audio/Visual Room	Board Room	Children's Library	Circulation Desk
Computer Room	Fiction	History Room	Lobby
Meeting Room	Non-fiction	Parking Lot Entrance	Reading Area & Magazines
Reference Desk	Storytime Room	Union Street Entrance	Young Adult

Figure 7-1   River Falls Public Library Virtual Tour, Young Adult Area

Berea High School in Greenville, South Carolina, offers an very nice on-line tour of its Web site. Users can click their way through the tour, which demonstrates an Infotrac search, explains how to use the catalog, shows users which magazine subscriptions the library offers, then ends with the option of using a search engine to find information. Try it at www.greenville.k12.sc.us/bereah/Media/net1.htm.

IDEA #49: GIVE AN AUDIO OR VIDEO TOUR

For more on using audio and video on your Web site, see Chapter 3

Take the tour idea even further by offering an audio or video rather than photographs or graphics.

You might let teens download an "audio tour" of your library, much the way some museums do. Teens would need iPods or other portable MP3 players for this activity, and also software such as iTunes to download the presentation. A librarian could also pre-load the MP3 players before the tour.

Numbered, laminated cards posted around the library could tell a teen where to stand or what to look at for each part of the tour. Instead of de-scribing a painting and its history, as museums do, the audio presentation might discuss how to get a library card as the teen approaches the check-out desk, or guide students to the catalog computer and introduce some of the li-brary's databases. This idea would probably work best for large, central pub-lic libraries with multiple floors and a great many services.

A video version of your tour could be posted on the Web site for teens to watch at their leisure, from home or school. Currently, many university li-braries are offering this service. For example, the University Library at Cali-fornia State University, Long Beach, features student tour guides and many videos to choose from at www.csulb.edu/library/video/.

IDEA #50: OFFER DOWNLOADABLE E-BOOKS

Why even come in to the library to get a book? That's the idea behind e-books, a service more and more libraries offer. While it's unlikely that most patrons will want to read the latest bestseller online or on their PDAs, unless they happen to own an e-book reader, downloadable books are a good way to access how-to instructions, technical data, ready reference, and other types of more specialized information.

Most libraries offering e-books pay for the service. Two of the most popular providers include:

- ebrary

    www.ebrary.com/corp/index.htm
- netLibrary

    Available at: www.netlibrary.com

There are also free, public domain titles available at sites such as Project Gutenberg (at www.gutenberg.org).

If your library offers e-books, think about using your Web site to promote appropriate titles to teens, much the way you do with print titles. You might mention e-books and explain how to access them as part of a pathfinder or bibliography, or a subject guide, if they are titles that are likely to be popular for school assignments.

If you know that teens in your community or at your school are researching a particular topic, use your Web site to publicize any e-books that might be useful. These will be especially popular for students who do their research at the last possible moment, when many print resources are borrowed and the library is closed.

IDEA #51: PROVIDE DOWNLOADABLE AUDIO BOOKS

Many libraries also offer downloadable audio books to their patrons. This is a fairly recent development, one that makes sense, given the popularity of portable MP3 players. Instead of checking out CDs or cassettes, library users browse the audio book collection from home or work, then "borrow" an audio file that they can listen to on their computers or on an MP3 player. The audio books generally "expire"—are no longer playable—after a set period of time.

Two popular companies that provide audio books for libraries are Over-Drive (at www.overdrive.com) and Recorded Books (at www.recordedbooks .com). While there are still some compatibility issues to work out—not all audio books will play on all MP3 players—this seems likely one day to become the primary way that people access audio books.

If your library or school offers downloadable audio books, you can use your teen Web pages to promote the service, offer instructions, and highlight certain titles. Review new titles, for instance, on your Web site or blog. If possible, offer samples.

New York Public Library's TeenLink site lets teens hear samples of audio books. Recent titles featured include "Sisterhood of the Traveling Pants" by Ann Brashares, "Feed" by M. T. Anderson, and "Whale Talk" by Chris Crutcher. To see the featured samples, go to http://teenlink.nypl.org and scroll down the page to "Listen Up! Hear Audio Book Samples Online."

Listen to these brief samples of audio books online. If you like what you hear you can reserve either the book or the audio book from your local branch library. All audio is provided in the RealAudio™ format.

BEFORE WE WERE FREE
Alvarez, Julia

Listen UP!

In the early 1960s in the Dominican Republic, twelve-year-old Anita learns that her family is involved in the underground movement to end the bloody rule of the dictator, General Trujillo.

Reserve this title.　Reserve the Audio Book

SPEAK
Anderson, Laurie Halse

Listen UP!

A traumatic event near the end of the summer has a devastating effect of Melinda's freshman year in high school.
FIC A
Reserve this title.

FEED
Anderson, M.T.

Listen UP!

In a future where most people have computer implants in their heads to control their environment, a boy meets an unusual girl who is in serious trouble.

Reserve this title.　Reserve the Audio Book

THE SISTERHOOD OF THE TRAVELING PANTS
Brashares, Ann

Listen UP!

Four best girlfriends spend the biggest summer of their lives enchanted by a magical pair of pants.

Reserve this title.　Reserve the Audio Book

A GREAT AND TERRIBLE BEAUTY
Bray, Libba

Listen UP!

After the suspicious death of her mother in 1895, sixteen-year-old Gemma returns to England, after many years in India, to attend a finishing school where she becomes aware of her magical powers and ability to see into the spirit world.

Reserve this title.　Reserve the Audio Book

Figure 7-2　New York Public Library's Young Adult Audio Book Samples

Interview
Sandra Payne Coordinator of Young Adult Services The New York Public Library New York, New York **How Did You Decide to Offer Samples from Audio Books Online?** We were actually just inspired with the idea of having excerpts read aloud. **How Long Are the Samples?** About five minutes. **How Did You Decide on the RealAudio Format?** As this is our first foray, we asked Tim Ditlow of Listening Library if there were such an animal as short excerpts, and were pleased to know that Listening Library had such an animal! **What Kind of Permission Did You Need from the Publishers to Offer This?** Going straight to the top with Timothy P. Ditlow, Vice-President and Publisher of Listening Library, we were given permission to use excerpts from CD titles in NYPL's young adult collections. **Are You Finding That This Is a Popular Service? Do You Think It Increases Circulation of Your Audio Books?** As librarians introduce Listen Up!, we have heard that it is a good thing. We do hope that ListenUp! brings young people to the audio books and to the actual books. Right now, it's a bit difficult to measure. **What Kind of Feedback Have You Gotten about This Service, from Teens or Others?** The responses from teens, librarians, and educators have been very positive. **Do You Know of Any Other Libraries That Are Offering Something Like This?** Several months ago, Tim Ditlow said that NYPL was the sole public library that acquired Listening Library's RealAudio clips. That may have changed, though.

IDEA #52: PRESENT DOWNLOADABLE VIDEO

This is the next step in providing remote services—allowing users to download video directly to their home computers or portable devices. Denver Public Library is already providing this service, called eFlicks. Users can download video from a collection of titles, which so far are mostly documentaries and classic movies. They are able to watch them on computers, Pocket PCs, or some cell phones. Video iPods, unfortunately, are not yet an option.

This is an idea with wide teen appeal, since so many teens already enjoy watching video clips and music videos online. The trick will be providing content that they want to see, and then promoting it in the teen area of the library Web site.

IDEA #53: ISSUE LIBRARY CARDS ONLINE

If your library can issue library cards online, or at least allow teens to print the application form at home, teens can also show up at the library prepared to get borrowing privileges. Receiving an actual library card in the mail might be just the incentive some teens need to visit their public library.

Many libraries are already using or testing online library card applications. Some libraries issue card numbers to online users so that these patrons can access databases immediately. Others provide an application and a list of acceptable ID, so that patrons can prepare to get a card before they arrive at the library. This service might be especially helpful for teachers who want to take their classes to the public library.

Denver Public Library allows patrons to register online. Users of the service immediately get a temporary library card number that gives them access to the library's databases. Patrons then have fourteen days to go physically to a library, where they are asked to show ID and verify their addresses in order to get their permanent card. The library offers adult and children's cards, with applications in either English or Spanish. Imagine how useful this service would be for a teen who, late at night, realizes she needs to look up something in the library's database, but has never had a library card! The application is at http://denverlibrary.org/card/register.html.

The Carnegie Library of Pittsburg, Pennsylvania, also has an online form that allows new users to request a library card. Their patrons can actually have the card mailed to them, which takes two to four weeks. Patrons then must present ID and address verification when they go to the library to borrow materials. This service is at http://carnegielibrary.org/borrowing/cardrequest.html.

Home — Books, DVDs, and More — Research Tools — Services — Hours - Locations — Unique Collections — Online Learning

Search Our Website: [_____] [Search]

Search the Catalog by: [TITLE ▼] [_____] [Search the Catalog]

Your Online Helpdesk:

Browse all the help topics in our site

Apply for a Minneapolis Public Library Card

First Name: [_____]

Middle Name: [_____]

Last Name: [_____]

Street Address: [_____]

City: [_____]

Zip: [_____]

County: [_____]

Phone: [_____]

E-Mail: [_____]

I have had a card from the Minneapolis Public Library before: ○ Yes ○ No

Number: [_____]

I want to register a card from another Minnesota library: [_____ ▼]

Number: [_____]

Birthdate: [-- ▼] [____] , [____]

Please read the following and click "Send Application" if you agree to these terms and conditions of having a library card.

- My library card is for my personal use. I am responsible for all use of this card (including its use to access the Internet).
- For most materials borrowed, I will be charged a fine if I do not return items by the date they are due.
- I will be charged for items I do not return (based on average replacement cost).
- If my card is lost or stolen, I will report it to the Library immediately to prevent unauthorized use. (If I fail to report a lost or stolen card, I will be held liable for any overdue fines or replacement charges).
- If I lose my card there will be a $1.00 fee to replace it.
- The Library may suspend or limit service if I have fines or billed material.
- I understand that fees and charges are set by the Library Board and may be changed without prior notice.
- I will report any name, address, telephone or e-mail address changes to keep my record current.
- I can use my card at any public library in the 7-county metro area (MELSA) and at most public libraries in Minnesota.
- I understand that my card is needed to obtain full library service (service might be limited if I do not present my card).

[Send Application]

Once you have received your card in the mail and you visit a Minneapolis Public Library for the first time, you now have full borrowing privileges.

If you have registered a card from another Minnesota library with us, you must present a current Minnesota Driver's License, State or Tribal Identification that verifies identity and current residency before you are allowed full library privileges. In the absence of current Minnesota Driver's License or State Identification, a combination of items can also be used. For example, old license, state identification, passport, school or work identification with photo verifies identity and a checkbook, utility bill or mail with a recent postmark verifies current address. Although photo identification to verify identity is required, the receipt from the Department of Motor Vehicles listing the current address is acceptable. Minors under the age of 18 who apply online, will have their library card mailed "Attention Parent or Guardian of" and will include an insert that states the card was "applied for by a minor" and are allowed full library privileges.

If the applicant is under 18, the parent or guardian is responsible for use of the card to access the Internet or borrow library resources. In compliance with the Minnesota Data Practices Act, minors may request that information on their records be withheld from their parents or guardians. The request may be granted only if it is in the child's best interest to do so.

Please contact the Access Services Department (612-630-6040) if you have any questions about library cards.

Figure 7-3 Minneapolis Public Library's Online Library Card Application

Minneapolis Public Library, in Minneapolis, Minnesota, offers library card sign-ups online. Patrons fill out a Web form and receive their cards by mail within two weeks.

Minneapolis Public Library, in Minneapolis, Minnesota
Available at: https://www.mplib.org/cardapplication.asp (see Figure 7-3)

Part III. Information

Chapter 8

Reference Help

OVERVIEW

Once in a while I get calls from teens who clearly need in-depth help on homework, but are obviously reluctant to come to the library. The telephone is limited, however; I can answer quick, factual questions, but more comprehensive help is difficult. These conversations often end with me asking the teen if he or she can come in to pick up a book or a printout of an article.

Reference help is a basic library service, but some teens may not want to visit the library. They may lack the time or the transportation to come in. Luckily, new technology is making it easier to surmount those obstacles.

Not only can librarians now chat online with teens, they can also send pictures, text, video, or audio. They can also direct teen patrons to good online resources such as Web sites or electronic books in the library's collection. Some reference programs allow users to draw or write on an online "whiteboard" as they also communicate using text. Others allow voice communication using instant messaging or other voice services.

Eventually, online reference services may take their inspiration from the gaming world and build virtual libraries where librarians create avatars—graphical representations of themselves—that can interact with "visiting" patrons. A few enterprising librarians are already creating a library in the Second Life online community; read more about the project and see what the virtual library looks like on the Second Life Library 2.0 blog (available at http://secondlifelibrary.blogspot.com/).

Online reference services will appeal to teens who want answers fast, and without the inconvenience of actually going to the library. Better yet, if the service is available twenty-four hours a day, as some are—often through a statewide cooperative effort among libraries—even a teen working late into the night on a last-minute term paper can get librarian assistance. A few of these services include:

AskNow
Available at: www.asknow.org
Staffed by California librarians during library hours, and by librarians around the country the rest of the time, AskNow is available twenty-four hours a day, seven days a week. You can even request a Spanish-speaking librarian or a medical, law, or business librarian. This service uses chat, and afterwards sends users a follow-up e-mail with a transcript of the session, including suggested links.

MassAnswers
Available at: www.massanswers.org/
This is a cooperative project of Massachusetts Regional Reference Center libraries and other participating libraries. The Web site offers chat and also allows the librarian to "show" the patron where to look online for answers based on a "co-browsing" feature.

L-Net
Available at: www.oregonlibraries.net
Oregon's live reference service for state residents answers questions using chat or e-mail. It is open twenty-four hours, seven days a week, except for certain holidays.
Other services include www.qandanj.org/, which serves New Jersey residents. Illinois also offers a service for residents, at www.myweblibrarian.com.
However, librarians who work with teens need not launch quite such an ambitious project. Instead, they can simply make themselves available online, in a variety of ways, during the hours they are staffing service desks. They can use e-mail, chat, instant messaging, text messaging to and from cell phones, or VOIP—Voice Over Internet Protocol—to make themselves accessible to teens who use all of these technologies, not just the telephone, to seek information.
Librarians who do this will reap several benefits. First, they will develop relationships with teens who might not otherwise use the library. Second, they will show that they are open to new technologies and willing to reach out to teens using the medium that teens find most appealing.
Since most libraries can't offer reference services 24/7, another alternative is to create a teen Web site that guides users toward online help. Pathfinders on popular homework projects, for example, give students a place to start.

Library Web sites can also link to homework help sites, indices to the Internet, and lists of search engines to try. Web sites can also offer help with building a search strategy. These pages may not take the place of help from a real, live librarian, but they can serve as a starting point and a guide.

IDEA #54: OFFER IM REFERENCE

> For more on instant messaging, see Chapter 3

Lansing Public Library, in Lansing, Illinois, currently offers virtual reference services via instant messaging. Icons on the Web site show which staff members are online and available for IM conversations. The icons indicate the particular librarian departments, so that teens can contact the teen librarian if they choose. The site also includes a Frequently Asked Questions page that explains instant messaging and describes the different services, such as Yahoo! and Windows Live Messenger.

Instant messaging is a type of communication that involves two users who are online at the same time and exchanging real-time messages. When you "IM" someone, if that person is online they are immediately notified. You can then chat back and forth by typing (or speaking, if the IM software and your computer setup allow voice communication). On some services, users can also exchange photos and graphics. Video is the next step.

Lansing Public Library, in Lansing, Illinois
Available at: www.lansing.lib.il.us/im.htm (see Figure 8.1)
Framingham Public Library, in Framingham, Massachusetts, includes the following information on their teen page at www.framinghamlibrary.org/teen/teenpage.htm:

> **Teen Chat Reference**
> Come chat with the YA librarian online with comments or questions you have (or just to say hi!). Find her on AIM and MSN Messenger under the handle: fplteenlib (@hotmail.com).

This is a very simple but effective way to implement IM reference service. Teen librarians can simply download the free software and then publicize their IM names. Yahoo! Messenger, AOL Instant Messenger (AIM), and Windows Live Messenger are three of the most popular services. There are also "aggregators" that allow users to communicate with users on multiple services.

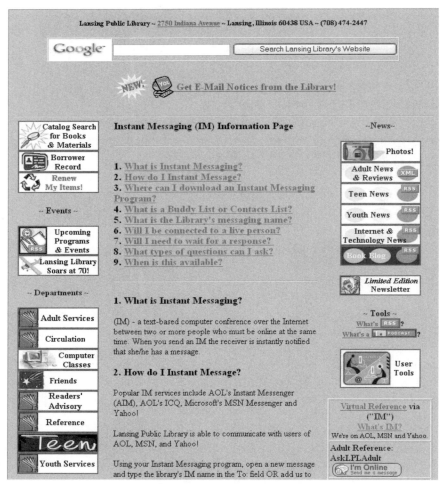

Figure 8-1 Lansing Public Library's Instant Messaging Information Page

Some considerations for librarians who are considering offering IM reference include:

1. Availability—Few librarians can be available and at their desks at all times. Make sure your Web site explains that the librarians are often helping other patrons on the phone or in person but will respond Instant Messages as quickly as they can. This way, teens won't get discouraged if they don't get a response within seconds. It's also a good idea to provide other ways to get questions answered—by phone or e-mail—in case staff can't be online during certain hours.

2. Privacy—Decide whether you will save transcripts of chats or clear them each time you sign off of the IM service. Transcripts could be useful—imagine the teen who IMs you a second time because she lost the link you gave her to that Web site on medieval footwear—but they also raise privacy concerns. Different services may have different default settings.

3. Time—Instant Messaging is fun and useful, but it can also be distracting. If you find that teens are using it as a social tool, to contact you without a question in mind, just to chat, you might want to set some time limits or come up with a polite way to sign off when you have patrons in line or other duties waiting.

Interview

Liz Zylstra
County of Prince Edward Public Library
Teen Services Head
Teenroom.blogspot.com
www.peclibrary.org

How Long Have You Been Offering Reference Using Instant Messaging?

Since the beginning of 2006.

Why Did You Decide to Try It? Why Do You Think It's an Important Service to Offer?

I saw that the vast majority of teens coming into the library were using MSN to talk to each other, and I thought this was a way that I could conveniently provide reference service to teens. It also lets the library "come into" another space in their lives, reminding them of our presence and services every time they log in and see the Teen Room online.

How Did You Choose MSN [Now Called Windows Live Messenger] over Other IM Services?

Primarily, it is almost the only IM service that I see teens in my community use—when I began promoting it, I offered to set up an account at any free IM service, and the only response I got was from MSN users. It's the only IM service that I have ever had a patron ask me to install on the few computers it wasn't on already.

How Many Librarians Are Involved in Using Instant Messaging, or Was It Something You Decided to Do on Your Own?

As head of teen services, I do all the teen reference work (time permitting, of course). I am the only one currently using instant messaging, as I'm able to help teens from all branches.

How Do You Let Patrons Know That the Service Is Available?

Posters, advertisements on our Web site and blog, and word of mouth.

How Often do Teens Use IM to Contact You?

I would say I receive, on average, messages from three or four teens a day.

What Kinds of Questions Do You Get?

We get a lot of questions about what the library's hours are and requests for specific information about programming. We also get requests for homework help and for books to be put on hold.

What Are Some of the Advantages of Offering This Option (Compared to Phone Reference, for Example)?

For many teens, this is a very easy and common way to communicate. Not only can I talk to them while they are at home on their personal computers, but I can talk to them on their cell phone through SMS and while they are at other branches of the library. Many teens would be hesitant to call the library when they might get someone they don't know, but they can message me and know exactly who will be on the other end. Also, they know it's confidential—they seem to be less embarrassed to ask for potentially controversial or private subject books because they don't have to face saying it out loud.

Have You Had Any Problems or Issues So Far?

The only "problem" is teens who think I can sit and chat with them for hours. However, it's easy enough to deal with by being honest—I just tell them that I'm a bit busy to chat, but if they have any specific questions they can message me.

Would You Recommend That Other Libraries Do This?

YES—if there is someone on staff who can do it, then absolutely.

What Advice or Suggestions Do You Have for Implementing IM Reference Service?

Get the word out about who you are and what you are doing. Ensure that staff members are entirely familiar with the service so they can promote it.

Interview

Kelli Staley
Head of Information Technology Services
Lansing Public Library
Lansing, Illinois

How Long Have You Been Offering Reference Using Instant Messaging?

We began in October 2004.

Why Did You Decide to Try It?

I saw a presentation at ILA (Illinois Library Association) where they mentioned another library in our consortium was doing it; I thought, if they can do it, we can too!

Why Do You Think It's an Important Service to Offer?

It's where our users are. There is no quirky virtual reference software for the patron to learn, since they already use IM. It is another mode of contact. DSL [which allows for high-speed Internet access] isn't as widespread in our area yet, so if you're online and have a question, you'd have to log out to call the library. And it's cheap.

What IM Services Do You Use (Yahoo!, AOL, Others)?

We use Trillian [www.ceruleanstudios.com] to connect to all three at once.

Did You Do Any Special Training for Staff?

I trained staff pretty much on a one-to-one basis. A few staff members were already IM users, so they helped us have "practice conversations."

How Do You Let Patrons Know That the Service Is Available?

This wasn't publicized heavily in the beginning. We advertise on our Web site (we're becoming almost "famous" for our use of the IM status icons on our home page!) We took small sheets (business-card size) to the high school. Now we include IM names in the newsletter, on brochures, anything we print up.

We added a screen name for readers' advisory in May 2005. We have a "What's IM?" page on our Web site, and our custom library toolbar has a link as well.

How Often Is the Instant Messaging Reference Used?

We average one or two messages a month per department. It could probably be more, but often the staff who are more comfortable with IM aren't scheduled at what would likely be peak times.

We are a little unique in that we have separate screen names for each department, so patrons can contact the specific department desk they need to talk to. Our teen librarian is out of the building frequently in the evenings as she attends MLS classes. Nobody fills in on the teen screen name while she is away. (Note: we don't get a large number of e-mail requests either, and we've offered that for quite a while.)

Do You Think Teens Are Using It?

Despite the teen librarian being offline a lot (which will change after this summer!) the teen name gets the most IMs. I keep stressing to the adult reference and adult readers advisory that the teens grow up quickly, and will rapidly expect consistent IM service from the adult departments, and usage will increase. One teen IMs to request books (teen romances mostly) and one day the librarian was in when she came in to pick up the books. She had never seen her in, browsing the collection, so we think she just requests via IM, then picks them up at the circulation desk.

Have You Had Any Challenges or Issues So Far?

Challenge: training. It's not hard to train, you just need the support from management that has decided to integrate IM as a service. Other challenge: getting people into the habit of signing on (and off at night).

We just began offering Meebo.com [a Web-based IM service] on our public terminals, so it will be interesting to see if IM numbers go up.

Would You Recommend That Other Libraries Do This?

Yes. Check the libsuccess.org wiki for a list of other libraries that do IM reference:

www.libsuccess.org/index.php?title=Online_Reference#Libraries_Using_IM_Reference

IDEA #55: PROVIDE LIVE HOMEWORK HELP

Many libraries are now using paid services such as Tutor.com to provide live homework help. Tutors are available online—usually during certain after-school hours—from the library or from the student's home. They use instant messaging, voice communication, and online "whiteboards" to communicate.

San Francisco Public Library offers Tutor.com services to children and teens, in English and Spanish. Tutors are available from 2:30 p.m. to 9 p.m., with more limited hours for Spanish-speaking tutors.

San Francisco Public Library, San Francisco, California
Available at: www.tutor.com/sfpl/default.asp

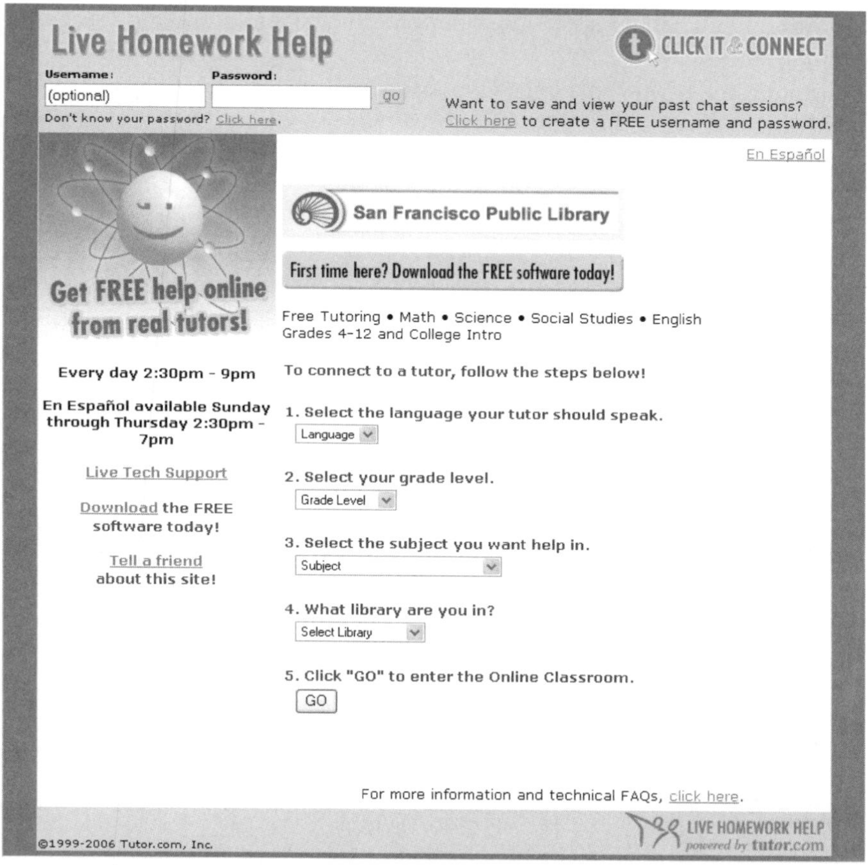

Figure 8-2   Live Homework Help from San Francisco Public Library

IDEA #56: GIVE GUIDANCE WITH PATHFINDERS

Even with 24/7 reference and instant messaging making librarian assistance more available, there will be times with teens are left on their own with a project. Ideally, they will turn to the resources available on their school or public library's Web site. Most libraries offer some kind of "homework help" guidance.

Carefully crafted online pathfinders are one way to provide virtual guidance to teens. School librarians may find it particularly useful to add pathfinders to their Web site, since they have closer contact with teachers and the curriculum and are more likely to know about upcoming assignments.

However, public libraries can also offer pathfinders for common projects and research topics.

Springfield Township High School, in Erdenheim, Pennsylvania, offers many outstanding pathfinders. They incorporate the library's print resources, catalog, and databases as well as Web sites.

Springfield Township High School, Erdenheim, Pennsylvania
Available at: http://mciu.org/%7Espjvweb/pathmenu.html
Before adding pathfinders to your library Web site, it's worth considering how much time you want to put into the project.

1. Will students use your pathfinders? How will you promote them? Maybe the teacher giving the assignment will require that students access the resources on the library Web site. Maybe you will need to make a flyer or bookmark, or simply guide students to the pathfinder Web page whenever they come to you with a relevant question.
2. Is this an assignment that teachers will give over and over, or is it a one-time topic? If it will be used year after year, it's worth putting in more time and fine-tuning the resources.
3. Do the resources align with state curriculum and standards? For a school library, this might be a particularly important aspect, but public

Figure 8-3   Pathfinders from Springfield Township High School

libraries can benefit, too, by looking into state guidelines to see what students are supposed to learn in each grade level.

Interview

Terese Chevalier
Online Media Computer Teacher
Lakewood High School, Lakewood, Ohio
Available at: www.lkwdpl.org/lhs/lhspath.htm

The pathfinders are created by the Lakewood Public Library. According to Chevalier, the public library has always worked closely with the schools. She explained the beginning of their collaboration this way:

> Several years ago, before our school libraries had Web pages, Lakewood Public Library generously offered to put together pathfinders to help with research on the Internet. Internet research was just becoming popular in our schools. We still encourage our teachers to make use of them. It is so easy for them. They have the option of doing it via e-mail, phone call or stopping in to Lakewood Public Library. There is an online form that can be completed. Turnaround is about a week.
>
> The site is faxed to the teacher for their review and comments prior to it being posted. Teachers are encouraged to include Web sites, vocabulary words, assignment sheets or whatever else they want. Or they can simply give a topic and grade level and let Lakewood Public Library do all the work. We have used several pathfinders repeatedly throughout the years.
>
> Prior to a class using it, we (Lakewood High School) ask Lakewood Public Library to update broken links if any are found. The teacher who did the Foreign Foods pathfinder has received e-mail from a teacher in Australia who has used it. What a thrill for her! Several of our student teachers have also made use of the pathfinders. Once they see how easy it is, they encourage others to do the same. Having a Web page with credible links on a topic saves so much time for our classes.
>
> Lakewood Public Library manages their pathfinders. All I have done is link to them on their site as a convenience for our students and staff. As far as advice for other librarians interested in starting a similar project: definitely, go for it! Keep your eyes open for copyright free clipart that could enhance the pages. Promote the pathfinders with local schools and teachers. It is a great way to reach out into the community and truly make your library useful 24/7.

Lakewood High School
Pathfinders

Resource Guides for
Class Assignments

- Lakewood City Schools
- Lakewood High School
- LHS LRC
- Middle Schools
  Pathfinders
- Elementary Schools
  Pathfinders
- Lakewood Public Library

- Crime and Punishment - Grade 10 Mrs. Schafer
- The Things They Carried - Grade 11 Mr. Strauss
- Public Opinion and Polling - Grade 12 Mrs. Schafer
- Voting and Voting Behaviors - Grade 12 Mrs. Schafer
- Presidents of the United States - Grade 12 Learning Resource Center
- Supreme Court Decisions - Grade 12 Mrs. Schafer
- Civil Rights - Learning Resource Center
- Creativity Through Visual Imagery - Grade 12 Ms. Jones
- Personality Inventories - Grade 11 Ms. Scheer
- Literary Magazine - Grade 9 Ms. Blackie
- Film - Grade 12 Ms. Israel
- History of Furniture - Grade 11 Ms. Hale
- Greater Cleveland Research - Grade 12 Mr. Ebner
- Afghanistan - Grade 12 Mrs. Schafer
- Women in the Middle East - Grade 12 Mrs. DeCapua
- Diego Rivera - Mexican Muralist - Grade 10-12 Ms. Sosnowski / Ms. Gonzalez
- Romanticism - Grade 11 Mr. Stupiansky
- Industrial Revolution - Grade 9 Ms. Flynn
- Enlightenment Thinkers - Grade 9 Ms. Scheer
- Middle Ages & Renaissance - Learning Resource Center
- French Literature - Grade 12 Ms. Braquet
- French Language/Francophone Countries - Ms. Braquet
- French Revolution - Grade 12 Mr. Sack
- Life and Times of Cyrano de Bergerac - Grade 10 Jacoby
- Art History - Grade 10 Ms. Smith
- German Architecture - Grade 12 Mr. Sent
- German Art - Grade 12 Mr. Sent
- Beowulf - Grade 11 Mr. Rhee
- Life in 19th Century England - Grade 9 Pearce/Blackie
- British Authors - Literary Criticism - Grade 12 Mrs. Perttu
- Oscar Wilde Grade 11 Ms. Gliha
- Roman Colonies / City Planning - Latin One & Two Dr. Abrahamsen
- Roman Emperors - Latin Dr. Abrahamsen
- Roman Art, Architecture, and Technology - Latin Dr. Abrahamsen
- AP Latin Vergil - Grade 12 Latin Dr. Abrahamsen
- The Ancient Olympics - Latin Dr. Abrahamsen
- The Roman Forum - Grade 9-12 Latin Dr. Abrahamsen
- Mythology - Learning Resource Center
- Symbols and Culture - Grade 9 Gliha / Wightman
- Monuments And Memorials - Grade 9-12 Ms. Nazelli
- World War One New Weapons - Grade 9 Mrs. Scheer
- Harlem Renaissance - Grade 11 Mr. Thornsberry / Mrs. Scheer
- History of CIA Covert Operations - Grade 12 Ms. Scheer
- American Culture in the 1980s - Grade 10 Mr. Demro
- Life in the 1960s - Learning Resource Center
- The 50's Project - U.S. History - Grade 10 Hinshaw/Ingham
- The 1920s - Grade 10 Ms. Nazelli
- Disabilities in Early Childhood - Grade 11 Ms. Tobin
- Deaf Education - Mrs. Macmillan & Mrs. Espenschied
- Biome Web Page Project - Grade 10 Ms. Smith / Ms. Zaremba
- Plate Tectonics - Grade 12 Mr. DeLong
- Celebrated Chemists - Grade 11 Ms. Eckert
- Cellular Respiration - Mr. Poulos
- Immunology - Grade 12 Ms. Eckert
- Genetic Disorders - Grade 10 Ms. Smith
- Infectious Diseases - Grade 10 Ms. Smith
- Rockets - Grade 12 Ms. Eckert
- Energy - Grade 9 Learning Resource Center
- Energy: The Pros and Cons of Our Decisions - Grade 9 - Rathge/Virost
- Mathematician Diversity Project - Ms. Weliczko
- American Historical Recipes - Grade 9 Learning Resource Center
- Cuisine and Culture - Intercurricular Project - Foreign Language/Culinary Arts - Sosnowski/Nagele
- Mrs. Salipante's Foreign Food Recipes - Gourmet Foods Class, Family and Consumer Sciences
- Mrs. Salipante's Creative Cooking Class - ANNUAL CHICKEN CONTEST - Winners and Recipes

Figure 8-4   Lakewood High School Pathfinders

Interview

Mary Ellen Stasek
Systems Librarian
Lakewood Public Library, Lakewood, Ohio
Pathfinders discussed:
High school: www.lkwdpl.org/lhs/lhspath.htm
Middle school: www.lkwdpl.org/schools/midschl.htm
Elementary: www.lkwdpl.org/schools/schlpath.htm

How Did This Project with Lakewood High School Start?

In 1996 we began this initiative with the middle schools media specialist. The intention was to catalyze use of electronic resources in the classroom. Our public library had more technical know-how and resources than teachers and LRC staff.

How Do You Communicate with the Teachers?

Teachers can submit a request for a pathfinder using our online form at www.lkwdpl.org/schools/pathreq.htm. Sometimes teachers phone or visit in person with a request. We communicate mostly via e-mail, sometimes by telephone. Sometimes the request comes from the LRC rather than a teacher.

How Many Pathfinders Have You Created?

We have done at least a couple hundred pathfinders since 1996. Some are used every year. We try to check links and keep them up-to-date but it is not always possible because of the number of pathfinders and how busy we are at the Library.

What Is the Process?

We are always prepared for collaboration but usually the teacher is satisfied with our product. Teachers sometimes have a few starter URLS [universal resource locators, or Web addresses] they want included. When we complete a pathfinder we ask the teacher to review the page and notify us if they want any changes. It is rare that they do.

Who Creates the Pathfinders?

Electronic Services staff in the Library Technology Center—typically, a librarian or para-professional. Occasionally it is a technician/assistant or student assistant with review by a librarian.

What Are the Factors You Consider in Choosing Web Sites?

The same factors used in general reference work for directing patrons to trustworthy information. In addition, we try to choose age-appropriate Web sites. This is a lesser concern with pathfinders for upper grades and AP classes.

Have You Had Feedback from Teachers and/or Students? Do They Find the Pathfinders Useful?

We often have feedback from teachers. They are very appreciative of the service. Offhand, I would say the three most common comments from teachers are:

- we make their job easier;
- we make learning more enjoyable for the students;
- we work fast (they often give us very short notice).

Here's an example of a comment from a middle school teacher:

> I just wanted to thank you for the Pathfinders page. My students have been researching for the last two weeks and it was great for them to have the reliable Web sites. The kids thought it was cool to have our own "special place" to get info. Thanks so much!
>
> And a high school (French) class:
>
> *Merci beaucoup*!!!! It is super! I have no idea how you managed to do all of that, and so quickly, but thank you a thousand times! I purposely took long to respond back to you because I "played" with the site and then had a few students try it as well to see if we could come up with any needed corrections. The feeling is unanimous . . . it is terrific! Thank you so much!

What Advice Would You Have for Other Librarians Who Wanted to Attempt a Similar Project?

Getting started:

- Public libraries have always worked with the local schools to assist students with assignments.
- Librarians have always made print pathfinders to materials in our collections.
- Librarians are now accustomed to steering our users to Web information.
- It's both practical and practicable to prepare a pathfinder and post it online for a class assignment.
- Everyone benefits—school and library staff, parents, and students.
- If the local schools are not particularly tech-savvy or tech-equipped, pathfinders are terrific joint undertakings that create a lot of good will.

Doing a project:

- A pathfinder doesn't have to be elaborate.
- Content rules.
- Include print resources from your collection.
- Guide students to your high-quality subscription databases when appropriate.

IDEA #57: TRY A PATHFINDER WIKI

As a variation on the previous idea, why not let students build their own pathfinders? A wiki, which allows all users to act as editors and add or delete content, is an ideal way to make this collaboration happen.

Students could—as they locate great resources for a project—add links and annotations to the class wiki. If you're worried about students adding substandard information sources, require them to go through the steps you've already taught them for evaluating Web sites. You might ask them to explain, in each annotation, how they decided that the site was a reliable one.

This type of project could result in terrific lists of resources for each assignment. Even better, it would give students a chance to collaborate, evaluate information, and take responsibility for contributing to the library Web site.

IDEA #58: ADD ASSIGNMENT LINKS

When students forget their assignment sheets, or lose their class notes, a quick way to access their assignments can be a lifesaver. The school or public library can provide a page that links to new assignments, organized by teacher or by the type of project. This way, students who forget what they're supposed to do still have the details at their fingertips, even from home or the public library.

Many teachers now have their own Web pages, where they post details of their latest assignments. That way, students no longer have an excuse to forget requirements or due dates. It's also handy for librarians, who can also access the sites. Many public and school library Web sites include links to teacher Web pages and to specific assignments.

Since updating online assignments can be time consuming for already overwhelmed teachers, consider suggesting to teachers that they use blogs to keep their homework sites current. Because blogs are quick and simple to update, this is a great approach for maximum teacher participation. Blogs also allow students to respond by asking questions or leaving comments, making this approach more interactive than a more static Web page. Teacher wikis, with passwords so that only the teachers or their most trusted students can make changes, are also a possibility.

Another quick solution is to use a site such as SchoolNotes (available at http://schoolnotes.com). Teachers register on the free, ad-supported site, then create home pages where they can easily update assignment information. Users enter the school zip code to find their teachers, but if many teachers at a school use the service, the school library Web site could also link to the pages.

Interview

Maggie Schmude
Library Department Chair
New Trier Township High School, Illinois
Available at: www.newtrier.k12.il.us/library/teacher_assignments/ASSIGN.HTM

The assignment pages are primarily created by the librarians, Schmude said, although teachers may ask librarians to post an assignment or add a particular link. The assignment links include descriptions of tasks, worksheets, and grading criteria as well as suggested resources.

What Is the Process for Adding an Assignment to Your Site?

Generally, when a librarian gets an assignment, she decides whether or not it would benefit from an electronic pathfinder. If so, she then creates it and posts it, sometimes with suggestions from other librarians.

For Assignments with Lists of Databases or Web Sites, Who Chooses the Links and What Are the Criteria?

The librarians choose the links (with occasional suggestions from teachers).

Are Most of the Assignments Repeated Each Year, or Are They One-time Assignments? How Long Do You Leave the Assignments on the Web Site?

Many are repeated from year to year, but we often do one-time shots for particular assignments. We usually leave them up until the assignment is handed in, but some go on for a good portion of the school year, and we leave them up as needed. Sometimes, we just forget to take them down and then I'll ask the librarians to check them to see which need to be removed.

How Much Time Does It Take to Add and Maintain the Assignments?

It varies with the assignment. It can be as simple as just posting a collection of links, or it can include far more extensive materials.

What Kind of Feedback Have You Had from Teachers and Students about Putting Assignments Online?

It's mostly been positive. The kids expect it, and sometimes I think the teachers feel we give the students too much help, but they also like it. It cuts down on the junk resources from the Web that they might get otherwise.

What Advice Would You Give to Other Librarians Who Want to Start a Similar Project?

Work with your teachers and your tech people. We can post our own assignments directly and this makes it much easier.

| class links | catalog | databases | style manual | web reference | audio-visual | reading & lit |

Class Links

Northfield Assignments	Winnetka Assignments
	Counterculture Project -- Mr. Forrest
	AIS Movement/Group Project - Licata/Plank
	Cold War Project
	AIS Project- Zwirner & Yang
Africa Research	Time Warp 'Zines: 1920s ---Ms. Horwitz
Beeler -- Africa	Reading Portfolio Project - Mr. Weiler
Christense -- Africa upfront	Psychology Topics
Muir -- Africa Project -- p. 2	Poetry Project - Mr. Virkus
Africa ... In the News	Spanish Speaking Cities
Muir -- Africa Current Events -- p. 6 & 7	Segregation Project - Mortier
Jackson -- Africa Upfront	Finding Scholarly Articles
Gilchrist - MyPyramid.gov Tracking	Finding Research/Studies
Gilchrist - MyPyramid.gov	Civilian Targets: World War II & Today
Fullenkamp - Oceans	Chinese Idioms & Proverbs
Ward -- Biomes	Provinces of China
Cowan/Buckingham/Meyer - Shakespeare Research	Age of Anxiety Humanities Project
Haskell - Poetry Project	Africa Project
Roaring Twenties - Ms. Theodore	AIS Junior Theme--Campbell/Maxman
TREV. EXPO	Hamlet: Literary Criticism
Tricoli -- First Aid	World War II Scrapbook
	Researching Countries
Neptun - Rocks & Minerals	Jr. Theme - American Literature
Nakayama - Medieval and Edo Japan	AP Junior Theme
Feiertag/Jaffe - Greek Myth & Culture	AIS Jr. Theme
Moretta/Schmittgens - Rome	Company Information
Neptun -- Earthquakes	Spanish Cities
Mythology	Katrina: The Aftermath
Sowa - Diseases	Civic Engagement Project
Gilchrist - Emotional Health	Researching Constitutional Issues
Gilchrist - Substance Abuse Project	Third Party Forum
Kim--Maori Project	U.S. History - DVD Video Project
Feiertag/Jaffe--Maori Project	Hurricane Relief - Parks
Wurth - Space and Reality TV	Genetic Disorders - Ksiazek
Neptun - EcoVillage	Spring Chemistry - Goral
Gilchrist -- Emotional Intelligence	Elizabethan England
Molzahn -- Animal Kingdoms	Energy Project - Goodspeed
Woodruff -- zooquarium	Angola Project- Geraghty/Ksiazek
Mauer -- Invertebrates	Shakespearean Drama - Licata
Social Studies Demo	Spanish Artists - Tamuzian
	French Travel Project
	Hot Air Balloon Project - Druger
Archived Class Links	
New Trier High School Website	

Figure 8-5   New Trier High School Library's Class Links

IDEA #59: INCLUDE RESOURCES FOR PARENTS/TEACHERS

Teens aren't the only ones served by library Web sites. Parents and teachers are also an important audience. Many school and public library Web sites feature parent or teacher pages that contain resources for those groups. A parent's page might include links to parenting help, articles on Internet safety, links to college information, and much more. A teacher page could include Web sites and blogs of interest to teachers, curriculum guides, information on using technology in the classroom, Web design for teachers, tools such as online grade books, and so on.

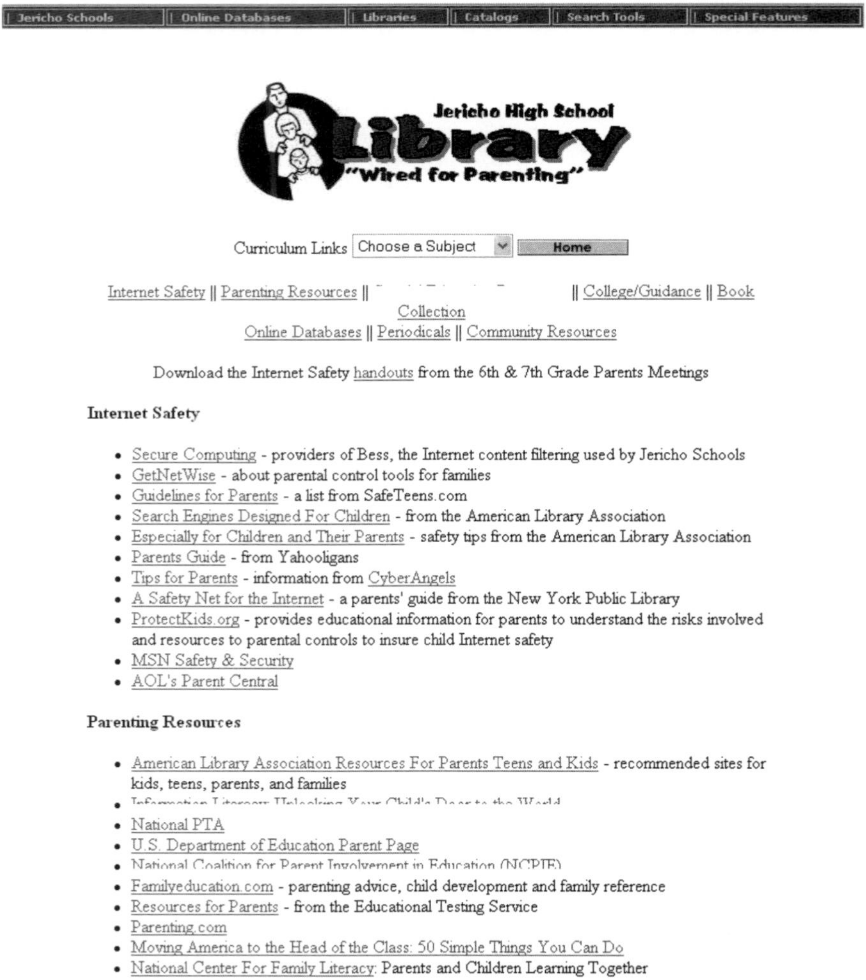

| Jericho Schools || Online Databases || Libraries || Catalogs || Search Tools || Special Features

Jericho High School Library "Wired for Parenting"

Curriculum Links Choose a Subject Home

Internet Safety || Parenting Resources || || College/Guidance || Book Collection
Online Databases || Periodicals || Community Resources

Download the Internet Safety handouts from the 6th & 7th Grade Parents Meetings

Internet Safety

- Secure Computing - providers of Bess, the Internet content filtering used by Jericho Schools
- GetNetWise - about parental control tools for families
- Guidelines for Parents - a list from SafeTeens.com
- Search Engines Designed For Children - from the American Library Association
- Especially for Children and Their Parents - safety tips from the American Library Association
- Parents Guide - from Yahooligans
- Tips for Parents - information from CyberAngels
- A Safety Net for the Internet - a parents' guide from the New York Public Library
- ProtectKids.org - provides educational information for parents to understand the risks involved and resources to parental controls to insure child Internet safety
- MSN Safety & Security
- AOL's Parent Central

Parenting Resources

- American Library Association Resources For Parents Teens and Kids - recommended sites for kids, teens, parents, and families
- National PTA
- U.S. Department of Education Parent Page
- Familyeducation.com - parenting advice, child development and family reference
- Resources for Parents - from the Educational Testing Service
- Parenting.com
- Moving America to the Head of the Class: 50 Simple Things You Can Do
- National Center For Family Literacy: Parents and Children Learning Together

Figure 8-6 Jericho High School Library Parenting Resources

Jericho High School in Jericho, New York, has an excellent page for parents. It includes resources on Internet safety, parenting resources, special education resources, college, and community resources.

Jericho High School, Jericho, New York
Available at: www.bestschools.org/hs/library/parents.html (see Figure 8-6)

Interview

Vicki Builta
Librarian
East Side Middle School
Anderson, Indiana
www.esmslibrary.com/categories.php?view=9

Why Did You Decide to Add a Page for Teachers to Your Web Site?

As a media specialist, I provide services for all of the members of my school community. There are many things that I do for staff members that serve to promote literacy, reading and instructional technology; a special section of the Web site that is devoted to staff development and professionalism just seems to be a natural outgrowth of that mission.

Many staff members truly want to use more technology sources in their classroom, but lack the time to find appropriate resources. By offering choices for them to use that relate to their teaching areas, all of them benefit, and our students benefit as well.

How Do You Choose the Resources? What Kinds of Sites Do You Include?

In addition to having a separate section for Teacher Resources on the site, I also send weekly e-mail updates to the staff on exemplary Web sites. I subscribe to several professional magazines and online weekly update sources that review a variety of Web sites and are used to glean items for the site and for the e-mail updates. Sites are chosen based on our middle school curriculum. The sites also have to have information that correlates with our Indiana Academic Standards in the various subject areas.

How Do You Let Teachers Know about the Page?

At the beginning of the school year, all staff members are given a folder called Library Lines that includes information on all types of services and programs sponsored by the school library. The Web site is mentioned there.

Each week, a Tech Tuesday e-mail is sent to all staff members. In this e-mail, sites are featured that deserve special attention from the teachers.

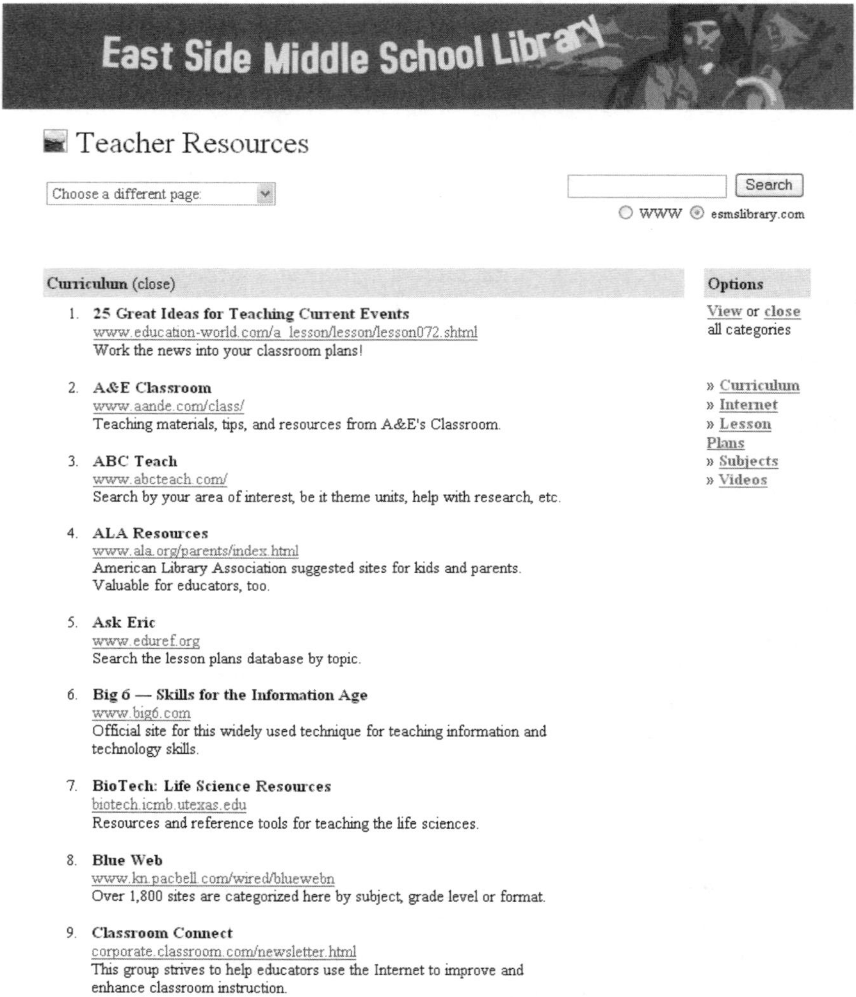

East Side Middle School Library

✉ Teacher Resources

Choose a different page: ⌄   [   ] [Search]
                                    ○ WWW ◉ esmslibrary.com

Curriculum (close)   **Options**

1. **25 Great Ideas for Teaching Current Events**   View or close
   www.education-world.com/a_lesson/lesson/lesson072.shtml all categories
   Work the news into your classroom plans!

2. **A&E Classroom**   » Curriculum
   www.aande.com/class/   » Internet
   Teaching materials, tips, and resources from A&E's Classroom.   » Lesson
                                                            Plans
3. **ABC Teach**   » Subjects
   www.abcteach.com/   » Videos
   Search by your area of interest, be it theme units, help with research, etc.

4. **ALA Resources**
   www.ala.org/parents/index.html
   American Library Association suggested sites for kids and parents.
   Valuable for educators, too.

5. **Ask Eric**
   www.eduref.org
   Search the lesson plans database by topic.

6. **Big 6 — Skills for the Information Age**
   www.big6.com
   Official site for this widely used technique for teaching information and
   technology skills.

7. **BioTech: Life Science Resources**
   biotech.icmb.utexas.edu
   Resources and reference tools for teaching the life sciences.

8. **Blue Web**
   www.kn.pacbell.com/wired/bluewebn
   Over 1,800 sites are categorized here by subject, grade level or format.

9. **Classroom Connect**
   corporate.classroom.com/newsletter.html
   This group strives to help educators use the Internet to improve and
   enhance classroom instruction.

Figure 8-7   East Side Middle School Library Teacher Resources

In the library's monthly newsletter to the staff, additional mention is made of the Web site and appropriate and worthy information technology sources.

Have You Had Any Feedback on It from Teachers?

The staff has been very supportive and appreciative of the site. Student teachers, teachers from other buildings, and colleagues that I meet at professional conferences also like to receive updates on sites that are added to the site. Many professionals from other school buildings have asked to be added to my mailing list for Tech Tuesday.

What Advice Would You Give to Other School Librarians Who Want to Add a Teacher Resource Page to Their Web Site?

The Teacher Resource section of my Web site is a vital component of my mission for my school. A school library is a resource for all stake holders in our school community. To me, there is no one section of the site that is more important than another. But the site and its various components must be maintained. This is time intensive. Checking to make sure that sites are still working and still being updated is vital to having a tool that is useful to all staff. Also, you must be willing to spend time checking new sites for possible inclusion. To save needless effort, subscribing to various weekly (free) e-mail updates on new or interesting sites is a tremendous help.

Interview

Thomas Kaun
Library Media Teacher
Redwood High School
Larkspur, California
http://137.164.143.46/library/teaching.htm

How Did You Come Up with Your List of Resources for Teachers? How Are They Organized?

I now have the sites organized by our curricular departments.: English, Social Studies, Science & Math, Visual & Performing Arts, World Languages, and physical education. I combined science and math because often sites have both subjects combined and it's harder to untangle them. Right now the P.E. and language lists are not complete because I haven't had the time really to explore for resources.

How Much of a Time Commitment Does It Take to Keep the List Current?

That's a tough question to answer. I don't do it regularly, though I have tried various methods. Basically I find that when I think patrons are going to use a page (it's been promoted in some way or someone has asked me about something specific), I will go in and make sure links are live. I'd love to have some kind of automated process for this task but because of firewalls (which most schools have) it's difficult to use the available tools out there.

How Do You Find New Sites to Add?

I try to find good starting points such as the state resources and sites that I already know about (such as Marco Polo, in the case of curriculum resources). Then, as I'm looking at those links, they lead to other places that seem good, and I will add those as well. You have to be judicious in adding links because if you have too many it becomes overwhelming and people won't use them.

The sites I provide are mostly gateways—other things I hope can be of use. I also subscribe to Librarian's Internet Index weekly new sites list, and that gives me a lot of ideas for adding to my Web site in general.

How Do You Promote That Part of Your Site to Teachers?

I am mostly promoting the site to students, and indirectly to teachers. I wish I had more staff development time one-on-one with teachers but it's hard to come by. I also send an occasional e-mail to teachers with lists of new materials, and I often will promote some particular thing I've heard about that I think will interest or help them. A recent article was about specialized search engines. (I also published that article in our parent newsletter.)

What Kinds of Responses Have You Had?

A couple of teachers recently have told me they found some interesting things using the resources on the page.

What Advice Would You Give to Other Librarians Who Want to Create a Resource Site for Teachers?

Take a look at what others have done. Make sure you are paying attention to your school's curriculum. Be very selective. Make sure the sites you select are of the highest quality.

IDEA #60: HELP WITH REAL-LIFE DILEMMAS

Teens require help finding answers for life problems, not just school assignments. Whether it is health issues, relationship dilemmas, or something else entirely, teens need access to books, Web sites, and other materials. Problem is, they may be too embarrassed to ask a librarian. Or they may not even think of the library as a place to find information. Instead, they may ask their friends or turn to less-than-reliable sources.

On your library Web site, you have an opportunity to provide solid resources to help teens make informed decisions. You can also provide links to sites where they can find support and see that they are not alone in dealing with their problems.

Areas where teen library Web sites often provide information include:

- General health
- Drugs, alcohol, and cigarettes
- Substance abuse
- Eating disorders

- Puberty
- Sexual health
- Gay, lesbian, bisexual and questioning teens
- Pregnancy
- Abortion
- Dating
- Abusive relationships
- Mental Health
- Divorce
- Family issues
- Child abuse
- Homelessness
- Teen legal rights
- Work issues
- Consumer and financial issues
- Online safety
- Self defense/personal safety
- Links to local resources—teen health clinics, support groups, etc.
- Crisis hotlines

Before you offer links to help teens with their "real lives," you should consider:

- What are your criteria for selection? Having a written collection development policy that includes Web resources is particularly important if you include links on sexuality or other controversial topics that might invite challenges.
- How much time will you need to select the resources?
- How often will you check/update links to make sure the URL (universal resource locator, or Web address) is still valid, and that the site is still up to date and appropriate?
- How will you publicize this resource? It could be as simple as a link from your library home page, or you could include references to it in your e-mail newsletter, blog, or other avenues of communication.
- Will you let teens participate in the initial selection of links and/or design of the page?
- Will you give teens and other users the opportunity to suggest additional links, through a feedback form or e-mail?

Denver Public Library, in Denver, Colorado, offers a great list of resources on their Web site. They divide their links into twelve categories, from "Mind" and "Body" to "Rights" and "Money." See the list at http://teens.denverlibrary .org/life/index.html.

IDEA #61: ASSIST WITH COLLEGE AND CAREERS

Few decisions have as much impact on a teen's life as the choices they make about college or a career path. As librarians, we're lucky to have a role in providing good information on this subject.

Many library Web sites for teens provide college and career information. Your Web site can link to:

- Individual college Web sites
- General college information sites
- Test sign-up information, such as a link to the Educational Testing Service
- Paid test preparation databases, such as LearningExpressLibrary.com
- Financial aid databases, including those that focus on scholarships for particular groups—African-American students, students with disabilities, and so on
- A FAFSA (Free Application for Federal Student Aid) link
- Internship programs
- Military career information
- Summer jobs
- The *Occupational Outlook Handbook* online

And much more!

Salt Lake County Library in Utah offers a nice "Career Launch" page that pairs Web site links with lists of print resources available in their teen center. Their resources are at www.slco.lib.ut.us/teen/teen_college_career.htm.

Mansfield High School, in Mansfield, Texas, also offers a good list of college and career resources on their library Web site. The annotations for each link tell users what to expect from each site on the resource list.

Mansfield High School, in Mansfield, Texas
Available at: www.mansfieldisd.org/mhs/library/college_info.html (see Figure 8-8)

IDEA #62: EMBED SEARCH ENGINE TOOLBARS

One decision library Web site designers have to make is whether to embed a search engine toolbar in their home page. It's fairly simple to add a Google Web search box, for example, to your site. Just go to http://services.google .com/searchcode2.html?accept=on and choose from three options:

- Google Free Web search. This allows you to add a Google Web search box to your Web page. Users type in their search terms and are taken to their Google search results.

ANSFIELD HIGH SCHOOL
TIGER PRIDE THROUGH EXCELLENCE

Library Links - College & Career Info

Business & Economics | College/Career Information | Cultural & Ethnic | Fine Arts | Homework Tools | Internet Tutorial
Just For Fun! | Languages & Literature | Mathematics | MLA Sample Entries for Works Cited | News, Sports, & Travel
Online Library Resources | Research Tools | Social Studies | Space | Teacher Links

**These sites are not part of the Mansfield High School website
and we have no control over their content or availability.**

College/Career Information

America's Job Bank	This site is a partnership between the U.S. Department of Labor and state operated Employment Services. This is a comprehensive source of occupational and economic information.
Best Jobs USA.com	Salaries for states by job category, best places to live and work, career fairs, corporate profiles, post your resume.
Brass Ring	Students benefit from seeing how professionals go through the job search process.
Career Development Manual	From the Department of Career Services at the University of Waterloo, Canada. This site provides an interactive guide to career planning with a multi-step self assessment inventory.
Career Exploration Links	Links to various career info.
CareerBuilder.com	Provides a searchable jobs database, resume posting service, online job fair information, and industry specific employment information.
Career Questionnaire	Complete the online Career Questionnaire and submit it(on computer). Your answers will be used to find careers that match your interests and abilities.
College Bound	Provides links for tips dealing with dorm survival, college profiles, aid, etc. The college connection has internship information and employment resources for college and graduate students, as well as high school students who are planning ahead.

Figure 8-8   Mansfield High School College/Career Information

- Google Free SafeSearch. Same as above, but Google claims that "Web pages containing adult themed and explicit sexual content are excluded from Web search results." Of course, no system is foolproof, and you're leaving it up to Google to define "adult themed."
- Google Free Web search with site search. This option allows users to search your site as well as the Web.

For all three options, Google gives you a few lines of code to copy from their box and paste to your HTML document or Web design software document. If you choose to search your own site as well as the Web, you'll need to make a couple of quick substitutions in their code.

Of course, Google is not the only search engine you can add to your site. Most major search sites offer this option.

Before adding a search tool like Google to your library Web site, however, consider the drawbacks. The advantages are pretty clear: teens who can't find what they need on your site have a simple way to look for resources on the Web. They don't even have to type in the name of a search engine or click on a link before choosing their search terms.

However, is providing a search engine box on your site's home page sending a message? Are you telling teens that your site can't help them, and that they might be better off going straight to Google (or another favorite search site)? Users might be tempted to take the "easy way" out with a Google search, rather than navigating the links you've so carefully chosen or instead of using your library databases. Furthermore, many teens find searching the Web to be an exercise in frustration, since they often have trouble choosing the right search terms and evaluating the results.

On the other hand, a site search might help your users quickly find what they need, and a Web search might assist them when they've exhausted other options. You'll have to weigh the pros and cons before making use of Web search boxes on your site.

Chapter 9

Online Learning

OVERVIEW

Assignments, tests, research papers—every day, middle and high students pour into libraries looking for resources. School librarians deal even more directly than public librarians with teens in their "student" mode. Teen library users need guidance in finding information, using it, citing their sources, and much more.

Many school and public library Web sites boast features that help students deal with their workload. Some, like assignment alerts, are a means of managing mass assignments, giving librarians a heads-up about a project whole classes (or whole schools) need to complete. Others, like advice on citing sources or evaluating Web sites, are aimed at the students themselves, so that they have the tools to do effective research.

The Web has incredible potential as a teaching tool. The simplest sites will provide information for students to read and ponder, while more advanced library Web sites can offer interactive features like test-taking practice or WebQuests. Features like audio or video lectures take things one step further, giving students twenty-four-hour access to personalized study tools.

IDEA #63: ASK FOR ASSIGNMENT ALERTS

For more on using feedback forms, see Chapter 3

There's nothing worse than having thirty or forty teens pour into the library, all looking for books on Abraham Lincoln—especially when you realize you already gave all three of the library's Lincoln biographies to the first student who asked. Equally daunting is trying to pry assignment details out of a student who needs help, only to realize that even he isn't clear on what he wants: "Uh, it's sort of about the Civil War. Or something. I think."

If you provide an assignment alert form on your Web site, however, teachers can communicate directly with the library. They can let you know about assignments in advance, so that you can place books on reserve if necessary. You can also print out details of the assignment, so that when the confused student arrives, you know exactly what he needs. Another advantage of having a heads-up is that, if the assignment calls for something the library doesn't have, you can contact the teacher in advance to discuss ways in which he or she might want to modify it.

Though school library media specialists work in closer proximity to teachers than public librarians, school library Web sites can also benefit from assignment alert forms. Instead of physically coming to the library, teachers can submit information from home or their own classroom. You can also customize the assignment form to make sure you get the information you need—not just a vague, one-line e-mail.

Multnomah County Library in Oregon has an excellent example of an assignment alert form. The library offers several services, including personalized Webliographies, pathfinders, and booklists. Teachers can pick up the books on a booklist from their nearest branch, if they so desire. See the form at www.multcolib.org/schoolcorps/assign.html.

Central Rappahannock Regional Library, in Virginia, has an attractive assignment alert form. It asks for the teacher's name, e-mail address, school, grade level, and the dates of the assignment. Teachers can describe the assignment and indicate the services they would like, whether it is having librarians place books on reserve, create pathfinders, or schedule an instructional session for the class.

Central Rappahannock Regional Library, Virginia
Available at: www.answerpoint.org/teachers_place/assignment_alert.asp

To add an assignment alert to your Web site, you will be designing a feedback form. (For more on how to do this, see the section on forms in Chapter 3). You'll want to ask for the bare minimum of information you need, since a long, complicated form might scare off teachers.

Also, make sure it's clear what your response will be once the form is submitted. Maybe no response is required, if the form is just a way for the teacher to let you know what to expect. Maybe the teacher expects you to perform specific services, in which case your Web page should include information on how much advance notice is required (for example, at least a week for compiling a booklist, at least two weeks to plan a visit from a librarian, etc.).

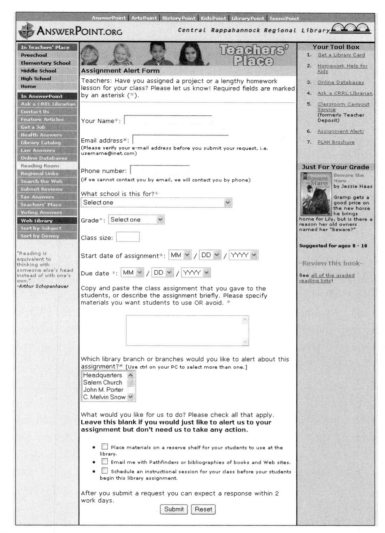

Figure 9-1   Central Rappahannock Regional Library's Assignment Alert Form

Some information you might want to ask for on the form:

- Teacher's name
- Teacher's contact information (phone, e-mail)
- Preferred method of contact
- Teacher's school
- Grade level

- How many students will be doing the assignment?
- Assignment due date
- Space for a description of assignment
- Special requirements—if there is any specific type of materials or sources students may not use, such as Web sites or Wikipedia; if they must use at least three different sources; if students must select novels of at least 100 pages; and so on
- Branches to place "on alert"
- Actions teacher would like the librarian to take—place books on reserve, create a booklist, plan a library orientation for the whole class

Generally, as soon as the teacher clicks the "submit" button, the information will be mailed to the e-mail address you have chosen. For a public library, that might be the teen librarian's account, or a general account that librarians take turns checking. For a school library, it would probably go directly to the school library media specialist. You will want to make sure that alerts get responses within the specified time limit even if the librarian who is usually in charge is absent or on vacation.

You might want to prepare a generic e-mail response to send back to the teacher immediately. This e-mail would acknowledge receipt of the assignment alert and describes the action the library will take. It might read something like this:

Dear teacher,

Thank you for submitting an assignment alert to Anytown Public Library! We appreciate the fact that you are keeping us informed so that we can provide better service to you and your students.

As requested, we will compile a booklist for your students on the topic you described. You should receive the booklist by e-mail by (date here). We will also set aside books on your topic on a reserve shelf at our Third Street branch from (date) to (date).

We look forward to working with you and your students on this project and future assignments. Please contact (name here) at (phone, e-mail) if we can be of any further assistance.

This would also be the time to let teachers know gently if the library will likely be unable to fill their request. You might insert a paragraph like this:

> One of your requirements for the assignment is that students choose a young adult novel of at least 500 pages. Unfortunately, Anytown Public Library has a limited number of books that meet your criteria, since most teen novels tend to be shorter. However, our teen librarians

would be happy to recommend many high quality adult novels that might be appropriate for your students.

Also, you might want to consider adding a checkbox to your assignment alert form that gives the library permission to post the assignment details on their Web site. This way, librarians at any public library branch can access the details, and students can look at their assignments from home as well. At schools, students can confirm the details of their assignments while in the school library.

Also, if you do come up with booklists for specific assignments, consider posting those on your Web site as well. Students, teachers, and librarians will be able to access the list from anywhere. You can also link each title to the library catalog, so that by clicking on the title the student can see whether it is available or checked out.

Some libraries choose to make their assignment alert forms available as PDF or Word documents. Teachers click on the document, print it out, and then fax or mail it to the library. This might be an option if your teachers are not very Internet savvy, or if you prefer a paper version (though you can always print out the e-mail if this is the case). It's also a nice touch to offer teachers the option of e-mailing, faxing, or phoning with a request, if they are more comfortable with one of those less high-tech methods.

IDEA #64: TEACH EVALUATION SKILLS

"Why can't I base my entire research paper on a Wikipedia entry?" "It was the first link that came up on Google, so it must be okay." "But it says right here that if you buy this product, you'll lose twenty pounds in one week."

Teens may feel confident about using the Internet, but that doesn't mean they're savvy enough to evaluate what they find there. Teaching teens to take a critical look at online information is one of a librarian's most important jobs. Your Web site can provide guidance, checklists, and even detailed tutorials and lessons in this area. While school libraries tend to offer this information more often, public libraries can do so as well.

The Chico High School Library, in Chico, California, offers a comprehensive list of resources to help students and educators learn about the Internet, at http://melvil.chicousd.org/wdev.html#Learning. Chico High School's site also links to a page where students can practice for the district's proficiency test on analyzing Web sites. A Web site evaluation form is included, plus links to thirty sites students can use to test their proficiency. Access it at http://dewey.chs.chico.k12.ca.us/info-lit.html.

School librarian Joyce Valenza of Springfield Township High School in Erdenheim, Pennsylvania, has designed a WebQuest for ninth to twelfth graders that leads them through a lesson on evaluating Web sites. The WebQuest requires students to look critically at sites that address controversial topics such as cloning and smoking/tobacco. Students complete an evaluation chart and rank sites according to four criteria, including bias, usability, authority, and content. The WebQuest is available at: http://mciunix.mciu.k12.pa.us /~spjvweb/evalwebstu.html.

IDEA #65: HELP STUDENTS AVOID PLAGIARISM

With the advent of the Internet, plagiarizing is easier than ever—students can just cut and paste. Worse, they may not even fully understand that they are doing anything wrong. Teachers and librarians need to be vigilant not only about detecting plagiarism, but also about teaching students how to avoid it.

Many library Web sites for teens, especially school library Web sites, include information on plagiarism. This kind of information is a natural to pair with tools and instructions for citing sources, which are addressed in the next idea.

A terrific presentation on plagiarism comes from the Marathon Middle/ High School Library Media Center in Marathon, Florida. The PowerPoint presentation defines and explains plagiarism, paraphrasing, summaries, and citing sources. It also gives examples and asks students to decide whether they constitute plagiarism. Find it at www.monroe.k12.fl.us/mhs/media/Why%20am%20I% 20in%20trouble%20for%20plagiarizing/Why%20Am%20I%20Trouble% 20for%20Plagiarizing_files/frame.htm.

The Downers Grove North High School Library, in Downers Grove, Illinois, takes a slightly different approach by providing information aimed at teachers. The page explains how students buy papers from online "paper mills," and links to some of those sites. The page also provides strategies for detection, articles about plagiarism, and tips on how to structure assignments to make cheating more difficult. The page is at www.csd99.org/north/library/plagiarism.htm.

IDEA #66: ENCOURAGE CORRECT CITATION

Your library Web site can help teach students how to cite their sources properly. This can range from a simple one-page checklist or list of links to detailed, interactive resources. In creating this part of your Web site, you'll probably want to consult with teachers to find out what citation styles they prefer. Citing Internet sources is another area you'll want to be sure to address.

Many library sites also link to online citation tools, where students can enter information about their sources and automatically create a properly formatted list of citations. These tools include:

Citation Machine
Available at: http://citationmachine.net

A free tool that generates APA or MLA-style citations for various types of resources.

EasyBib

Available at: www.easybib.com

This tool allows students to create bibliographies, upload journal citations, and choose between MLA or APA style. EasyBib offers a free service as well as a subscription service with more features.

NoodleTools

Available at: www.noodletools.com

Created by a teacher-librarian, this site provides tools to help students use APA and MLA style. It includes a free "express" citation tool, but more sophisticated tools require a subscription.

The Ganada Library at Ruben A. Cirillo High School in Walworth, New York, offers extensive information on citing sources. The page on citations links to a rubric and also to a printable slip that students can use to record information about their sources. It also links to many Web sites with information about MLA style, APA style, and citing electronic sources. Finally, the "bibliography makers" section provides links to tools such as NoodleTools and EasyBib. A disclaimer notes that the automatic citation tools may not create citations in the exact format the students' teachers require.

Ruben A. Cirillo High School, Walworth, New York

Available at: www.gananda.k12.ny.us/library/mshslibrary/Webcite.htm

Public libraries also can and should provide information on citing sources. The Saint Paul Public Library in Saint Paul, Minnesota, has a nice page on writing tools that includes links to style guides such as APA, MLA, and the Chicago Manual of Style. Available at: www.stpaul.lib.mn.us/weblinks/writing-tools.html.

IDEA #67: OFFER TEST-TAKING PRACTICE

Taking tests, especially standardized tests, is a fact of life for most students. They're probably familiar with acronyms like PSAT, SAT, ACT, and AP, or have heard of the GED and ASVAB tests, as well as high school entrance exams such as the ISEE and COOP/HSPT. Library Web sites for teens can easily provide links to test-taking resources, such as the College Board or Educational Testing Service.

Some libraries go farther to also provide test-taking practice sites. SAT classes can be prohibitively expensive for many teens, and while there are test books available at school and public libraries, online practice tests may have

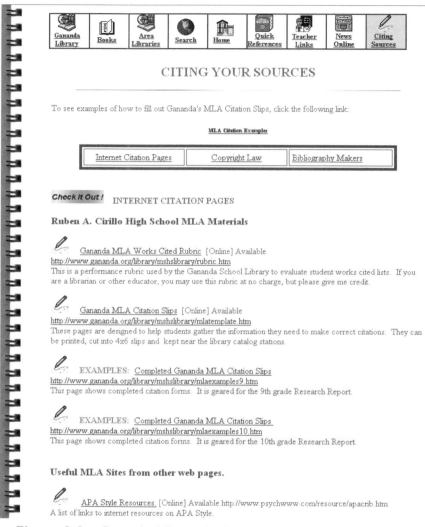

Figure 9-2   Ganada Library's Citing Your Sources Page

more appeal. For one thing, online test practice can provide instant results as well as analysis of a students' areas of strength or weakness.

Some libraries offer subscription services such as Learning Express Library, at www.learnatest.com/. Teens can use the service to practice for certain state reading and math tests as well as the ACT or SAT, the Catholic High School entrance exam, AP exams, and more. The Carthage Media Center at Carthage High School in Carthage, Missouri, is one school library that offers test practice through Learning Express Library. Many public libraries do the same.

IDEA #68: ASSIGN WEBQUESTS AND ONLINE LESSONS

A WebQuest is a research assignment where most or all of the activity takes place online. Students usually complete WebQuests as part of a group, where each student in the group has an assigned role. The term originated with Bernie Dodge, a professor at San Diego State University, in 1995. A well-constructed WebQuest requires students to construct their own meaning from the information they find, rather than simply to gather facts.

For more on WebQuests and the educational theory behind them, as well as many examples, see the following Web sites:

- Best WebQuests
  Available at: http://bestWebQuests.com/
- Taming the Internet with WebQuests
  Available at: www.greece.k12.ny.us/ath/library/WebQuests/taming_internet_with_WebQuests_files/frame.htm
- WebQuest Definition and Foundations
  Available at: http://eduscapes.com/sessions/travel/define.htm
- WebQuest Portal (Bernie Dodge's site)
  Available at: http://WebQuest.org/

Once you've read up on the structure and purpose of WebQuests, you'll be ready to create your own. There are several helpful tools on the Web for this purpose, such as:

- InstantWebQuest, a free site for creating and hosting WebQuests
  Available at: www.instantprojects.org/WebQuest/main.php
- Quest Garden, Bernie Dodge's new authoring tool
  Available at: http://WebQuest.org/questgarden/author/
- WebQuest template, for those who like to use HTML
  Available at: http://ozline.com/templates/WebQuest.html
- Filamentality, a tool for creating online learning activities
  Available at: www.kn.pacbell.com/wired/fil/

Chico High School Library, in Chico, California, provides educators with an extensive list of links and information about WebQuests at http://melvil.chicousd.org/WebQuest.html.

The media center at Greece Athena Middle School in Rochester, New York, offers excellent resources on WebQuests, as well as several examples of WebQuests created in collaborations between Library Media Specialist Will Haines and teachers at the school. The site is at www.greece.k12.ny.us/ath/library/WebQuests/default.htm.

Springfield Township High School in Erdenheim, Pennsylvania, offers many online lessons and WebQuests on its Virtual Library site. There is even a WebQuest about building a school library Web site. Find the library's many WebQuests at http://mciu.org/%7EspjvWeb/jvles.html. Below is the beginning of a WebQuest about the Ancient World, where students must act as "travel agents" to sell a trip to their particular ancient civilization.

Springfield Township High School in Erdenheim, Pennsylvania
Available at: http://mciu.org/%7Espjvweb/ancientwq.html

Images from Pics4Learning

Introduction

Welcome to the annual convention of ancient travel agents! You are gathered to sell your best product--your own, very impressive, civilization. Get ready to sell it!

The Task

A large group of ancient tourists is planning a trip. As members of a travel agency, you have been brought it to "sell a trip" to your own ancient civilization. Not only do you want to land this big account and prove your culture the very best destination, you are also a proud citizen. You want to encourage tourism, to show this group of early tourists all your civilization has accomplished.

Your group will be assigned one of the following cultures to promote:

- Ancient Egypt
- India
- China
- Rome
- Israel
- Greece

Each group member will be responsible for **two** products: a two-page persuasive essay and a section of a PowerPoint travel brochure.

Figure 9-3   Travel Agent to the Ancient World: A WebQuest

Interview

Will Haines
School Librarian
Greece Athena Middle School
Rochester, New York

Why Should Librarians Learn about and Create WebQuests?

I think we're the logical ones in our school to do so—we are the information specialists, and we collaborate with classroom teachers on various research projects.

How Do You Collaborate with Teachers to Create WebQuests?

The same way I collaborate with other projects we create. It is more time intensive, so one has to allow for plenty of time.

Have You Had Any Feedback from Students about the WebQuests You've Designed?

Over the years, students have responded that they enjoyed the activity, and that initially they were intimidated by the task, but once they "got into it," they were fine. Students have liked some of the graphics that we've incorporated with our WebQuests.

What Advice Would You Give to Other Librarians Who Wanted to Learn about WebQuests?

Bernie Dodge and Tom March were the creators of the concept, and they maintain Web sites that discuss the whole concept. I've bookmarked their links and other resources to learn more about WebQuests at: www.greece.k12.ny.us/ath/library/WebQuests/default.htm. My advice would be to dive into the Dodge and March sites and learn there!

IDEA #69: VENTURE INTO AUDIO/VIDEO LECTURES AND LESSONS

For more on using audio and video, see Chapter 3

The growing use of audio and video on Web sites has many exciting implications for teaching and learning. As more users have access to high-speed Internet services, it also becomes easier for the average person to access these kinds of files. As you design and enhance your library Web site for teens, think about how you might use these formats.

One feature library Web sites could offer is audio or video lessons on information literacy topics. These short lectures could be linked to assignments so that students work at their own pace. Students also have the option of listening or watching from home, or downloading the lectures to portable devices such as iPods.

A school librarian, for example, could record a lecture on the steps involved in the research process. Students could then listen to or watch the lecture on their own time, pausing or rewinding as needed. They could return to the lecture later if they felt unsure about the information. They might then go on, at their own pace, to complete a related assignment. The audio lesson could also be linked to an online PowerPoint slide presentation so that photos, illustrations, diagrams, and word definitions could be included in the lesson.

Another great teaching tool is a "screencast," which is basically a movie that shows what is happening on a computer screen. Librarians can make a digital recording as they demonstrate a new database, for example—capturing every movement of the mouse, each click of a link, and all of the keywords they type into a search box. They can also add a voice track where they narrate each step in the process. By adding a screencast to your Web site, you give students and teen patrons the ability to access your lesson at any time, and to watch as you demonstrate on the computer screen. This is much more effective, obviously, than a PowerPoint demonstration where each step is illustrated with a motionless screenshot. To make a screencast, you can download free software such as CamStudio (available at: www.camstudio.org) or buy commercial software packages such as Macromedia Captivate or TechSmith Camtasia Studio.

School librarians might also encourage teachers to record and post their lectures and class materials online. This would allow students who miss class or need a refresher to go back and listen again. This kind of service might be especially helpful to students with learning disabilities or those who have trouble taking notes.

The University of California, Berkeley, recently announced that it is making audio and video of selected lectures available on iTunes, and used the term "coursecasting" to describe the free service. Users sign up for a course and use iTunes to subscribe to future lectures. "Berkeley on iTunes U" has a Web site at http://itunes.berkeley.edu/, but users need to download free iTunes software to take advantage of the lectures. Other universities offer similar services, but often limit them to enrolled students.

IDEA #70: INITIATE FACULTY/STUDENT WIKIS

> For more on wikis, and how to set one up, see Chapter 3

A wiki—an online space that allows users to edit and add information as they see fit—has tremendous potential as an educational tool. Librarians are just now beginning to explore that potential. One of the most obvious uses is to allow school faculty and staff to collaborate and share information online.

School Library Journal, in February 2006, reported that the Bering Strait School District in Alaska had launched a wiki to allow teachers—separated by many miles—a way to discuss curriculum. At Springfield Township High School in Erdenheim, Pennsylvania, teachers can use a password-protected faculty wiki.

Before long, I expect to see more schools using wikis with their students. Librarians are likely to be at the forefront of this experiment. For more on the pros and cons of wikis, be sure to see the wiki section in Chapter 3. To join the discussion on using wikis for education, try—what else?—this wiki, created by Joyce Valenza of Springfield Township High School in Erdenheim, Pennsylvania: http://teacherlibrarianwiki.pbwiki.com/.

Chapter 10

Readers' Advisory

OVERVIEW

Helping teens find books they'll enjoy is one of my favorite parts of being a librarian. Reading widely is, of course, the best way to get good at suggesting books. However, when you're really stumped, it's nice to have a wealth of resources available online—from the expertise of colleagues to the information on Amazon.com to online databases like NoveList. Querying the teen librarians on listservs like YALSA-BK, an e-mail discussion group, is also frequently helpful. I also find the booklists published online by various library systems and individual teen librarians very useful.

I use many of these resources to find books for my own leisure reading. I particularly enjoy novels about time travel, for example. I've read most of the "obvious" titles, so now I'm digging deeper, going online to find more obscure books or to see what's just been published. Teens with very specific reading interests may find it necessary to do the same.

School and public library Web sites for teens can organize readers' advisory information for easy access, or contribute new lists and reviews that may be particularly relevant to their particular community. For example, my former branch library serves many African-American patrons, so information about African-American interest titles tended to catch my eye and were an obvious area of focus for my readers' advisory services.

Librarians can write their own reviews and create booklists for their patrons. They can also give teens the opportunity to share their suggestions and reviews with the world. Since teens are generally more responsive to suggestions from peers, this is a very effective way to interest them in reading. Written reviews, audio recordings, videotaped reviews—the possibilities are wide open in terms of what format to use.

Library Web sites can also provide virtual meeting spaces where teens can chat about books with their peers. Through this type of forum, teens can meet and talk to others with similar enthusiasm about reading or about a particular genre or author. Librarians can also arrange for virtual discussions with authors, an easier—and often less expensive—alternative to in-person visits.

Of course, a Web site can never take the place of a well-read librarian who can do a readers' advisory interview and then enthusiastically booktalk several relevant titles. Online booklists with annotations can, however, aid the memory of the librarian and give teens a wider range of titles to select from.

One question that often comes up in relation to promoting reading on library Web sites is whether you can use book cover images without violating copyright. Adding a digital image of a book's cover definitely enhances an accompanying review and adds visual appeal to Web pages. Librarians also often want to create a virtual "display" of new books on their sites. Carrie Russell, the American Library Association's copyright specialist, has addressed this issue several times in her column for School Library Journal. In the August 2004 "Carrie on Copyright" column, for example, she tells a school library media specialist that "Reproductions of book covers for school or library Web sites is fair use" and that "The purpose of the use is nonprofit and has an educational focus—the encouragement of reading."

In her January, 2002 column, she gave the same opinion, and adds that she believes that copying images from Amazon.com or other sources is also fair use, as long as the intention is not to make money. "I would argue that even though the digital book cover copy is 'ripped' from another Web site, the use is fair," she writes. However, she also notes that her comments are not to be considered legal advice.

IDEA #71: PROVIDE ONLINE BOOK LISTS

This is the simplest and most obvious idea for readers' advisory, but also one of the most useful. Most libraries that have teen Web sites include lists of suggested books somewhere on their sites. These lists often have themes—"Romance," "Sports," "Resources for Gay & Lesbian Teens," "Tearjerkers," "Survival Stories," "Multicultural Books," and so on.

One very helpful thing to do if you possibly can is to link the titles on booklists to the same item in your library catalog. This way, teens can immediately see whether and where the book is available. If you offer online reserves, teens may also be able to reserve any title they want quickly. An online booklist that has only text, no links, is something of a "dead end" for users.

Many libraries offer excellent book lists for teens on their Web sites:

- Boston Public Library offers booklists for teens in its Teen Lounge
      Available at: www.bpl.org/teens/booklists/
- Plymouth District Library in Plymouth, Michigan, has a nice selection of booklists in their "Teen Zone" Web site
      Available at: http://plymouthlibrary.org/yabibs.htm
- Seattle Public Library also offers a good selection of book lists for teens
      Available at: www.spl.org/default.asp?pageID=audience_teens_ categorybrowser

The New York Public Library also offers many book lists, with topics ranging from "When Bad Things Happen" to "Taffeta, Tuxedos and Tulle: Books and Movies About Prom Night." Each list is attractively designed and features book covers and links to the catalog. Visit the site at http://teenlink .nypl.org/index.html and find lists on the left-hand side of the page.

The New York Public Library, New York, New York
Available at: http://teenlink.nypl.org/index.html (links to lists are on left-hand side) (see Figure 10-1)

Interview

Sandra Payne
Coordinator of Young Adult Services
The New York Public Library
New York, New York

How Do You Decide on the Topics for Each List?
    Monthly selections are chosen by the Materials Specialist in the Office of Young Adult Services. For the Books for the Teen Age titles, members of our administrative young adult librarian team select the titles and prepare the annotations.

Who Puts Together the Lists?
    Our Materials Specialist is a committee of one for the monthly lists. Selections are based upon the titles reviewed by young adult librarians across the NYPL system. A majority of young adult librarians serve as members of our book committee team.

Why Do You Think It Is Important to Offer Teen Booklists?
    Our booklists, whether they be online or in hard copy, such as Books for the Teen Age, are a feature of the core services that we offer to teenagers.

The New York Public Library has published Books for the Teen Age since 1929 and our online booklists and other booklists are a complement. We are convening a committee of young adult librarians to develop a booklist based upon the classics. The classics booklist will also be featured on TeenLink.

Taffeta, Tuxedos and Tulle: Books and Movies about Prom Night

AMERICAN PIE

Four "unlucky in love" friends gear up for prom night. 1997 – starring Jason Biggs and Alyson Hannigan.

Reserve this title.

BUFFY THE VAMPIRE SLAYER

Cheerleader Buffy becomes a vampire slayer ruining her plans for prom. 1992 – starring Kristy Swanson and Luke Perry.

CARRIE

Classic horror film of the book of the same name.

DRIVE ME CRAZY

Popular Nicole remakes slacker neighbor Chase into the perfect prom date. 1999 – starring Melissa Joan Hart and Adrian Grenier.

FOOTLOOSE

Rebellious boy moves to a town where dancing is outlawed. 1984 – starring Kevin Bacon and Sarah Jessica Parker

Figure 10-1   New York Public Library's TeenLink Book List

IDEA #72: PROMOTE YOUR NEW BOOKS

Many libraries with Web sites feature new titles on their teen home pages, often with graphics showing the books' covers. Other sites let users click on a link or graphic that says "New Titles," or something similar, to see a list. Just like the shelf of new books in a physical library space, this is a way to promote fresh, exciting titles in cyberspace.

Salem Public Library, in Salem, Ohio, has a very attractive list of new teen books on its site.

Salem Public Library, in Salem, Ohio
Available at: www.booksite.com/texis/scripts/bookletter/showlist.html?sid=
    6071&list=CNL6

The Carthage High School library in Carthage, Missouri, has an excellent list of new titles, with graphics showing book covers and a link to the catalog for each title.

Carthage High School, Carthage, Missouri
Available at: www.carthage.k12.mo.us/hs/media/New%20books.htm

IDEA #73: BLOG ABOUT BOOKS

> For more on blogs and how to create one, see Chapter 3

Blogs work well for providing readers' advisory services because they are so easy to create and update. It's also fairly simple to add graphics, so you can include book covers with your reviews. If you allow teens to comment on your blog, you'll also be able to start a discussion about books that will generate excitement and interest.

Some teen librarians focus on books in their blogs, while others talk about a wide range of subjects and throw in a book review or a list of new titles every once in a while. You'll have to decide on the focus of your library blog.

Salem Public Library

Newsletter Signup   Events Calendar   Author Directory

Home

New Teen Books

May 23, 2006

The following Non-fiction titles and Graphic Novels are now available for circulation at Salem Public Library:

Click on the book jackets for title details and to reserve your copy.

The Two Swords
By *Salvatore, R. A.*
2005/08 - Wizards of the Coast
0786937904 Check Our Catalog

The third and final title in the latest "New York Times" bestselling trilogy from R.A. Salvatore, this book once again features his popular dark elf character Drizzt Do'Urden. ...More

The Thousand Orcs
By *Salvatore, R. A.*
2003/07 - Wizards of the Coast
0786929804 Check Our Catalog

Key Selling/Marketing Points:
- R.A. Salvatore is a perennial New York Times best-selling author and commands an avid and ever-growing fan base.
- This title features striking cover art by award-winning fantasy artist Todd Lockwood, who has rendered many of the recent best-selling Salvatore covers.
- Product listing, editorial content, and free downloads featured at wizards.com. ...More

Go Ask Alice
By *Anonymous*
1971/09 - Simon & Schuster Children's Publishing
0671664581 Check Our Catalog

A fifteen-year-old drug user chronicles her daily struggle to escape the pull of the drug world. ...More

Demon Thief
By *Shan, Darren*
2006/06 - Little Brown and Company
0316012378 Check Our Catalog

Kernel Fleck sees lights--strange, multicolored patches of light. It's not until a window opens into a demon world, with horrific consequences, that Kernel discovers his powers. As a Disciple, his mission is to hunt vicious, powerful demons to the death in this follow-up to "Lord Loss." ...More

Figure 10-2   Salem Public Library's New Teen Books

Hours:
Monday - Thursday
7:30 am - 4:30 pm
Friday
7:30 am - 3:30 pm

Carthage High School   714 South Main St.   Carthage, MO 64836   417-359-7036   Fax 417-359-7037
Card Catalog   Online Resources   Search Engines   Citation Formats   New Books
Libraries   Ready Reference   CHS Classes
Home   Teacher Tools

NEW BOOKS

FICTION

Names will never hurt me	F Ado
The camel club	F Bal
Friends of the heart : amici del cuore	F Ban
Breaker's reef	F Bla
Ready or not : an all-American girl	F Cab
Reunion	F Cab
Shadowland	F Cab
Twilight	F Cab
Honey, Baby, Sweetheart	F Cal
Artemis Fowl : the opal deception	F Col
Balzac and the little Chinese seamstress	F Dai
Safe house	F Car
Fade to black	F Fli
Wrecked	F Fra
Tending to Grace	F Fus

Figure 10-3   Carthage Media Center's New Books

Interview
Meg Canada Web Services Librarian Hennepin County Library, Minnesota   Hennepin County Library offers a summer book blog as part of their Teen-Links Web site. According to Meg Canada, the Web Services Librarian who

oversees TeenLinks, the blog has been extremely successful 2005 was the second year it was offered.

At first, Canada said, the library system offered the blog for eleven-to-fourteen-year-olds—who "love it." They also tried a blog for twelve-to-eighteen-year-olds for Teen Read Month, but that one "didn't take off." The blog updates automatically and is available twenty-four hours a day, so it's offered on the honor system, with a list of rules that include:

- Respect everyone's right to an opinion.
- Profanity, inappropriate language, or put-downs are not allowed.
- Personal information such as phone numbers, IM screen names, or e-mail addresses are not allowed.

Canada said the library system has been lucky in that the blog hasn't had major problems or been vandalized. Library staff does monitor the blog, and has removed a few posts (four to five each summer) because they included personal information or inappropriate language. Teens must create a login before beginning to post. In the summer of 2005, the blog had 254 postings.

Each week, library staff posed a question, Canada said. They might ask the young teens whether they liked series fiction, what catches their eye when it comes to book covers, or what author they would most like to meet. The two questions that generated the most discussion, Canada said, were "Where is your favorite place to read?" and "Are you a Harry Potter fan?" The blog was linked to both TeenLinks and KidLinks, and about half the blog's visitors came from each site, Canada said.

IDEA #74: SOLICIT TEEN BOOK REVIEWS

While I'd like to think that teens value my book suggestions, I also know that book recommendation from peers mean much more to them. When I've visited high school classes to do booktalks, that fact makes itself clear. I'll hold up a book, only to hear a voice from the back pipe up, "Hey, I read that! It's really good." Suddenly the whole class perks up, and everyone wants that title before I've said a word.

We know that teen habits and choices are very much influenced by their peers. Why not use that fact in a positive way, to "sell" the books in your library?

Many teen library Web sites gives users a chance to write their own reviews and post them or have them posted. Some librarians set up sites where teens can add their reviews instantaneously, but most seem to have a screening system. Before you add teen reviews to your Web site, consider the following factors:

- Will you screen the reviews first for inappropriate language, etc.?
- Will you include negative reviews, or only the titles readers recommend?

- Will you feature only books, or also accept reviews for movies, music, and other materials? Must materials be owned by your library if they are to be reviewed? Will you link to the item in your catalog, so that users can see where to find it or even reserve it online?
- Will you edit reviews for grammar, spelling, etc.?
- Will you set up guidelines as far as who can submit reviews? What ages do you consider "teen?" Will teens need to attend your school or live in your community to submit reviews? How many can they submit per week/month/year?
- If you solicit reviews to build up your site, who will you ask to write reviews? Any teens who visit the library, only teens on your advisory board, students taking English classes, or other groups?
- How will you publicize this feature of your site?
- Will you use an online discussion board, a blog, a Web page, or find some other way to display the reviews?

Interview

Meg Canada
Web Services Librarian
Hennepin County Library, Minnesota

Hennepin County Library offers a form on their TeenLinks site that allows teens to submit their reviews online. Teens write a review, rate the book, and click "submit." According to Meg Canada, who oversees TeenLinks, reviews are added to their site daily, five days a week. Library staff adds an ISBN to each review so that the book's cover art is displayed. They also create a link to the library catalog so that Web site users can click to see where the book is available, and can reserve it if they choose.

The library system receives reviews every day, Canada said. During the summer of 2005, for example, they received 242 reviews in a three-month period. Teens are limited to two reviews per week, and to keep staff from being overwhelmed, a note above the form warns:

> Attention Teachers: Due to staffing we are unable to post reviews from a whole class or handle a large volume of reviews at one time.

Form for Submitting Book Reviews
Available at: https://www.hclib.org/teens/ReaderReviews/Add.cfm

During the summer reading program and also Teen Read Month at the library, Hennepin County Library offers prizes for those who submit reviews. Canada said that, to be eligible, teens must live in the county. Library staff enters the writer of each posted review in a random drawing. Teens can win anything from books to small incentives to $10 Barnes & Noble gift certificates. If

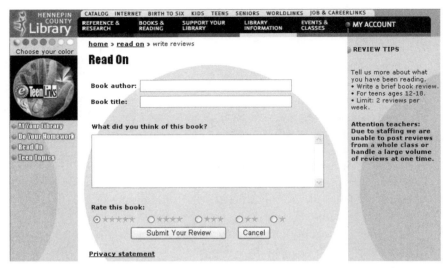

Figure 10-4 Hennepin County Library's Reader Reviews Form

they win a book, Canada said, they can choose from a list of available titles. Prizes are mailed to winners.

On the review site itself, reviews are very attractively displayed next to book covers. Star ratings—one to five—are included. Book titles link to the library catalog. In addition, users can click on the reviewer's name to see more reviews by that person. They can also click on "Read more reviews of this book" to see what other readers thought.

Teen Reviews at Hennepin County Library

Available at: www.hclib.org/teens/ReaderReviews/Reviews.cfm

Hennepin County Library has offered this program for about four years, Canada said. Eighty-one percent of the reviews are sent from computers outside the library's buildings. The only challenge they've faced is when a review is clearly copied from Amazon or from the catalog description, and Canada said that has only happened with one reviewer. When it does happen, she said, it is easy to recognize that the teen did not write the review.

Running the program requires an investment of time, since staff must check for submissions daily and then enter the ISBN so that the cover art will be included with the review. However, Canada said the book review feature is "a wonderful draw" and that teens get the gratification of seeing their work published.

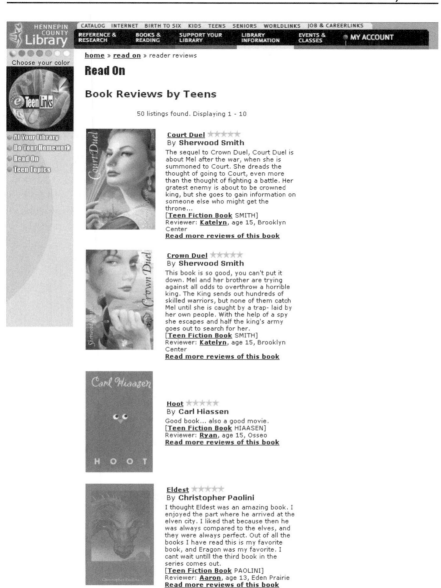

Figure 10-5   Hennepin County Library's Reader Reviews

Interview

Maggie Schmude
Library Department Chair
New Trier Township High School, Illinois
Available at: http://nths.newtrier.k12.il.us/library/reviewslist/listofreviews.htm
 	
How Long Has the Library Offered Student Reviews on the Web Site?
   About four years.
 	
How Do Students Submit Reviews?
   This is done primarily at the freshman campus. The students submit their
reviews through their English teachers to Anne O'Malley, our department

Figure 10-6   New Trier High School Library's Student Book Reviews

coordinator at the freshman campus. She reads them, makes any corrections and posts them.

How Do You Publicize This Part of Your Web Site?

Mostly through the English classes.

How Often Do You Add Reviews? How Much Time Does It Take to Update and Maintain the Review Area?

We add them as they become available. I think the startup time is fairly heavy, but it's easy to add them.

What Kind of Feedback Have You Had?

We've not had lots of feedback. I think that the students like it because they get feedback from a classmate and that could determine whether or not they read the book.

What Advice Would You Give to Other Librarians Who Want to Start a Similar Project?

Work with the teachers. We usually do book talks for them before the students read the books, and the teachers require them to write short reviews.

Interview

Emily M. Ugino
School Media Specialist
Athena High School Media Center, Rochester, New York
Available at: http://www.greece.k12.ny.us/ath/library/book_reviews/submit ted.htm

I joined the Greece Athena library media center team as a school media specialist last year, and was immediately impressed with the quality of our Web site, and the amount of use that it regularly generates.

One of our first tasks this year was to create an "Athena Reads" campaign where we made posters of both faculty and students reading their favorite books as a way of promoting our district-wide literacy initiative. In addition, I was having an extraordinary number of students inquiring about whether or not our media center had any "good books" for them to read. As a result, I decided to create a binder of "Athena Reads" student-written book reviews to be displayed on our library circulation desk. Other students could then refer to this binder when looking for a book suggestion, and actually read something that their peers had recommended.

Thus, the feature of our Web site that I would like to comment on is the

"Athena Reads" student book reviews link that we began approximately one month ago. Although it is certainly nice to have a binder of paper reviews on our library circulation desk, I wanted to make those reviews available electronically so that students could also peruse them when they are online in any location. I am hoping that as we add more titles to this Webpage, it will spark even more student interest. Several of our teachers have kindly volunteered to have their students fill out our review forms in class, which has been extraordinarily helpful in developing this link from our homepage.

I hope that the "Athena Reads" reviews continue to pile in next year.

IDEA #75: ASK FOR STAFF BOOK REVIEWS

You don't want your students and teen patrons thinking that only librarians read. So why not think about soliciting reviews for your Web site from others in your community? The school principal, your city's mayor, local athletes, the police officer who patrols your block, janitorial staff, parents of students—anyone is fair game for this idea. You could feature one recommendation at a time, with a short blurb about the book and why the person likes it, on your Web site. Or you could add new recommendations each month to a growing list of book suggestions.

Wyandotte High School, in Kansas City, Kansas, has reviews from school staff on their Web site. Teachers, counselors, the assistant principal and the school social worker all contributed to the site, which is at http://kancrn .kckps.k12.ks.us/wyandotte/library/bookreviewsstaff.html.

IDEA #76: INCORPORATE AUDIO/VIDEO BOOKTALKS

For more on audio and video content, see Chapter 3

Written book reviews are great, but imagine being able actually to "talk" to a teen who visits your library Web site. Now, with audio and video files on your Web site, you can reach teens in an entirely new way. Or, even better, you can have teens record their reviews and then add those to your site.

For an audio booktalk, a teen might click on the title or cover graphic for a book. They would then hear an oral booktalk through headphones or on their computer's speakers. They could then click on a link to the catalog that would tell them if the book is on your library's shelves, and if not, they can reserve the book online. You could also set this up as a podcast, so that users "subscribe" to your audio files. Whenever you create a new booktalk, subscribers' computers automatically download that file.

The Thomas Ford Memorial Library in Western Springs, Illinois, offers audio reviews of books, movies, and music on their teen Web site at www.fordlibrary.org/yareviews. Hennepin County Library, in Minnesota, is also offering teen reviews by audio podcast at www.hclib.org/teens/Podcasts.cfm.

Another great example of using a podcast for booktalking is available on Nancy Keane's "Booktalks—Quick and Simple" Web site. The audio booktalks are available at http://nancykeane.com/rss.html, or you can subscribe at iTunes by using this URL: http://www.nancykeane.com/rss.xml.

Video is another option. If you don't have access to a video camera or Webcam, many digital cameras will record a few minutes of video, which you can then download and add to your Web site. While video files require more memory than most other types of files, it's hard to beat letting your teens actually watch each other talk about books, especially if the quality of the video is high. It's also appealing to the teens who appear and get their fifteen minutes of fame on your Web site.

Interview

Doug Achterman
Library Media Specialist
San Benito High School, Hollister, California
Available at: www.sbhsd.k12.ca.us/sbhslib/bestbets/vids/pickofweek.htm

How Long Have You Offered Video Reviews on Your Site?

I've done video reviews with students and teachers for the past few years.

What Gave You the Idea to Do This?

I bought a digital video camera that circulates out of the library and just thought it would be fun. In addition to promoting reading and student participation, it's a great plug for using technology.

How Do You Recruit Students and Staff to Do Video Reviews?

Recruiting almost always starts with a conversation about a book. "Mr. A.," a student will say, "that was such an awesome book!" After chatting a few minutes, I'll suggest a "Baler Best Bet" review. Library "regulars" are always a target. Some students can't wait to get in front of a camera; others take some encouragement and persuasion. The same is true for teachers and other staff. I like to include all members of the school community to show that we're all readers.

What Are the Costs Associated with Offering This Feature—Time, Equipment, and So On?

Digital video cameras are falling in price every day and should be part of the audio visual equipment available through any school library. Microsoft and MacIntosh offer simple, intuitive editing software whose basics can be learned in under an hour. Another cost is server space. We are rapidly running out of room on our server, and I cannot archive as many videos as I'd like.

Video is an increasingly common format for the Web, so it's important to encourage those who make technology decisions at the site and district level to account for growing demand.

Time is by far the greatest cost, though. Arranging filming, setting up the equipment, doing the filming, downloading to a computer for editing, completing the editing and some simple graphics add up to a fairly substantial commitment.

Occasionally a capable and reliable student will help me with shooting or editing. This year we shot a "poem of the day" during April, which is poetry month, and for part of it, the drama teacher worked with her students to do dramatic readings of poems, and the teledramatic arts class filmed and edited the best few for publication on the Web. Next year we're going to plan poetry month in February, shoot and edit in March, and publish in April. The drama and teledramatic arts classes will be doing everything; all I have to do is post their final products on the library Web page. This really is the best of all possible scenarios: the drama students have a venue for their performances, the teledramatic arts class has a real project for publication, and the library program promotes the love of poetry!

What Other Video Clips Have You Added to Your Site?

In addition to "Baler Best Bets," which are readers' advisories, we've included Poetry Slam winners and this year we did a "Poem of the Day" for Poetry Month. Since a substantial portion of our school population speaks Spanish, we offered Spanish language poems, too. Teachers, students, and staff all volunteered to read their favorites, which ranged from the prologue to the Canterbury Tales—recited in Middle English—to simple nursery rhymes. A campus supervisor read a beautiful nineteenth century love poem, and that gave our school community a completely new and different look at a person whose role is to keep students in line all the time.

What Kind of Response Have You Had from Students and Staff?

Every video we've ever posted on the Web has produced a positive response. It's been a great promotion for the library program and for reading in general. In addition, teachers have started filming on their own. Our sign language teacher videos her students as they sign a contemporary poem. A reading teacher has had her students produce their own video book recommendations for her class.

Would You Recommend That Other Librarians Try This? If So, What Advice Would You Offer Them?

This is one of the activities that returns the school community to the library Web page repeatedly. One of my tricks in promoting the library page is to e-mail staff about a new feature—a video, a display of student work, an art project— and rather than providing a link directly to that page, send users to the library homepage with the message, "Just follow the link from the library homepage at www.ourschoollibrary.k12.ca.us." Yes, it's an extra click for users, but it's also a reminder of all the other resources available through the library Web page.

Interview

Ed Wilson
Teen Librarian
Manchester Public Library, Manchester, Connecticut
Available at: http://feeds.feedburner.com/primesboxlive and http://feeds.feedburner.com/primespeaks

How Did You Come Up with the Idea to Do Book Review Podcasts?

The idea just seemed a natural extension to advertising my Box O' Good Books. Basically I try to review/booktalk what I have enjoyed.

How Many Episodes Have You Done So Far?

I did my test episode about a year ago. Overall I have done ten episodes, of which there are eight still available. At this point I am going to try for two per month, minimum, but I'm sure there will be more during the summer.

Are the Reviews by Teens, Librarians, or Both?

The person who talks about the book is the one who "writes" the review. Most of the reviews are completely spontaneous, which adds a bit of fun to the mix. It doesn't sound rehearsed because, obviously, it isn't.

How Do You Recruit Your Reviewers?

Some of the reviewers are regulars who keep coming back for more. They go by the names of Merv and Spellcheck. I also try and recruit kids at all of my programs. A lot are reluctant because they are shy or don't know which book to talk about.

How Do You Record the Podcasts?

I use an Apple iBook running Audacity to record audio from the built-in microphone, though I am trying a Bluetooth headset for myself. I will eventually need to get a USB microphone.

How Do You Publicize Them?

There is a link through the main teen Web site. I haven't done full-blown publicizing yet, waiting until I get a better production record going.

Have You Had Any Feedback from Listeners or from Those Involved in Making the Podcasts?

The ones who are involved really like doing it. Whether or not they subscribe to the podcast is a different story. What I have heard from the few people I know have listened seems fairly positive.

When and Why Did You Add Video Podcasts (Vodcasts)?

Manchester has a local television station that is dedicated to municipal use. In the past we have broadcast various library-related items on the channel. The initial idea was to record book reviews until there were enough of them to splice them all together to make a thirty minute show. It was after the fact that I realized I could use them for vodcasts.

How Do You Record Those?

I use a regular digital camera to record them. However, I would ideally use the library's DV camera and transfer it to the iBook to edit using iMovie.

Have You Had Any Problems or Challenges So Far on This Project?

The challenge is finding time to record the reviews that I do, as well as getting teens in who want to take part. At the very beginning, it was a small hurdle, writing the XML code required, but that passed. It is even easier now that there are so many software options available for podcast production.

Would You Suggest That Other Library Systems Try This?

It can't hurt, really. Anything that will help us reach these kids, I'd suggest.

What Advice Do You Have for Librarians Who Want to Start Podcasting or Video Podcasting Book Reviews?

Finding kids to participate is key. Going all out and just jumping in helped when I started mine.

IDEA #77: INVITE AUTHORS FOR VIRTUAL VISITS

For more on VOIP, instant messaging, chat, and audio files, see Chapter 3.

Author visits are a wonderful way to get teens interested in reading. Meeting an author in person is likely to spark excitement about that person's books. But these visits can be expensive, especially if the author is from out of town and requires travel expenses as well as a speaker's fee.

One way for libraries with smaller budgets to get around this problem is to offer virtual author visits. You could do this using instant messaging, chat, or by using VOIP (Voice Over Internet Protocol) to call the author on the phone. If you save a transcript of the IM or chat sessions, you can then add that to your Web site for future browsing. If you record an audio version of the visit, that audio file can be added to your site for users to access.

If you're lucky enough to have live author visits, ask if you can record their speeches and their answers to questions from the audience. These can also become audio files on your site that users can access later.

Once you have an archive of author visits, teens can visit the library Web site to click on a favorite writer and experience that visit again. You can also include links to the author's books in the library catalog, so that teens can view the availability of titles that interest them.

Interview

Sandra Payne
Coordinator of Young Adult Services
The New York Public Library
New York, New York

The New York Public Library offers live author chats on its TeenLink Web site. Visitors can also read the transcripts of previous "Author Chats." For example, here is the beginning of an Author Chat with Meg Cabot, author of "The Princess Diaries" and many other titles, from the summer of 2005, available at: http://teenlink.nypl.org/cabot_transcript.html.

According to Sandra Payne, Coordinator of Young Adult Services, more events are planned for the summer of 2006, including chats with Gary Soto, Sharon Draper, and Kate DiCamillo. She also said that, for 2005 and 2006, "our summer reading program is now partnered with the Brooklyn Public Library and Queens Library, thereby expanding our audience for the online chats. We try to include authors whose books are represented on our jointly prepared summer reading lists."

How Long Have You Been Offering Online Chats with Authors?

The New York Public Library has offered online chats with authors since the summer of 2002. The authors that summer included: Sharon Creech,

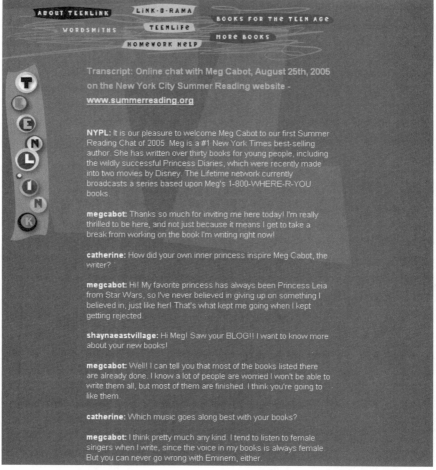

Figure 10-7   TeenLink Transcript of Online Chat with Author Meg Cabot

Chris Crutcher, Christopher Paul Curtis, and Sharon G. Flake. During the fall of that year, Judy Blume offered a chat.

How Do You Arrange the Chats? Do Most Authors Have Access to the Technology They Need?

We either contact the authors directly or work closely with publishers. Most of the authors have had access to computers. For the Ann M. Martin chat—she had some computer challenges for the day of the chat—we transcribed her responses by telephone.

How Many Participants Do You Usually Get, Approximately?

It's difficult to know exactly, as many library branches sign on as a group project. We would, though, love to have increased participation from young people throughout New York City or wherever they are in the world.

How Do You Decide Who Will Get to Ask Questions?

The questions are selected by a librarian.

Who Moderates the Chats?

The chats are moderated by The New York Public Library's Youth Web Editorial Coordinator.

What Kinds of Responses Have You Had to This Program?

The response has been very positive from librarians, teens, authors, and publishers. Last year Meg Cabot was inspired by a set of questions from teens at Teen Central to send along a special package just for the teens at that library. She truly enjoyed the series of questions that really had New York attitude and spirit, as she was sending responses from Key West, Florida.

Do You Have Any Advice for Other Library Systems That Would Like to Try This?

Author chats are really a terrific way for young people to ask those questions that may not even be answered on the author's Web site. I would encourage libraries to speak with other public libraries about the technical and programmatic pieces. We are always exploring ways of reaching out to more young people with these events. One of our goals is to increase the audio chats as a year round experience.

You will need the buy-in of librarians and support staff as well as those in the community to assure that the chat is a success.

Other tips from The New York Public Library for promoting and managing online chats include:

Before the event:

- Display the books of the author in multiple formats (hardcover, paperback, audio book) with a flyer promoting the event.
- Have children and teens visit the terrific Websites of the participating authors.
- Encourage the participation of summer camps and other community-based organizations.
- Recruit volunteer youth to assist! Here are a few suggested roles for youth:

Orator—Reads aloud the incoming questions and answers for the group;
Questioner—Takes notes and collects threads of the conversation for follow-up;

Evaluator—Reads and researches information on the authors and their books, helps the group to craft intriguing questions.

- Remind those who will be out of the city that they are able to participate wherever they are in the world!

On the day of the event:

- Display the author's books.
- Coordinate the day's events with branch staff and volunteers.
- Play a fun game using the content of the author's books or information about the author's life.
- Encourage youth to craft questions prior to the chat!
- There may be slow periods during the time the author is answering questions—this will be a perfect time to have filler activities to keep the momentum and excitement level up.
- Ask the participants, upon sign-in, to identify the name of their library. This will allow the moderator to assure that there is citywide representation among the participants.
- Provide incentives for youth participating in the chats at your branch.
- Take photos to document the good times.

IDEA #78: PROMOTE AN ONLINE FORUM

An online forum or discussion board is a great way to let teens "gather" online to discuss books. Libraries can also run teen book clubs entirely online.

A great example of an online book discussion forum is sponsored by Cleveland Public Library in Cleveland, Ohio. Called "YRead?," the program is subtitled "Youth Unite Through Books." Each month, the site features one multicultural title. Teachers can reserve multiple copies of the chosen book to read with their classes, if they choose. Next, participants have the opportunity to chat online or to participate in a discussion forum about the book.

Interview
Annisha Jeffries YRead? Librarian Cleveland Public Library, Cleveland, Ohio Available at: http://www.yread.org/index.asp

What Is YRead? and What Are Its Goals?

YRead? is an interactive, virtual community of teens, educators, librarians,

Figure 10-8   Cleveland Public Library's YRead?

students and youth advocates who enjoy reading and discussing acclaimed young adult books.

Each month the site features a young adult fiction or nonfiction title. Educators can reserve multiple copies of the featured title from our Main Library to read with their classes and incorporate young adult literature into their curriculum. Participants can then log on to the Web site for comments and start a discussion.

The goal of YRead? is to merge multi-cultural literature and technology while furthering and strengthening a strategic partnership with the local schools and community organizations. It is our goal to have featured discussions of multicultural young adult books, where teens can share ideas about books they have read, and learn more about themselves and their peers by connecting through books and with technology. YRead? also provides participants with access to multiple copies of featured books for educators and community leaders.

The Cleveland Public Library wants to put quality multicultural young adult literature in the hands of these teens and give them a forum on the Internet to communicate with each other their thoughts, emotions, and opinions that come from their reading.

Who Can Participate?

Anyone who enjoys reading young adult fiction and nonfiction books.

How Do You Choose the Book to Be Featured Each Month?

Recommendations from teens, educators, our children's and Youth Services staff at the Cleveland Public Library.

What Are the Participation Rules and Guidelines?

We have guidelines that are posted on the Web site:

1. People who do not follow the "Chat Participation Rules and Guidelines" will be eliminated from the chat room.
2. Inappropriate language is strictly prohibited. Chat discussions should relate to the topic/theme for the scheduled event. No offensive or racist remarks are tolerated. No name-calling or use of profanity with regard to another person. No personal insults, threats, or harassment.

How Often Do You Offer Discussions in Your Chat Room? How Many Participants Do You Usually Get?

We offer online discussions every month. If we get a special guest to participate in an online chat, we offer two chats, one in the morning and another in the afternoon. Teachers use the chat room with students to have in-depth discussions about the titles.

We may get from twenty to a hundred participants in an online discussion.

How Does the Discussion Forum Work? What Kinds of Comments Do Participants Post?

Once teens have read the book, we ask for their real and honest comments about it. The message board is entitled "Speak Out!" and that's exactly what we ask them to do. They do not need to log in or use a password to have access to the forum.

Most of the feedback we receive has been very positive. Any criticisms of the books, or unrelated posts, receive a response from the moderators. If someone sends a post such as "I did not like this book" we ask for elaborated feedback. We make sure to reply to anyone that posts on the board because we know that their opinion is essential.

What Kind of Feedback Have You Had from Users, Teens, Teachers, Etc.?

We have received tremendous response. Educators have embraced YRead? from the very beginning. We have book sets that they can borrow and a Web site that is inviting and easy to navigate. Educators will use the message board as part of their curriculum and this feature has given students another outlet to talk about books. Parents have sent us positive comments, too.

Why Do You Think It's Important to Provide an Online Community for Book Discussion?

The Cleveland Public Library—"The People's University"—has grounded its mission of service in a recommitment to the book and the fostering of life-long reading. The Cleveland Municipal School District, meanwhile, has developed programs with the educators are working to raise the proficiency scores of their students who are at great risk of dropping out of school.

A collaboration between the public library and the public school system is both critical and timely. YRead? has allowed Cleveland teens, librarians and educators to discuss the books that are part of the public school curricula in a fun, interactive and high tech way.

How Do You Publicize the Program?

As the YRead? Librarian, I promote YRead? by visiting the middle schools, high schools and, community centers. I also meet with educators at school meetings, career fairs, etc.. Colorful bookmarks that appeal to teen population help with promoting the Web site and our extensive booklist for educators.

What Challenges Have You Faced So Far? Would You Like to See Other Libraries Create Similar Programs?

The challenge is to get teens to visit not just one time, but every month to see what books are featured, and get them excited about taking part in a online discussion. Yes, I would love to see other libraries implement a similar program like YRead?.

What Advice Do You Have for Librarians Who Want to Create Online Book Discussions for Their Library Systems?

Do it now! Within the four years since YRead?'s debut, we have had support of The Cleveland Public Library, Youth Services Department, educators and students from the Cleveland Municipal School District, private and parochial schools, and well known young adult authors.

Anything Else You'd Like to Add?

I hope I can motivate librarians to create an online book discussion Web site. Teens are well informed about technology, and once we introduce them to books with substance, and get them motivated about reading, our goal is accomplished. We can honestly say that YRead? has made non-readers into readers.

Interview

Margo Schiller
Reference Librarian
Kamloops Library
Thompson-Nicola Regional District Library System, British Columbia, Canada
Available at: http://www.tnrdlib.bc.ca/teens/onlinebookclub.php

How Long Has Your Library Offered an Online Book Discussion Group for Teens?

Since September 2005.

How Did You Get the Idea for an Online Book Club?

We envisioned a library program that all teens living within the Thompson-Nicola Regional District could participate in, rather than one that would be limited to those living within a certain geographic area. The online environment is perfect because teens can participate from any location. If they don't have a computer, they can visit the library branch closest to them and use the computers there.

How Did You Choose the First Book (*The First Stone*, by Don Aker)?

One day, I was talking with the Head of the Children's Department who was processing some new books. She picked one up and said "How about this one?" I read the book, and I thought that it would be good. It is meaty enough to discuss, and I thought that it would appeal to both males and females. It is also a Canadian book, and we are always trying to promote Canadian content in the library. I was very excited when I contacted the author and he was interested in participating.

How Do You Publicize the Book Discussion?

Posters. Bookmarks. Most publicizing has been in-library. We had a listing in the local Activity Guide as well. We have recently created a listserv function for the library system, so I am hoping to have a teen listserv and to advertise it there.

What Prizes Are You Offering as Incentives?

A $15 dollar gift certificate to Chapters. The winner will be drawn at random. All teens who join the club and participate online are entered in the draw. We haven't had any other prizes yet.

Are There Any Other Costs for This Program, and How Are You Funding Your Program?

Staff time has been the biggest cost. Planning the project and figuring out all of the details took quite a bit of time. Designing promotional materials (posters, bookmarks, writing a press release), figuring out the technical details of the chat, and designing a questionnaire and an introductory booklet for the teens also took some time.

Now that all of that has been done, however, to continue running the club requires much less staff time. We have run the program for most of the '05/'06 school year and now it takes very little staff time (just reading the book, preparing questions, and moderating the live chat).

The library decided to use some money it received from a literacy grant to pay for the books. Initially, we purchased ten copies of each book. After the second book, we began purchasing twenty copies, as we had quite a few teens signed up.

How Do Teens Sign Up?

Teens sign up online. They fill in their name, e-mail address, library card number, and library branch on an online form. I send each of them of confirmation e-mail that welcomes them to the club, and tells them what to expect next and who to contact if they have any questions.

How Many Teens Do You Have Signed Up So Far?

Sixty-one teens from one of our smaller communities have registered, and we've averaged about four teens from our other communities.

What Is the Next Step? Do You Contact Teens with Information about the Discussion?

Each teen is sent an e-mail after they register, welcoming them to the club. Then, the teens are sent a copy of the book, a questionnaire for them to fill out at the end of the first book, and a booklet explaining the ins-and-outs of the club (how to participate online, for example).

Now that we have been running the club for a while and many of the same teens participate month to month, we send out a bookmark with the necessary information about the book (we no longer send out a package). We sent out the questionnaire only with the first book. We are hoping to develop another questionnaire to get further input from the teens.

How Long Have You Had a Discussion Board for Teens?

About one year. I came across another library (Pike's Peak) that had one, and I thought it was such a good idea, we decided to try it out. The library currently pays for the message board. (It is really cheap, however.) In the future, I hope that our library can create its own message board. The message board is not as heavily used as I had hoped.

Have You Had Any Problems with Inappropriate Content? How Do You Monitor the Board?

Teens must follow the Rule of Content, or they will be banned. We preview all messages before they "go live." As a result, we know what is being posted, and we can delete anything inappropriate. We have not had very many problems with inappropriate content.

Our most common problem has been teens that provide personal information (for example, e-mail addresses). We will edit a post if it contains any information that may identify a teen.

Who Manages the Technical Aspects of the Book Club, Such as Creating the Sign-up Form?

Our technical services staff manage all of this (except for the message board, which is managed by an outside company). They have been really helpful in this regard.

How Do Teens Discuss the Books Online?

Teens can discuss the book on a message board and through a scheduled chat. The message board is great because teens can log in anytime of night or day to read postings and post their own. I really like that aspect of it because teens are often so busy.

The message board was not used much for the online book club. We have kept a forum for teens who want to post, but the live chat seems to be a lot more popular. I thought it would be interesting to have a live chat to see if teens would participate. Our first chat was the most popular, likely because the author participated. The other chats have been somewhat successful, with an average of four to ten participants.

How Did You Schedule the Live Chat?

An evening time was selected as it was thought that this would fit in well with the teens' schedules. Tuesday was selected because it is the evening I work, and I would be moderating the chat. We got comments from teens and parents that an earlier time would be better. We are now holding the chat between 4:00 and 5:00 P.M.

Will a Librarian Lead the Discussion? Will You Have Questions Prepared or Just See Where the Discussion Goes?

A librarian led the discussions initially (myself), and I do have questions prepared ahead of time, but I also try to see what happens. As I became involved in other projects, I was unable to lead the discussion. A Reference Assistant has been leading the discussions for the last three books.

What Kind of Time Commitment Does a Program Like This Require?

Initially, it took a lot of staff time to get started. Now that it is becoming an ongoing program, however, there is not too much work—reading the books and preparing questions, continuing to market the program. I would like to do more marketing and promotion in high schools.

What Are Your Hopes for the Online Book Club?

I hope that it will become part of the library's regular programming. I also hope that we can work with schools and parent groups to help get the word out about it.

What Kinds of Responses Have You Had from Teens?

Teens filled out a questionnaire after reading the first book and we had a lot of positive input from them. It was especially rewarding to get comments such as, "I never liked books before the book club." We also had some excellent feedback from parents.

What Are Some of the Challenges So Far?

The biggest challenge has been getting the word out about the book club. Another challenge has been getting teens involved. We have had a lot of success in one of our smaller communities (Ashcroft) because of a very dedicated Parent Advisory Council member. She spread the word and encouraged teens to join. I think it would be ideal if other parent groups or teachers could do the same thing. Developing these partnerships would really help the club along and help to motivate teens to join.

What Advice Would You Offer to Other Librarians Interested in a Similar Program?

It was a lot of working putting it together, but now that it is up and running, it is easy to do and fun! Spend a lot of energy promoting the program to teens and to parent groups. That may really help to boost the success of the program and I think our library needs to do more of that.

IDEA #79: OFFER A READERS' ADVISORY WIKI

For more on wikis, and how to set one up, see Chapter 3

Wikis are perfect for collaborate projects like booklists and book reviews. If you've been wanting to add one to your site, readers' advisory is a good way to start. Using a wiki, you can tap into the collective knowledge of your teens and find out what they're reading.

You may want to start small, by limiting the wiki to your teen advisory group or to one class, under the guidance of a teacher. You can add password protection to the wiki so that only this small group can access and edit it. You'll probably want to set a purpose for the group, such as:

- Create a list of the best twenty-five fantasy novels of all time, with brief reviews. What's fun about a project like this is that opinions will differ, so some titles may get knocked off the list or added back as the process continues.
- Create a wiki page for your favorite author, including biographical information, books they've written, and suggestions for "read-alike" titles. Then add titles and information to the pages others in the group have created.
- Use the wiki to create and continually update a log of what the class or advisory group is reading this month.

IDEA #80: ADD REVIEWS AND BOOK LISTS
TO YOUR CATALOG

Where is your readers' advisory headed next? I believe the next step is to make our library catalogs more like Amazon.com and similar Web sites. On Amazon, users can make a wish list, create subject-specific booklists for others, and add their own reviews to the site. Users are providing readers' advisory service to each other.

As most avid readers know, there's nothing as wonderful as meeting someone who shares your tastes. You grow to trust that person and their book recommendations. Amazon is one place to find readers with similar interests. Whatever you think of the reviews on Amazon (and many librarians find them amateurish), they can be useful, at least to gauge popularity. I also like seeing what people who bought a certain title also bought or looked at. It often gives me a beginning point for finding a title that's like the one I just read and loved.

Libraries are beginning to catch up. Many catalogs now allow users to create a "shopping cart" or "wish list." Some catalogs are also beginning to have the capability to incorporate readers' advisory information and professional book reviews.

One teen library Web site is headed this way. At Minneapolis Public Library, in an area called "My Reads," the site allows teens with a library card from the system to post their own booklists, with short reviews and a "request a copy" option for the site's users. As on Amazon, a graphic of the book's cover appears as part of the booklist.

Minneapolis Public Library, Minneapolis, Minnesota
Available at: www.mplib.org/wft/yourreads.asp

Open WorldCat, from OCLC, now allows users to add their own content, including reviews, to the titles in its catalog. Try it by going to Google or Yahoo!. Type in, in quotes, "Find in a Library" and then the title of the book you're looking for. The WorldCat link should be the first hit. Click on the link and you'll see the title with multiple tabs. If you click on the "review" tab, you'll be able to add a review—fill out the short registration form first.

Another site of interest is Library Thing (available at www.librarything.com). This site allows users to catalog their own book collections and arrange them on a "virtual shelf." Users can then add their own "tags," or keywords. They can share their collections with others and get recommendations.

Most libraries may not have yet moved in this direction, but I'm looking forward to a time when I will go to the library catalog and find reviews written by my next-door neighbor, a teacher at my local elementary school, or someone from another country who was just passing through the library Web site with a recommendation for a book I'm sure to love.

Figure 10-9   Minneapolis Public Library's What to Read

Teens are a natural audience for this idea, since recommendations from peers carry so much weight. Of course, there is always the potential for abuse, but with a good system for reporting problems, I believe libraries should give this a try.

Part IV. Imagination, Inventiveness, and Ingenuity

Chapter 11

Spotlight on Teen Creativity

OVERVIEW

Many library programs give teens an outlet for their creativity, whether their interests and talents lie in poetry, art, crafts, music, performance, or another area. Both school and public libraries often make bulletin board space available to display the results. Teens usually like to see their work recognized and displayed. They can share their accomplishments with their peers, teachers, parents, and the general community.

Posting teens' creative work on the Internet takes this concept a step further. Creative work becomes available from any place with access to the library Web site. Teens can easily share their work with friends and relatives who live far away. Anyone, worldwide, can enjoy the site.

Library Web sites may create online student magazines or art and photography galleries. Libraries may also offer poetry, short stories, or teen zines. They may showcase contest winners—for example, the winning poster for Teen Read Week—or accept year-round submissions for posting. Sites that showcase teen creativity can be administered by librarians or created entirely by teens.

School librarians also have many sources for teen creative work. They may want to feature projects created by entire classes, or stories and poetry turned in as class assignments. They may also want to sponsor their own art or writing contests and both display the results in the library and publish them online. School library Web sites can also spotlight students' best academic work, using digital portfolios.

There are several factors to consider when adding creative work by teens to your Web site:

1. What kind of work will you feature? Will it be art, photography, poetry, prose, music, film, or some combination of more than one type?
2. Will the creative work be related to library services—for example, book reviews, poetry, or art created at a library program, posters for library events—or will the site be more open-ended? For a school library Web site, must creative work be part of a class assignment? Must it be related to a library poetry or art contest, or will it be accepted year round?
3. What kind of guidelines will you adopt? For instance, can poetry address any subject matter, even potentially controversial topics? Can drawings contain nudity, violence, or other possibly offensive images?
4. If you decide to include music or other audio files, or digital movies, do you have enough space on your server to accommodate large files?
5. Will you incorporate teen participation, and if so, how? For a teen zine, for example, will you appoint an editor or other staff members? Who is responsible for the project?
6. If you accept submissions, what are the age limits for contributors, and must they live in your city or county?
7. Will you publish a print copy of the teens' creative work, or will the Web site be the only place to access it?
8. How will you get permission to publish work? Must contributors will sign a permission form. What about their parents, if they are under eighteen? If all submissions will be published, how will you make that clear to contributors? Creative work can be very personal, and not all teens will want to make theirs public.
9. How will you identify contributors, while still protecting their privacy? Generally, it's better to identify minors by first names only, and possibly school and grade. Using photos can also be tricky. Be sure you know your school district or public library's policy.

IDEA #81: PUBLISH A TEEN E-ZINE

A teen zine provides a forum for creativity and also an excellent way to use teen participation in the library. A zine—short for "magazine"—is usually an informal, small circulation, self-published collection of poetry, art, short stories, opinion pieces, and anything else the publishers want to include. When posted online, zines become "e-zines."

Phoenix Public Library features a good example on their teen Web site. The site explains that the magazine, called *Create!,* was the brainchild of a member of their teen council. The first issue showcases the best of hundreds of entries to a contest sponsored by the library. Categories for submissions included art, writing, poetry, and photography. The zine was published both in print and on the Internet in PDF format.

San Francisco Public Library offers a Teen 'Zine program at its Chinatown Branch. Teens come together to learn about technology and about their community. They conduct interviews, write articles, and take photographs. The Web site includes walking tours of several San Francisco neighborhoods, interviews with members of the Chinatown community, and slideshows of cultural events like Chinese New Year. In addition, the site features a biographical Web site for each participant, video game reviews, short stories, jokes, poems, and horoscopes. The site is mostly in English, with some pages in Chinese.

San Francisco Public Library, San Francisco, California
Available at: http://sfpl.org/sfplonline/teen/sfteenzine/english/index.html

San Francisco Public Library's Teen Advisory Council also publishes a zine called *Hot Secret Files*, available at http://sfpl4.sfpl.org/Webroot/sfplonline/teen/zines.htm.

Figure 11-1   San Francisco Chinatown Teen 'Zine

IDEA #82: POST TEEN ART

An online gallery of teen artwork is a great way for teens to share their work. It's also relatively easy to set up and to update.

Teens at San Benito High School in Hollister, California, share their interest in manga on the school library Web site, at www.sbhsd.k12.ca.us/sbhslib/manga/index.htm.

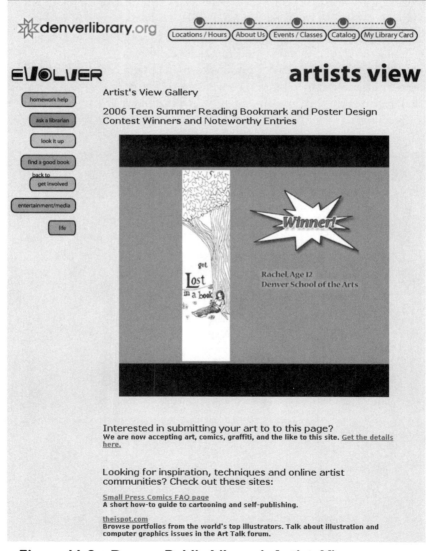

Figure 11-2   Denver Public Library's Artists View

Denver Public Library has an "Artists View Gallery" on their teen Web site. Their site includes a form that spells out submission guidelines and a release form that requires a student's and also a parent's signature (for those under eighteen). One of their latest galleries showcases the winners and some of the entries for their 2005 Summer Reading Bookmark Contest and also their Poster Contest. The gallery is displayed as a slide show, and the viewer scrolls through the artwork at his or her own pace.

Denver Public Library, Denver, Colorado
Available at: http://teens.denverlibrary.org/involved/view_links.html (see
    Figure 11-2)

IDEA #83: FEATURE CREATIVE WRITING AND POETRY

Another common feature on Web sites for teens is an area where student poetry and writing is on display.

Denver Public Library has "Writer's Realm," a chance for teens to publish their poetry and stories. The site features writing by teens, who must sign a release form when submitting their work. The site also features resources for young writers and other places to get writing and poetry published.

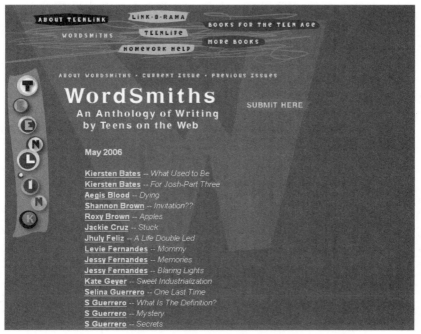

Figure 11-3   New York Public Library's WordSmiths

New York Public Library also has an excellent site featuring writing by teens. Called "Wordsmiths," it's described as "An Anthology of Writing by Teens on the Web." Teens submit their work using an online form. They must be between twelve and eighteen, but do not need to live in New York City. The site is updated frequently, and users can read teen writing submitted as far back to 1996.

The New York Public Library, New York, New York
Available at: http://teenlink.nypl.org/WordSmiths-Current.cfm (see Figure 11-3)

Interview

Sandra Payne
Coordinator of Young Adult Services
The New York Public Library
New York, New York

How Long Have You Had This Section?
WordSmiths was launched in December, 1996.

What Are the Rules for Submitting Material?
We accept original submissions from young people—poetry, essays, non-fiction pieces, stories.

How Many Submissions Do You Get?
The submission rates vary from month to month. We have issues of Word-Smiths archived on TeenLink.

How Do You Choose What to Publish?
There is very little that we don't publish. There are very few non-serious submissions. Our gates are open to even more submissions! I have to say that a few submissions have come from young people who clearly are putting out a cry for help. In those cases, we try to refer them to local hotlines. A couple of the young writers have actually thanked us for being concerned.

How Often Do You Update This Part of Your Web Site?
It's my pleasure to update WordSmiths daily!

Why Do You Think It Is Important to Publish Creative Writing by Teens?
Not only do we publish young people who submit work directly to the site, we also publish work created in poetry-writing workshops in branches of The New York Public Library. Clearly, some of our writers desire to have their

voices in the world at this time in their lives. Many speak of hard times with family and friends, others speak of broken-hearted love affairs; still others take the observational route, describing the world around them. Others give us deep fantasy and serious science fiction. Some speak with a hip hop/urban beat, and others are clearly inspired by the masters of the craft. For some young writers, WordSmiths is their first public venture out in the world.

What Kind of Responses Have You Had, from Teens and from Others?

It's interesting to see where young people say they come from—we have had submissions from the five boroughs of New York as well as from as far away as California, New Zealand, and Kuala Lumpur. Early on in TeenLink's history, The New York Public Library was approached by Orchard Books to produce a book of poems based upon submissions to WordSmiths. *Movin': Teen Poets Take Voice,* edited by Dave Johnson, was published by Orchard Books in 2000. It was a steady seller for a number of years in hardcover and paperback! I think it's time for a new edition—but that's just my opinion!

Have You Had Any Problems or Challenges?

Knock on wood—we have not had any challenges to the content of Word-Smiths. Marketing the site continually to teens and others is a challenge in a media-saturated city like New York.

What Advice Would You Give to Other Librarians Who Wanted to Start a Similar Project?

I consider WordSmiths as one of our teen development/teen programming projects. This is one project of the site that changes almost daily, giving the visitors something new to come back to. There are a number of teen writers out in the world searching for a place to land. What better place to land than at a library site! There is a challenge to continually marketing Word-Smiths in an ever-changing environment. When the writings come in, I do only a very gentle edit to correct for spelling and punctuation. We continue to have returning writers submitting. It's like seeing an old friend!

I think it is also very important to visit a variety of sites to get a sense of the artistry and appeal to young people. We know that teens steer away quickly from the unattractive and not-very-useful very quickly!

IDEA #84: USE AUDIO TO GIVE TEENS A VOICE

For more on using audio, see Chapter 3.

While most school and public library Web sites limit themselves to text and graphics, a few are beginning to experiment with audio and video. Sound files offer one more way for teens to express themselves. Spoken-word poetry, for example, would be an excellent addition to library Web sites. You might want to let teens record their poetry and offer that as part of a podcast or for downloading. Teens could also read their essays and fiction aloud. Audio files could also be used to allow teens to share their music, as in recording a Battle of the Bands program, or asking teens to submit recordings of themselves singing or playing instruments.

IDEA #85: CAPTURE CREATIVITY ON VIDEO

> For more on using video, see Chapter 3.

As downloading speeds increase, streaming video over the Internet grows more and more popular. You may have already noticed teens watching music videos and movie previews on library computers. Teens also have more access to digital video cameras, or your school or public library may be able to lend them one. Put the two together and you have an opportunity to let teens put their filmmaking talents to use.

One idea is to sponsor a contest. Teens could film and edit short "commercials" publicizing the library and all it has to offer. The best could be made available on your Web site. The contest could also ask teens to talk on camera about their best library memories or discuss their favorite books. They could recite poems, read stories they've written, or conduct interviews.

Interview

Meg Canada
Web Services Librarian
Hennepin County Library, Minnesota
Available at: www.hclib.org/teens/hmongpoetry.cfm

At the Hennepin County Library in Minnesota, the TeenLinks Web site features poetry by Hmong and Latino teens. According to Meg Canada, who oversees TeenLinks, the poetry is written by the teens in groups facilitated by outreach specialists. The poetry is also published in printed books, but making it available on the Web gives teens an easy way to share their poetry with others. Canada said that the library has received positive feedback through

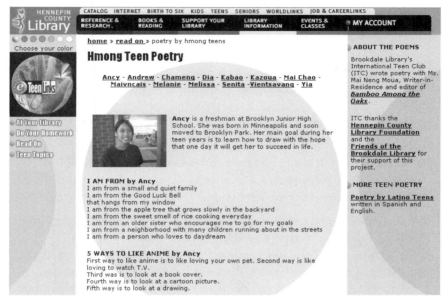

Figure 11-4 Hennepin County Library's Hmong Teen Poetry

their Web site. For example, people who are practicing their Spanish have said they enjoyed the bilingual poetry.

The poetry by Hmong teens includes photographs and brief profiles of the writers that identify them by their first names. TeenLinks also features "Nuestras Voces," published in both English and Spanish, at www.hennepin.lib.mn.us /teens/nuestrasvoces.cfm. This page offers bilingual poetry by high school students at the Center for Training and Careers in Richfield, Minnesota. The page includes photographs of the teens alongside their work.

Interview

Ginger Nelms
Young Adult Services Coordinator
Henry County Library System, Henry County, Georgia
The Henry County Library System sponsored a poetry contest for teens, then made the poems available on their Web site at www.henry.public.lib .ga.us/content/YApoetry.pdf.

What Were the Rules for the Poetry Contest?
The poetry contest was open to all students in grades six through twelve, ages eleven to eighteen.

Why Did You Decide to Make the Poems Available Online?

I didn't have the funds to offer print copies of the entries, but wanted to publish them. I felt the best way to publish the poems was through the Web site.

Have You Had Any Response from the Teen Winners or the General Public?

The teens, and their parents, love knowing their poems are published and that anyone can access them.

Why Do You Think It's Important to Showcase Teen Creativity?

Teens deserve recognition for their hard work. There is so much talent that largely is unseen, in teens and tweens.

What Advice Do You Have for Other Librarians Who Would Like to Put Teen Poetry or Other Creative Work Online?

As with laying out any newsletter, etc., typing each poem individually, so that the layout is comprehensible, is usually a challenge, but it's not impossible. Also, working with your IT department and knowing how they want things submitted to include on the Web site goes a long way.

Chapter 12

Teen Advisory Groups

OVERVIEW

Both school and public libraries often have groups of teens who act as formal or informal advisers to the librarian. This group may be called a Teen Advisory Board (TAB), a Teen Council, or something else entirely. These groups may help suggest purchases of library material, organize fundraisers or children's programs, assist with outreach to their peers, publish a zine, contribute to the library Web site, and so on. Although many of the examples in this section come from public libraries, they would work equally well for school librarians.

With the many commitments teens often have—school, sports, activities, and more—it can be difficult to get everyone together for regular meetings of a teen advisory board. Even if you do have frequent meetings, you may be looking for ways to let the world know about the teen advisory board's activities, to keep members up to date, to expand membership, or to get group members more involved.

The ideas in this section are intended to give your teen advisory group a presence online. Having a home page, a review site, a discussion forum, or even just a description and mission statement, gives teen advisory groups a place of their own on the library Web site. By enhancing communication, you'll make your teen advisory board a more cohesive group. A Web presence can also be a great tool for recruiting new members.

As always, it's a good idea to keep privacy concerns in mind, especially if you will be allowing teens to post to a blog or forum, or including photos of minors on the teen advisory board Web site.

IDEA #86: ADD A TAB WEB PAGE

Consider giving your teen advisory group its own section on your library Web site. The group's pages can include all kinds of information:

- An events and meetings calendar
- Photos and/or profiles of the members
- A description of the group's responsibilities
- Contact information for joining
- Application form
- Mission statement
- Meeting minutes
- Links to the teen advisory board's creative projects, such as zines or artwork
- Book reviews by board members

Ideally, you could have the teens themselves participate by agreeing on the components of the Web site, writing up the statements or profiles, and even designing the site themselves.

Haverhill Public Library in Haverhill, Massachusetts, dedicates a part of their teen Web site to the teen advisory board. The site includes a description of the group, a list of required qualifications such as age and commitment level, a list of TAB responsibilities, and a photo of the board members.

Haverhill Public Library, Haverhill, Massachusetts
Available at: http://teencybercenter.org/tab/tab.htm

The same site also provides a detailed task description for the teen advisory board. The task description includes duties, qualifications, time commitment information, and the benefits of joining.

At Phoenix Public Library in Phoenix, Arizona, teen advisory councils maintain their own Web sites using Geocities, a free, ad-supported online service. The library's teen page links to each site but includes a disclaimer that reads, "Note—The branch teen council Web sites utilize commercial Web space freely available on the Internet. The use of such space may involve the display of advertisements not endorsed by the Phoenix Public Library."

An obvious advantage of taking this approach is that teens can maintain and update the site without help from the library's technical staff. Teens can be more autonomous in designing the site and making decisions about what to post. The drawbacks include a less professional looking site and annoying ads.

HAVERHILL
PUBLIC LIBRARY

99 Main Street
Haverhill, MA 01830
(978) 373-1586
fax: (978) 373-8466
mhv@mvlc.org

Home
Ask a Question
Hours & Directions
Calendar
Museum Passes
Library News
Contacts
Library Policies
Online Catalog
Jobs at the Library
Friends of the Library
Volunteering
Donate to the Library
FAQs
Sitemap
Search This Site

 Teen Advisory
Board

TCC Home

Teens ages 13 to 18 are invited to join the Teen Advisory Board at the Haverhill Public Library. The teen advisory board will be responsible for planning programs for teens and ordering materials.

Upcoming Meetings:

Meetings are 3:15 - 4:45 PM in the Pentucket Medical Association room on the 1st Floor of the Library.

Thursday, January 12th
Wednesday, February 8th
Thursday, March 9th
Tuesday, April 4th
Wednesday, May 10th

Want to be a part of the Teen Advisory Board?
A complete task description is available; qualifications and responsibilities are posted below. If you are interested in joining the Teen Advisory Board, please fill out the application (opens in Microsoft Word) and return it to Alissa at the Reference/Information desk, or email it to alauzon@mvlc.org. Applications are also available at the Reference/Information desk at the library.

Qualifications for a Teen Advisory Board Member:

- Must be a Haverhill or Bradford resident between the ages of 13 and 18
- Must be willing to commit to 1.5 hours once a month for a meeting
- Must be able to fulfill the responsibilities of a Teen Advisory Board Member
- Must enjoy working with others as a team
- Should be interested in the library and improving library services to teens

Responsibilities of a Teen Advisory Board Member:

- Attend all meetings and be an active participant
- Attend as many programs as possible and help with setup and cleanup
- Be a responsible library user
- Set an example of appropriate library behavior for your peers
- Help promote participation in library programs for teens

As seen in the Boston Globe

The Haverhill Public Library's Teen Advisory Board was featured in the Boston Globe North Weekly section on Sunday November 3, 2003. Please take a look at the scanned article Youth Boom at the Library by Brenda Buote

Figure 12-1   Haverhill Public Library Teen Advisory Board

IDEA #87: LET TEENS APPLY ONLINE

Why not let teens who want to join your teen advisory board apply online? An online application makes the process easier and more accessible—leading, one hopes, to more applicants.

There are several ways to make your existing teen advisory group application available online. The easiest is simply to add a link to your Web page that brings up a Microsoft Word file. Haverhill Public Library, in Haverhill, Massachusetts, does this at http://teencybercenter.org/tab/application.doc.

Teens then have two choices:

- Print the application, fill it out, and take it in to the library; or
- Save the application, fill it out on their computer, and then send it to the teen librarian as an e-mail attachment.

You can also create your application as a Web page, as in the example, from Coshocton Public Library in Ohio, at www.cplrmh.com/application .html. Teens would still need to print this application out and take it in to the library.

Perhaps the best—though slightly more complicated—option is to create your application as an online form, so that teens fill it out on the Web and the information goes to your e-mail address as soon as they click "submit." See Chapter 3 for a discussion on creating Web forms.

IDEA #88: DISPLAY A MISSION STATEMENT

Several libraries include their teen advisory board's mission statement on their Web sites, as in this attractively displayed example from Kalamazoo Public Library in Kalamazoo, Michigan.

Kalamazoo Public Library in Kalamazoo, Michigan
Available at: www.kpl.gov/teen/TAB.aspx

IDEA #89: DRAW UP SOME BYLAWS

If your teen advisory group has a formal set of written bylaws, adding them to the Web site is a simple task. At the Grace A. Dow Memorial Library in Midland, Michigan, the Teen Advisory Board keeps its bylaws online, with a list of dates showing when the bylaws were updated. The bylaws address everything from membership, meetings, and officers to the TAB's code of ethics. See it at www.midland-mi.org/gracedowlibrary/teen/tab_bylaws.html.

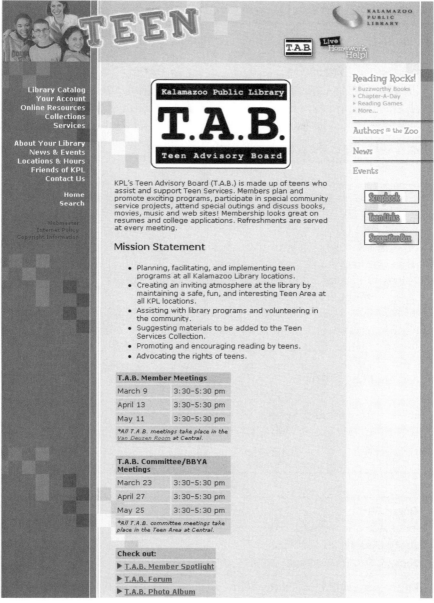

Figure 12-2   Kalamazoo Public Library Teen Advisory Board

IDEA #90: KEEP THE MINUTES

Keep everyone up to date with records of your teen advisory board meetings by posting your minutes online, as Appleton Public Library, in Appleton, Wisconsin, does. Their Teen Advisory Board site has a listing of meeting dates at http://teen.apl.org/tab_minutes/minutes.html. When Web site users click on a date, they see the minutes for that day's meeting.

IDEA #91: BEGIN A TAB BLOG

For more on blogs, and how to create one, see Chapter 3.

Another way to keep your teen advisory group up to date quickly and easily is to create a blog, a frequently updated online journal. Chapter Four covers blogs in general, in depth; but some teen librarians are specifically using blogs to communicate with teen advisory groups.

One excellent example of a blog that contains information aimed at a teen advisory board comes from Henry County Library System in Henry County, Georgia. "Henry TAB Talk" includes posts on the next scheduled meeting for the group as well as more general items such as book lists, community events, and more.

Henry County Library System, Henry County, Georgia
Available at: www.henrytabtalk.blogspot.com/

Interview

Ginger Nelms
Young Adult Services Coordinator
Henry County Library System
Henry County, Georgia
 	
Approximately How Many Teens Are on Your Teen Advisory Board?
    Right now we have Teen Advisory Boards at two branches of our system. Between them we have thirty-five to forty members.
 	
What Kinds of Projects Do They Do?
    They have participated in local community service projects, helped with summer programs—both teen and children's programs. They helped create

Figure 12-3   Henry County Public Library's "Henry TAB Talk" Blog

the summer schedule of teen activities this past summer, they suggest books and other materials, they offered input on the design and decor of future teen areas to be included at one of the branches after renovation, and are currently working on a float for the local Christmas parade.

Are They Excited about More Chances to Participate Online?

They really seem to like being able to access what is going on for them whenever they want to.

What Are Their Feelings about Technology and the Internet?

Since, by and large, they have grown up with the Internet, for most it seems just one more part of their everyday lives. And they know how to make it work for them.

How Long Have You Offered the Blog?

Since May, 2005.

What Kinds of Items Do You Post? How Often Do You Post New Items?

As often as possible, if there are things going on that need to be posted. I try for at least once a week, but sometimes fall short.

How Do You Promote Your Blog to Teens?

There is a link from the main library Web site. I've created bookmarks with the blog address, and I include it on any and all handouts and announcements.

Do You Get Feedback from Teens That Tells You They Read It?

Occasionally, but it seems to be growing all the time.

Do Teens Post Comments?

So far, the comments have been vague, more from adults.

Have You Had Any Problems with Inappropriate Comments?

No.

How Much Time Does It Take to Maintain the Blog?

The time depends on how much I need to post. It takes longer to post images and get the text just so than simply to type in text.

Why Did You Decide to Start a Discussion Forum?

The members of the TABs voted on starting the forum so they can communicate between meetings.

Who Is Allowed to Participate?

As of right now, forum members are only TAB members, but if a non-TAB teen asked to join, that might change.

What Are the Rules for the Forum?

All memberships are approved by the administrator. Of course, abusiveness won't be tolerated. Mainly, the goal is to have a safe online space for the teens to interact outside of meetings.

What Kinds of Discussions Do You Anticipate?

Programs, books and materials, and library advocacy.

What Are the Possible Benefits of Using Blogs?

They show that the library is not stagnant but ever-changing, willing to keep up with the growth and advances of electronic media, to meet the needs and interests of their patrons.

What Challenges Do You Foresee?

The biggest challenge is in keeping up with the teens. They are much more techno-savvy than I am.

Do You Have Any Advice for Other Librarians Who Want to Offer This Kind of Program?

As with anything, the hardest part is getting started. If you are in an area where the media outlets are limited, blogs and forums offer an easy access, with little or no cost to implement.

IDEA #92: ENCOURAGE ONLINE DISCUSSION

For more on forums or discussion boards, see Chapter 3.

An online forum or discussion board is a great way to keep in touch with your teen advisory group, and to allow the group to exchange ideas and information online.

Kalamazoo Public Library in Kalamazoo, Michigan, offers a TAB forum at www.kpl.gov/InstantForum/.

Henry County Library System in Henry County, Georgia, also has a discussion forum for its teen advisory group. The teen librarian is able to post information about meetings to the forum. Teens also discuss books, plans for upcoming events, and ideas for future projects.

Henry County Library System in Henry County, Georgia
Available at: http://xsorbit29.com/users5/henrytabforum/index.php/

IDEA #93: SHARE BOOK RECOMMENDATIONS

Some teen advisory group Web sites also give their members an opportunity to act as readers' advisors. Teen advisory group members may publish their book reviews, for example, or pick titles to recommend to their peers.

Arlington County Public Library in Arlington, Virginia offers attractive pages showing the Teen Advisory Board picks for each year, with book covers and brief summaries.

Arlington County Public Library in Arlington, Virginia
Available at: www.arlingtonva.us/Departments/Libraries/Teen/Tab/Libra
riesTeenTab2005.aspx (see Figure 12-5)

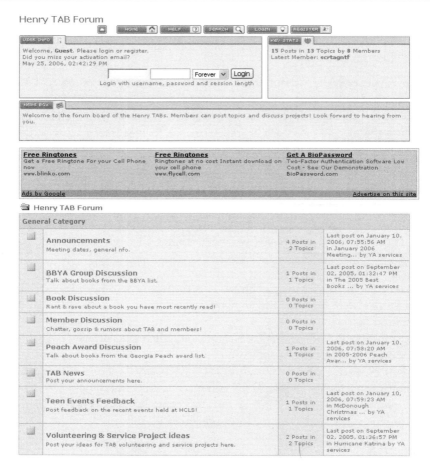

Figure 12-4   Henry County Public Library's Teen Advisory Board Forum

IDEA #94: PUBLISH A TAB ZINE

Another option is to have your teen advisory group publish an online zine. A zine—short for "magazine"—is usually an informal, small circulation, self-published collection of poetry, art, short stories, opinion pieces, and anything else the publishers want to include. When posted online, zines become "e-zines."

At Martin Memorial Library in York County, Pennsylvania, the Teen Advisory Board publishes an e-zine called *The Slant*. As they describe it on their Web site:

> We feature articles, creative writing, reviews, and comics by our TAB members, along with lists of great books organized by genre, useful links

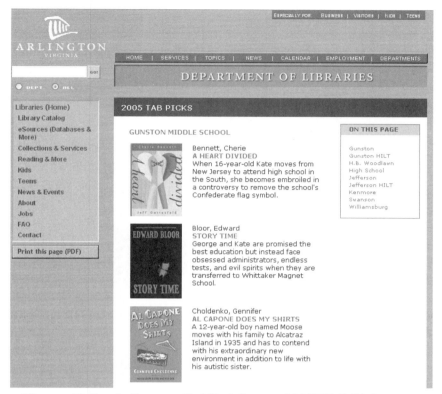

Figure 12-5   Arlington Public Library 2005 TAB Picks

about college and other subjects important to teens, and information about what the TAB has been doing.

Martin Memorial Library in York County, Pennsylvania
Available at: www.yorklibraries.org/teens/slant.htm

IDEA #95: LET TEENS SHAPE YOUR WEB SITE

If you're serious about developing a great Web site for teens, you might want to follow in the footsteps of Hennepin County Library in Minnesota. This library has created an advisory board for their teen Web site, called Teens Online. This not only ensures that the site is relevant and interesting to teens, but creates an audience and word-of-mouth campaign for it.

Teens Online brings together a group of teens each year, according to Meg Canada, the Web Services Librarian who oversees TeenLinks. Participants must be in grades eight through twelve.

Welcome to *the* Slant!

History of Books and Printing

The Slant is the e-zine by teens for teens, run by Martin Memorial Library's Teen Advisory Board (TAB). We're excited about our new layout, and we'd love to hear your feedback -- send your thoughts to teens@yorklibraries.org.

We feature articles, creative writing, reviews, and comics by our TAB members, along with lists of great books organized by genre, useful links about college and other subjects important to teens, and information about what the TAB has been doing. You can get to all of these sections of the site by using the menu at the top of the page.

Slant Updates

May 18, 2006

New this week is a story by Brandon, and a recap of this year's Youth Empowerment Summit by Sherry.

TAB: What's Happening

Looking for a job this summer? Want to learn what you need to do to get one? Martin Library is offering its third year of teen job training sessions, sponsored by Harley Davidson. All the information you need can be found at http://www.yorklibraries.org/teens/index.htm .

Summer Reading Club begins for teens on June 12th and will run until August 4th. This year the theme is "Paws, Claws, and Scales." Remember to sign up!

The winning entries from this year's poetry contest are now online (view the PDF)!

Figure 12-6   Martin Memorial Library's Teen Advisory Board Zine, *The Slant*

Next, according to Canada, teens are interviewed by phone or in person. The application and interview process ensures that the teens have the necessary level of commitment. The program has had from thirteen to sixteen participants during recent years. Applications—available online—are accepted in the fall, and then participants meet nine times during the year, on Sunday afternoons.

The students adopt projects, anything from blogging to designing pages on finding a summer job to providing college resources. In recent projects, one teen explains about wikis, while another reviews DVDs and a third interviews the new library director.

The program began in 2001, Canada said. One component is a contest organized and judged by the Teens Online volunteers. Past competitions have included Web site design and an online essay contest.

The main challenge of the program is getting the teens to attend meetings and keep their participation levels high, Canada said. She highly recommends that other librarians try similar programs. "Teen input is so important," she said, in finding out what teens want and need from the library's Web site.

She advises getting to know the students involved and building the program from year to year. "You won't accomplish all of your goals in the first year," Canada points out.

More on this program is available at www.hclib.org/teens/teensonline.cfm.

Chapter 13

Summer Reading

OVERVIEW

If the only goal of your summer reading program is to lure teens into the library, then online summer reading probably isn't for you. But if it's more important to get teens reading, regardless of where they do it, consider making at least some aspects of your program Web-based. The easier it is to sign up, the more likely teens are to participate. In addition, and online program gives them opportunities to interact with other eager readers, submit reviews, and become more deeply involved.

For school libraries, an online summer reading program could be even more beneficial. Since the school library is probably closed for the summer, an online program could give students an incentive to keep reading and give them a chance to discuss books with their classmates and teachers.

In addition, an online program might end up being easier to manage, since many of the functions can be automated. Public and school librarians can also use their Web sites to communicate with participants, publicize summer events, do readers' advisory, and much more.

Finally, and perhaps most importantly, a summer reading program that incorporates technology will seem more relevant and interesting to teens who might think of summer reading as something "just for kids." If your summer reading program isn't online yet, consider the following ideas and examples for your Web site.

IDEA #96: PROVIDE BASIC INFORMATION

At the very least, you'll want to provide basic information about the summer reading program on your Web site. This might include:

- Beginning and ending dates
- How to sign up
- Where to sign up
- Rules and requirements, including what ages are considered "teen"
- What types of materials participants can read (Books? Magazines? Graphic novels?)
- How much reading is required, and how participation is measured and documented
- What prizes will be awarded, and other benefits of participation
- Information about any contests or raffles
- Dates for and descriptions of special events
- How to find out more—contact numbers, e-mail, instant messaging information, etc.

IDEA #97: TAKE SIGN-UPS ONLINE

> For more on Web forms, see Chapter 3.

Why not let teens sign up for your summer program online? You can use a Web-based submission form to gather patron information, and either print out registration information or add it to a database using a program such as Microsoft Access. If that seems too daunting, you can make a form available online for teens to print, fill out, and then mail or take to their nearest branch.

Remember to remove the sign-up form once the reading program ends, and to put it back up for the next year. While the form is not available, your Web page can list the dates for next year's program and also a date when the Web form will be available again.

The British Columbia Library Association accepts online summer reading registration at www.teensrc.ca/signup.php. Denver Public Library allows teens to sign up for their summer reading program online beginning in late May.

Denver Public Library, Denver, Colorado
Available at: http://summerofreading.org/tsr/register.html

IDEA #98: ACCEPT ONLINE BOOK REVIEW SUBMISSIONS

Many teen summer reading programs require participants to submit short reviews. You can encourage participation by accepting reviews online, either by

Figure 13-1   Denver Public Library Teen Summer Reading 2006

e-mail or through a Web-based form. These reviews can also be published online as a readers' advisory tool for other teens, and as an ego boost for participants who will enjoy knowing that others are reading their comments.

Wichita Falls Public Library in Wichita Falls, Texas, offers a submission form for book reviews as part of its Teen Summer Reading Program. Teens who submit three reviews by a certain date can then go to the library to pick up their prize. The form is at www.wfpl.net/summerreading/teensummerform.htm.

Students at Tappan Zee High School in Orangeburg, New York, can also submit their summer reading book reviews online, using a form on their school library media center's Web site. The form is available at www.socsdteachers .org/lparkerhennion/breview.htm.

IDEA #99: ALLOW ELECTRONIC RAFFLE ENTRIES

If you offer a raffle as part of summer reading, consider allowing online entries. You might award one raffle entry for each book review, or ask participants to take an online survey in order to enter. You could also ask entrants to complete a quiz or answer trivia questions.

The online raffle could be a one-time event, but better yet, keep teens coming back once a week to enter again. Consider announcing the winner online (perhaps by first name and an initial) to spark additional interest. Raffles are an excellent way to build excitement about your Web site, since something cool is up for grabs—even if it's something inexpensive, like a CD or $5 gift certificate.

IDEA #100: START A SUMMER READING BLOG

> For more on blogs, and how to create them, see Chapter 3.

A blog is an ideal way to communicate with teens during your summer reading program. You can post book suggestions, remind teens about summer events, pose questions and solicit comments about the books they're reading, and announce any contest winners. You might also post photos from library events to show other teens how much fun they're missing if they aren't participating.

Garden Valley Library in Garden Valley, Idaho, started a simple blog for their 2005 teen summer reading program. This blog announced the program's rules and requirements, as well as providing book suggestions. Teens then posted their comments about the books directly to the blog.

Garden Valley Library in Garden Valley, Idaho
Available at: http://dragonsanddreams.blogspot.com/

IDEA #101: GET YOUR SUMMER READERS TALKING

> For more on forums and discussion board, and how to create them, see Chapter 3.

Creating a community of readers is an important goal for a summer reading program, but that can't happen unless those readers have a place to gather and talk. During the summer, teens may not be able to make it to the library regularly. Or they may not feel comfortable talking about books face to face with a librarian or a peer, especially if they have very specific tastes that aren't widely shared.

An online forum or discussion board can provide an easy, convenient place to connect with other readers. Of course, on any online forum that is open to all users, there are issues about appropriateness and safety. School librarians may want to limit their forums to their students only, providing sign-in names

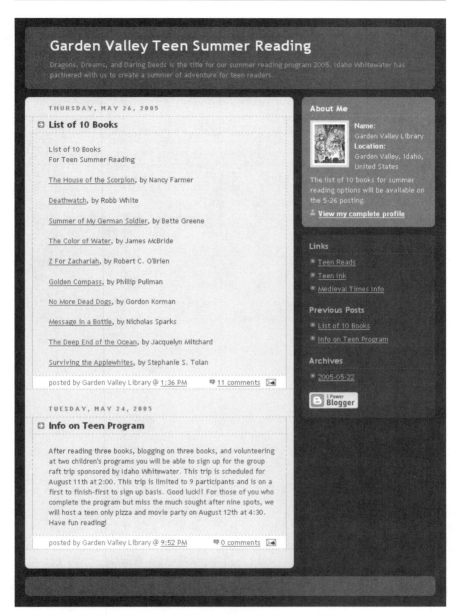

Garden Valley Teen Summer Reading

Dragons, Dreams, and Daring Deeds is the title for our summer reading program 2005. Idaho Whitewater has partnered with us to create a summer of adventure for teen readers.

THURSDAY, MAY 26, 2005

List of 10 Books

List of 10 Books
For Teen Summer Reading

The House of the Scorpion, by Nancy Farmer

Deathwatch, by Robb White

Summer of My German Soldier, by Bette Greene

The Color of Water, by James McBride

Z For Zachariah, by Robert C. O'Brien

Golden Compass, by Phillip Pullman

No More Dead Dogs, by Gordon Korman

Message in a Bottle, by Nicholas Sparks

The Deep End of the Ocean, by Jacquelyn Mitchard

Surviving the Applewhites, by Stephanie S. Tolan

posted by Garden Valley Library @ 1:36 PM   11 comments

TUESDAY, MAY 24, 2005

Info on Teen Program

After reading three books, blogging on three books, and volunteering at two children's programs you will be able to sign up for the group raft trip sponsored by Idaho Whitewater. This trip is scheduled for August 11th at 2:00. This trip is limited to 9 participants and is on a first to finish-first to sign up basis. Good luck!! For those of you who complete the program but miss the much sought after nine spots, we will host a teen only pizza and movie party on August 12th at 4:30. Have fun reading!

posted by Garden Valley Library @ 9:52 PM   0 comments

About Me

Name:
Garden Valley Library
Location:
Garden Valley, Idaho, United States

The list of 10 books for summer reading options will be available on the 5-26 posting.

View my complete profile

Links

* Teen Reads
* Teen Ink
* Medieval Times Info

Previous Posts

* List of 10 Books
* Info on Teen Program

Archives

* 2005-05-22

Blogger

Figure 13-2   Garden Valley Teen Summer Reading

and passwords before the end of the school year. Public libraries may want to require library card numbers or ask teens to register. Still, these concerns should not prevent libraries from offering these very important online gathering places.

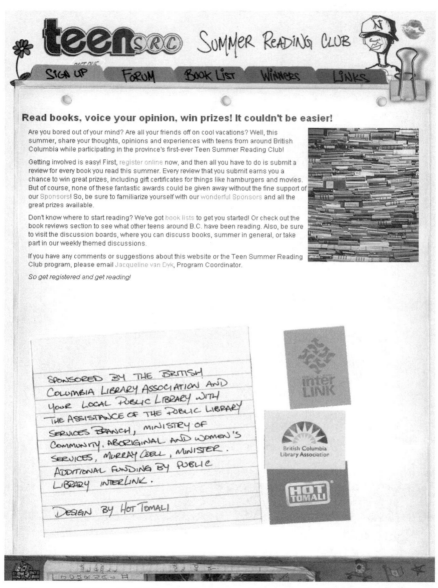

Figure 13-3 British Columbia Library Association's Teen Summer Reading Club

Home | Administration | Alumni | Athletics | Calendar | Departments | Guidance | Media Ctr | Search Engines | Students

BHS 2006 Summer Reading List

All Greenville County School District students will be tested during the first days of school.
Read the books from the appropriate grade level list below before you return to school in
August. You will be able to get these titles from the BHS Media Center, at county libraries,
& local bookstores. Many of these titles will be available for Berea students during the
summer months at school Monday-Thursday.

☆Assessment Instructions	9th Grade	10th Grade	11th Grade	12th Grade	Printable Reading List

- 9th Grade English (ONE book of your choice and ONE of the following)
(Click on Book or Title for Summary)

A Solitary Blue by Cynthia Voigt	*I Know What You Did Last Summer* by Lois Duncan	*Ender's Game* by Orson Card	*Silver* by Norma Mazer	*The Moves Makes the Man* by Bruce Brooks	*The Hobbit* by J.R.R. Tolkien

- 9th Grade Honors (ONE book of your choice and TWO of the following)
(Click on Book or Title for Summary)

Ellen Foster by Kaye Gibbons	*Walking Across Egypt* by Clyde Edgerton	*I Know Why the Caged Bird Sings* by Maya Angelou	*I Heard the Owl Call My Name* by Margaret Craven	*White Fang* by Jack London	*The Sword in the Stone* by T.H. White

Figure 13-4   Berea High School 2006 Summer Reading List

The British Columbia Library Association, in Canada, offers a discussion
forum for teens as part of its online teen summer reading club, which also has
an online application, a book list, contests, and suggested links.

British Columbia Library Association, Canada
Available at: www.teensrc.ca

IDEA #102: FEATURE ASSIGNED READING LISTS

Schools often assign summer reading, but often the booklists provided to students simply list titles and authors. Also, frequently, students lose their list of assigned books well before summer ends. So it's a great idea to add your school's summer reading lists to the library media center's Web site.

Even better, add reviews along with titles, so that students can make an informed choice, rather than going for the one title they remember—or, more likely, the book with the fewest pages. You might also want to link the book titles to reviews in Amazon or to the title in the public library catalog, so that teens can immediately see where it's available.

Berea High School in Greenville, South Carolina, offers an attractive list showing book covers and with brief annotations for each title.

Berea High School, Greenville, South Carolina
Available at: http://bereahigh.org/Media/honorsread.htm

Public libraries can also add schools' summer reading lists to their Web sites, to assist teen patrons in finding what they need. Boston Public Library does an excellent job of this, offering an extensive list of links to Boston-area schools. Their lists are at www.bpl.org/kids/summerlists/index.htm.

Chapter 14

Just for Fun

OVERVIEW

Once your site has all the elements you consider essential, consider adding some "just for fun" features. Of course, you don't want to overload your site with silly, distracting tidbits. You've probably visited sites where animated critters dance all over the screen, irritating music plays whether you want it to or not, and it's hard to find the functional parts of the site through all the clutter. This is not something you want to replicate. But one or two carefully chosen, entertaining ideas may make your site more welcoming and enjoyable for visitors.

IDEA #103: INCLUDE GAMES AND PUZZLES

Many library Web sites offer links to games, puzzles, and other "just for fun" sites. This would apply, of course, only to libraries where online games are allowed on the public or school computers. Also, you'll have to decide which sites to promote:

- Will you link to educational games only, like word games and puzzles, or include arcade-type games?
- Will you link to ad-filled commercial sites or choose non-profit sites only, which will limit your choices?
- How will you choose the games? Will you solicit recommendations from teens, or just notice what they seem to play?

Los Gatos Public Library, in Los Gatos, California, has a nice selection of game sites for teens at www.losgatosca.gov/index.asp?NID=271, about halfway down the page. Denver Public Library in Denver, Colorado, also offers links to games at http://teens.denverlibrary.org/media/games.html. The link on the

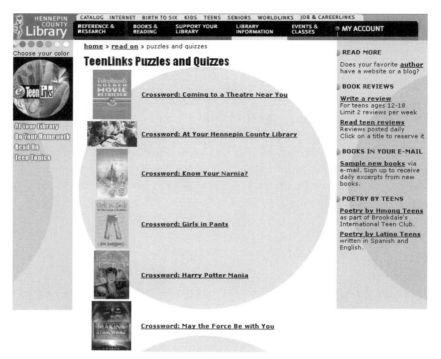

Figure 14-1   Hennepin County Library's TeenLinks Puzzles and Quizzes

bottom of the page, which lets teens suggest more games for the page, is a nice touch.

You can also choose to put the puzzles and games directly on your Web site. There are many Web sites that librarians can use to create crosswords, but a useful one is the tool at Edhelper.com, www.edhelper.com/crossword_free.htm. Hennepin County Library, in Minnesota, offers crossword puzzles—often book-related—on their TeenLinks site.

Hennepin County Library, Minnesota
Available at: www.hclib.org/teens/crosswords/index.cfm

IDEA #104: ADD A GAME BLOG

Any library with an Internet computer attracts them: the teen gamers. So why not embrace them? St. Joseph County Public Library, in South Bend, Indiana, does. They offer a Game Blog, which discusses gaming in general as well as the library's gaming tournaments, open play days, and other special events.

Teens can register and add comments, and judging from the number of comments on each post, they're embracing the opportunity. This is a great way to publicize the library's gaming events and to let teens know that you welcome them and their interests.

St. Joseph County Public Library, South Bend, Indiana
Available at: www.sjcpl.org/gameblog/index.php

Any other method you can think of that will encourage teen gamers to use the library and its services should be a welcome addition to your Web site. The more teen and school librarians learn about online gaming, the better they will be able to relate to their patrons and students. Projects such as the Second Life Library offer a glimpse of how gaming and MMORPGs—Massively Multiplayer Online Role Playing Games, where players create online worlds where their avatars can go on quests, buy and sell goods, form relationships, and more—might intersect with libraries and how they offer their services.

Figure 14-2   St. Joseph County Public Library GameBlog

IDEA #105: FEATURE BREAKING NEWS

When you go to Yahoo!'s home page, you see a box on the right-hand side with some of the main headlines of the day. I often glance at that "In the News" box to see what's happening in the world.

It's fairly simple to add similar breaking-news headlines to your library Web page, and have them update regularly and automatically.

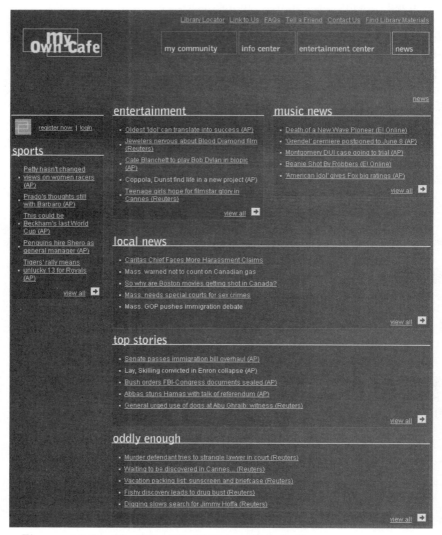

Figure 14-3   My Own Café News Feeds Page

This feature may make your Web page more dynamic and more of a destination for students, staff, or library users. You can select which news sources you'd like to include, or feature several sources together on one Web page, so that page becomes a place that library users check frequently.

For example, to add the latest New York Times headlines for free, go to www.nytimes.com/gst/nytheadlines.html. You'll fill in information such as your name, e-mail address, and URL for your Web site. Follow the steps to design your layout, then copy and paste the HTML code provided to your Web site. Headlines will update automatically.

Most major news sources offer similar services. You can also add this feature to your Web site as a scrolling "news ticker." Just beware of cluttering up your site in a way that's distracting or unprofessional.

MyOwnCafe.org, the teen Web site for the Southeastern Massachusetts Library System, uses news feeds for its site. They feature sports, entertainment, local news, and music news on their site, along with a section called "Strangely Enough," for offbeat stories. Because the site uses news feeds, little maintenance is required, and the feeds keep the site current with the latest headlines.

Southeastern Massachusetts Regional Library System
Available at: http://myowncafe.org/news/tabid/55/Default.aspx

IDEA #106: REPORT ON THE WEATHER

Similar to news updates, many online tools allow Web site creators to add weather reports to their pages. These features allow site visitors to track local weather with one quick glance.

There are many sites that allow you to add weather reports and forecasts to your site. One option is available at www.weather.com/services/oap.html. You choose a design, sign up, and then copy the HTML code to add to your site.

IDEA #107: FIND OTHER FREE CONTENT

If you're looking for other free, remotely hosted add-ons for your Web site, there are many options. You can set up a counter or ticker that shows how many people have visited your site, a guest book (beware of spam!), mini polls, and more to your site. There are many services that offer free—usually ad-supported—content, some with a paid, ad-free option.

A few services to consider include:

- Bravenet
    Available at: www.bravenet.com

- The JavaScript Source
    Available at: http://javascript.internet.com
- SiteGadgets
    Available at: www.sitegadgets.com
- StatCounter
    Available at: www.statcounter.com

If your school or library system has a Webmaster, it would be best to consult with that person about how you might be able to accomplish the same goal without off-site hosting or commercial services. The Webmaster will likely prefer to install software directly on the library's server. Also, be wary of making your site look amateur or unprofessional—you'll want to avoid ads, for example, and other graphics that will clutter your pages. Some of the free services may also slow down the loading time for your pages, since they are accessing information from the commercial sites.

IDEA #108: ANIMATE YOUR SITE

The Calgary Public Library in Calgary, Canada, adds software tools to its Teen Zone Web site. Users click on "Move it!" to pull up a box that allows users to draw simple shapes to create short animations. The "Mix it!" option lets users create music using drum loops, bass loops, and speech sound effects. Try it at http://calgarypubliclibrary.com/teens/welcome.htm.

IDEA #109: DESIGN A PHOTO GALLERY

One thing teens love to do online is to share their photos. With digital cameras and cell phone cameras, it's easier than ever to take pictures or videos and store them online for others to look at. One extremely popular Web site that allows users to do this is Flickr, available at www.flickr.com. On this site, users can store, search, sort, and share their photographs. It's just one more way that teens "live" online, by creating digital scrapbooks that record their activities, friends, and adventures.

Flickr and similar sites allow users to do more than store their photos and arrange them into albums, however. Flickr, for example, lets users label their photos with "tags"—essentially, to catalog them informally. This makes it possible to search and categorize photos in many ways. Flickr users can subscribe to feeds, so that they are notified when new photos are available. Also, Flickr users can give their friends and family members permission to organize and reorganize the photos they've posted. Friends, family, or the general public

flickr

Learn More   Sign Up!   Explore ⌄

SEARCH

Gwinnett County Public Library's photos

pro

Sets   Tags   Archives   Favorites   Profile

Pooh Visits Dacula

Everyone lines up to see Pooh.

This photo is public.
Uploaded on May 5, 2006
0 comments

Pooh Visits Dacula

Pooh is greeted by Miss Paula.

This photo is public
Uploaded on May 5, 2006
0 comments

Pooh Visits Dacula

Everyone waits while Miss Robin talks
about Pooh's visit.

This photo is public.
Uploaded on May 5, 2006
0 comments

**Grayson April2006, along
RockSprings Rd**

This photo is public.
Uploaded on May 1, 2006

Grayson Branch Exterior April 2006

This photo is public.
Uploaded on May 1, 2006
0 comments

Grayson April2006 Stone Siding

This photo is public.
Uploaded on May 1, 2006
0 comments

**Dacula Branch
Library**
32 photos

**Grayson Library
Project**
6 photos

**Gwinnett Reads
2006**
20 photos

**Read Across
America 2006**
4 photos

**Rock the
Shelves 2005**
47 photos

Figure 14-4   Gwinnett County Public Library Flickr.com Photos

can add captions and comments. Users can add photographs online, but they can also add them from cell phones or PDAs.

Libraries can tap into teen interest in seeing and sharing photos of themselves and their peers by creating photo displays on the library Web sites. Making the sites interactive—allowing students to post, comment on, or reorganize the photographs—would make them even more appealing. Of course, librarians need to be sensitive about privacy and make sure they have permission to post photographs of teens.

Many libraries have added photos to their teen sites. University Laboratory High School in Urbana, Illinois, has a gallery of photographs at www.uni .uiuc.edu/library/gallery/library/index.htm. East Woods School in Oyster Bay, New York, promotes reading with a photo page called "Get Caught Reading," at www.eastwoods.org/ewslibrary/Interactive/GetCaughtReading.htm.

Several libraries are using Flickr for their teen photos, including Weymouth Public Library, in Weymouth, Massachusetts. Their teen photo album is at http://www.flickr.com/photos/wpl/sets/72057594063418062/. By using this service popular with and familiar to teens, the library increases the chance that teens will view their photos. In addition, using social networking software like Flickr makes it easy to use links, tags, and other networking features to connect to the rest of the community.

Gwinnett County Public Library in Gwinnett, Georgia, uses Flickr to display photos from library events, including teen events.

Gwinnett County Public Library in Gwinnett, Georgia
Available at: http://flickr.com/photos/gwinnettcountypubliclibrary/

Part V.   Tech Companion Pages

A: KEY TECH TERMS

Access—Microsoft Access is software for creating and managing data, available as part of Microsoft Office.

Adobe Acrobat—Software for opening and creating PDF files. PDF stands for Portable Document Format, and is a way to create files in which the text and layout appear exactly as the designer intended. It is often used for official forms and documents.

Adobe Audition—Software for creating, mixing, and editing digital audio files on a PC, perhaps for creating podcasts or adding online audio to your Web site.

Ajax—Asynchronous JavaScript and XML, a Web development technique which increases the speed at which Web sites respond to users' needs. It is a combination of existing technologies that allows Web pages to be more responsive. Ajax is commonly behind many Web 2.0 applications, such as maps that users manipulate or Web collaboration tools.

Apple Safari—A Web browser developed by Apple Computer and available on Macs as part of the operating system.

Audacity—Free software for recording and editing sound files. Most audio files will require some editing to remove background noise, amplify sound, and delete errors and silences. Download Audacity at http://audacity.sourceforge.net/.

Avatar—A graphical representation, usually used in the context of an online game, where each player selects or designs an image as their virtual representative on the screen.

BlackBerry—A wireless portable device that allows users to read and send e-mail.

Blog—Short for "Web log," a blog is an online journal. Blog creators frequently use Web-based sites that make updating the blog very simple.

Blogs usually consist of short entries that include links to other Web sites. Blogs are often chatty and opinionated in tone. They may have a "comments" link where readers can add their own opinions or suggestions.

Blogger.com—A free blogging service owned by Google. Blogger.com allows users to create personal blogs and update them easily.

Bluetooth—A short-range radio technology that allows for wireless communication between personal digital devices, cell phones, laptops, printers and more.

Bookmark sharing sites—Web sites that allow you to store and organize your favorite Web "bookmarks" and share them with others. Two examples are del.icio.us (http://del.icio.us) and Furl (www.furl.net).

Buddy list—A list of online friends, usually in association with Instant Messaging software. By checking their buddy list, users can see whether their friends are currently available to chat.

Bulletin board—One of several terms for an online space where users can leave messages that other users then respond to. They might also be called discussion boards, Web forums, message boards, discussion forums, or discussion groups. The site keeps a running record of what users have posted, so anyone joining can read the entire discussion from the beginning. Some boards allow anonymous posting, while others require registration. Usually groups have a moderator, who is able to edit or delete inappropriate messages.

CamStudio—Free software for recording all activity on your computer screen, creating a "screencast" that has many educational uses. For example, you can create of "movie" of your lesson on using library databases. Download CamStudio at www.camstudio.org.

Camtasia Studio—TechSmith Camtasia Studio is software that allows users to record activity on their computer screens in order to create a "screencast." Screencasts can be used to offer online tutorials and lessons. The Camtasia Studio software allows users to capture screen activity, edit the results, add special effects, and share the results.

Captivate—Macromedia Captivate is software used to record activity on a computer screen to create a "screencast." The software also allows users to add text, captions, narration, and more.

Chat/chat rooms/live chat—A way of interacting with others online by typing text messages that everyone involved can read. Two or more individuals can chat online, in real time. Groups often gather in chat rooms to discuss specific topics. In a library context, chat may also be used for virtual author visits, to answer reference questions online, or as part of a homework help program.

Content Management Systems (CMS)—A general term that encompasses software and Web applications that help organize information and allow users to work together to create documents. Blogs, wikis, online calendars or scheduling applications, software that facilitates online buying and selling, and systems that allow users to access training documents or instruction manuals could all fall under this category.

Dreamweaver—Macromedia Dreamweaver is software used for creating, editing, organizing, and maintaining Web sites. It is often preferred by experienced Web designers over Microsoft FrontPage because it generates cleaner code, doesn't favor the Internet Explorer browser, and allows for more flexibility. However, for beginners, there may be a steeper learning curve.

E-books—Electronic books, which users can download and then read on their computers or portable digital devices.

Facebook.com—A popular social networking site. Users must have a valid e-mail address from a high school, university, or approved corporation or nonprofit organization. Facebook is extremely popular with college students. As in MySpace, users create profiles and network with their friends and peers.

Feedburner.com—A free online service that converts feeds between the two different standards, RSS and Atom. By using Feedburner, you can ensure that all users will be able to make use of your feed.

Feeds—A feed is a way of subscribing to information and gathering it all together on one Web page. Using RSS—Real Simple Syndication—or Atom, Internet users can "subscribe" to a blog or any other Web site where content is added regularly. Users utilize either a desktop news aggregator such as FeedReader or, more likely, choose an online service such as Bloglines or MyYahoo!. They can then see the newest headlines all in one place, rather than checking their favorite blog or Web site every day. Web designers can also add feeds to their pages so that the pages are updated automatically with new content.

Form—An online form is an element of a Web page that allows users to send information directly to the creator or Webmaster. For example, a teen might paste his or her book review into an online form on the library Web site and then click "submit," rather than e-mailing the review to a librarian. A Web form can have many different parts, from check boxes to radio buttons to drop-down forms and boxes for text.

Friendster.com—A popular social networking site. Users fill out an online questionnaire and upload a picture, then start adding friends and friends of friends to expand their social networks.

FrontPage—Microsoft FrontPage is software for creating and maintaining

Web sites. While experienced Web designers often prefer FrontPage's competitor, Dreamweaver, those new to creating Web pages may find FrontPage easier to use. For those who use other Microsoft applications regularly, the look, feel, and navigation will probably seem simpler and more familiar.

GarageBand—Software used to create and edit audio files on a Mac, perhaps for creating podcasts or adding online audio to your Web site.

HTML—Hypertext Markup Language, the codes used to create Web pages. HTML "tags"—such as <b> for bold—tell the Web browser how to display text or where to access images.

Image map—A single graphic on a Web page that allows users to click on different areas to go to different parts of a Web site. For example, a user might click on an image of a book to go to online booklists, or on a picture of a computer to go to the library's databases. When Web designers create an image map, they designate areas on the image, called "hotspots," which are related to particular links.

iMovie—Software for the Mac used to edit digital video and create special effects. Teen librarians might use iMovie to create video booktalks, video library tours, or a video podcast program.

Instant messaging—Software or Web-based programs that allow users to type text messages back and forth in real time. Users can also send each other files, photos, video and audio. Some IM services also allow free voice chat.

Internet Explorer—Microsoft's Internet Explorer is the most widely used type of Web browser.

iPod—A very popular MP3 player sold by Apple. The iPod can be used to play music, podcasts, and other audio files. Newer iPods can also be used to watch videos.

iPodder—Like iTunes, iPodder is a podcast aggregator. It is a type of software that allows users to subscribe to podcasts. When a new podcast is available, the aggregator downloads it automatically for the user.

ISP—Internet Service Provider. A company that provides connections to the Internet.

iTunes—Software created by Apple (but available for PCs) that allows users to purchase, play, and organize music and video files. The iTunes software also allows users to subscribe to and download podcasts. It can be used with an iPod or another type of MP3 player, such as one from a company such as Dell, iRiver, Samsung, Rio, or Creative.

Juice—Like iTunes, Juice is a podcast aggregator. It is a type of software that allows users to subscribe to podcasts. When a new podcast is available, the aggregator downloads it automatically for the user.

Listserv—A listserv is an online group that discusses a subject, usually a predefined topic, by e-mail. A message sent by one subscriber goes out to all of the subscribers. Users subscribe electronically, either on a Web site (such as Yahoo! Groups or Google Groups) or by sending an e-mail message to a computer running special software. Listserv is another term for an e-mail discussion group. Popular lists for librarians include PUBYAC, YALSA-BK, and LM_NET.

LiveJournal—A popular blog hosting site, as well as a virtual community. LiveJournal offers many social networking features, such as a "friends list" as well as blogs.

MMORPGs—Massively Multiplayer Online Role Playing Games, where players create online worlds where their avatars can go on quests, buy and sell goods, form relationships, and more.

Moblog—Mobile phone blogs, or "moblogs," allow users to add photos and video taken with their mobile phone, often from a distance, without even logging onto a computer.

Movable Type—Blog publishing software that can be downloaded and installed on a library or school server. Movable Type offers many advanced features, and a great deal of flexibility in customizing the look and feel of a blog. Pricing varies.

Mozilla Firefox—A type of Web browser, Firefox is the most popular alternative to Internet Explorer.

MP3 player—MP3 is an audio format. An MP3 player, usually portable, allows users to download music or spoken word files and then listen to them on the go. While the iPod is the most popular type of MP3 player, there are many other brands. Companies other than Apple that sell MP3 players include Dell, iRiver, Samsung, and Rio.

MySpace.com—A social networking site that is incredibly popular with teens. Users set up a profile, upload a photo, and begin networking with friends, friends of friends, and other users who share their interests. Users can post comments, send e-mails, start a blog, and more.

Outlook—Microsoft Outlook is software for managing e-mail and other personal data, available as part of Microsoft Office.

PDA—Personal Digital Assistant. Any handheld device that offers computing functions or Internet access. BlackBerry, Pocket PC, Sidekick, and Palm are all examples of types of PDAs.

PDF—Portable Document Format. A file where the text and layout appear exactly as the designer intended. It is often used for official forms and documents. PDF files are opened using Adobe Acrobat software.

Photoshop—Adobe Photoshop is software used to edit and manipulate digital images. It is available for the Mac or PC.

Podcast—A combination of "iPod" and "broadcast." Many Web sites include audio—generally music or spoken word files—that users can click and listen to online. Podcasting takes this a step further by allowing users to subscribe to a series of audio files. When you subscribe to a podcast, your computer automatically downloads new sound files as they are added to a Web site. You can then listen to the files on your computer or on an MP3 player.

Podcast aggregator—A podcast aggregator is a type of software that allows users to subscribe to podcasts. When a new podcast is available, the aggregator downloads it automatically for the user. While iTunes is the most popular podcast aggregator, there are others, including iPodder and Juice.

PowerPoint—Microsoft PowerPoint is software for creating presentations, available as part of Microsoft Office.

RSS/Atom—RSS stands for "Real Simple Syndication." RSS and Atom are both formats that allow users to subscribe to data feeds from blogs, news organizations, and more. RSS and Atom also allow users to subscribe to podcasts and video podcasts.

Screencast—A screencast is a movie that shows what is happening on a computer screen. Software such as CamStudio, Captivate, or Camtasia can be used to create screencasts, which can then be made available online. Screencasts are great educational tools, perfect for demos and tutorials.

Server—A server is a computer that holds information—Web page files, graphics, audio, video, and so on—and then responds to requests from other computers for that information. When you create a Web site, you store those files on a server. When a web user accesses a link to your site, your server provides that information over a network.

Skype.com—A service that uses VOIP (Voice Over Internet Protocol) to allow users to make free Internet phone calls to other Skype users. For a fee, people can also use their computers to call regular telephones, a service called Skype Out.

SMS/MMS—Two types of services for sending messages to cell phones. SMS (short message service) allows users to send and receive up to 160 characters per message. It is used for sending text messages. MMS (multimedia message service) is a more advanced service that allows users to transmit graphics, video clips, sound files and text messages by cell phone.

Social networking sites—MySpace, Friendster, Tribe.net, Facebook, and other similar sites allow users to post profiles that may include photos and information on their interests. They can then "network" with other users who share their interests or link to them as a "friend of a friend."

These sites are often controversial for use by teens—some schools ban them, citing safety concerns, since users sometimes post their full names and contact information.

Text messaging—Sending text messages using cell phones. As with Instant messaging, users often abbreviate words or use acronyms.

Trackback—Trackback is a system used by one blogger to notify others when someone comments on the person's blog. The first blogger will send what is called a "trackback ping" to the second blogger. This allows readers to follow the "conversation" between bloggers and to read all comments on a topic that interests them.

Typepad.com—TypePad is a service for bloggers. The site uses the Movable Type platform but is aimed at less experienced users and offers blog hosting. A trial is free, but then users pay for the service.

URL—Universal Resource Locator, or Web address.

USB—Universal Serial Bus, a standard method for attaching devices to a computer. For example, many people now use USB flash or jump drives rather than floppy disks. The drives plug into any USB port. Other peripherals, such as mice, keyboards, scanners, and printers may also plug into a USB port.

Vlog—Combines the words "video" and "blog"—a blog that features video files rather than text. The creator of a vlog regularly posts video clips to the site, which users then download and watch.

Vodcasting or video podcasting—"Vodcast" combines the words "video" and "podcast." It refers to producing a series of video files, adding them to your Web site, and then allowing users to subscribe to them. As with podcasts, an aggregator such as iTunes can be used to download files to a computer or portable device.

VOIP—Voice Over Internet Protocol uses the Internet to transmit voices. Communicating by using Skype, the best known service, is similar to making a telephone call, except that users on both ends speak into a microphone on or plugged into their computers. VOIP could allow librarians to talk to patrons while also showing them Web pages or text files on their computers, enhancing reference services. It could also be a way to host virtual author visits or communicate with teens who don't want to make long-distance telephone calls.

Web 2.0—A term for the next generation of Web services. It encompasses the idea of the Web as a more interactive place, with user-created content, community building, social networking, and resource sharing. It can also be used to refer to Web services that replicate software applications such as word processing and databases. In this context, users go online to do all of their computing. In addition, Web 2.0 can refer to

Web-based applications that respond smoothly to the needs of the user, with no waiting and no software to download. Many people use this term to differentiate between "old" Web sites that simply provided information or links and newer, more interactive sites. Librarians are now using terms like "Library 2.0" and "School Library 2.0" to refer to the next generation of library Web services.

Webcam—A Web camera. Video images captured by this camera can be made available on the Web.

Web Hosting service—A company that hosts Web sites by "renting out" space on their server, generally for a monthly fee. Web hosting services also often provide tools for managing your site, checking your statistics, backing up your Web pages, installing discussion forums or chat rooms, and more.

Webliographies—Like bibliographies, but available on the Web, Webliographies gather lists of links to resources on a subject together on one page. A Webliography may be annotated and may list Web sites, electronic texts, and other online resources.

WebQuest—A WebQuest is a research assignment where most or all of the activity takes place online. Students usually complete WebQuests as part of a group, where each student in the group has an assigned role. The term originated with Bernie Dodge, a professor at San Diego State University, in 1995. A well-constructed WebQuest requires students to construct their own meaning from the information they find, rather than simply gathering facts.

WiFi—Short for "wireless fidelity," WiFi allows users to connect to the Internet using portable devices such as laptops. Users must be in a WiFi "hotspot," or a spot where they are able to access the WiFi network.

Wiki—A wiki is a collaborative Web site where every user is an editor. "Wiki" is short for *wikiwiki*, Hawaiian for "quick." (The first wiki was created in Hawaii in 1995.) Users of wikis can change, add, edit, or delete content. The best known wiki is probably Wikipedia, an online encyclopedia project where amateur editors contribute to the articles.

WYSIWYG—"What You See is What You Get." The term refers to computer applications that let users create pages that look on the screen just as they will look on the Web or once printed out. Dreamweaver and FrontPage are two WYSIWYG HTML editors. Instead of looking at text and code and guessing what it might look like as a Web site, users can see the actual Web page as they create it.

Xanga.com—A Web site, popular with teens, that hosts blogs and also serves as a social networking site.

XML—Stands for Extensible Markup Language. It is one of the tools used to make Web sites respond better to user needs.

B: CHOOSE THE RIGHT TECHNOLOGIES

There is no doubt that technology is quickly changing how Internet users get their information. Audio and video content is everywhere now. RSS feeds allow users to view all of their favorite news and entertainment sources in one place. Information is also becoming more mobile—laptops with wireless access are becoming common, as are wifi (wireless Internet) access in public places, including libraries. Teens don't even need to sit down at a computer anymore. Instead, they can access information on a cell phone or handheld PDA.

However, it's important that, in the rush to be trendy, you don't embrace every exciting new fad that comes along. Sit down and think about whether your teen patrons really need the service you want to offer. Will they actually make use of the format you want to adopt? We are lucky to work with teens because they adapt well to change—few teens walk into the library and complain because they can't find the card catalog—and they are very much willing to try new things. That doesn't mean, however, that they will stick around if you can't offer them something useful. If you start a blog because the whole world seems to be blogging, but you have nothing interesting to say, it will likely go unread.

Before adding the latest bells and whistles to their Web sites, librarians should take a close look at their own schools or communities. Knowing your community can help you rule out certain technologies, at least for now. If most of your patrons don't have high-speed Internet connections at home or at school, adding video files to your Web site might not make sense, since those files would take forever to download on a dial-up connection. Similarly, if few of the students at your high school have iPods or other audio devices, a daily podcast probably won't reach a large audience.

In some areas, teenagers may not own the latest gadgets—MP3 players, fancy cell phones, PDAs, etc.—or have broadband Internet access at home or at school. In other areas, teens may be on the cutting edge, with the latest video cell phones and mobile devices. Adding a communication option makes the most sense where at least some of your users can and will take advantage of it. You might also want to look at what other institutions in your community offer, and whether teens use those services. For example, if teens are creating and listening to podcasts at school, church, or other community organizations, they will probably be open to library podcasts as well.

It's also very important to know what modes of communication your teens prefer. If the teens in your community love instant messaging but consider e-mail a method of communication for "old folks," you might want to offer an IM reference service instead of answering questions by e-mail. If students at your school are crazy about blogging, it could be time to start one for the library.

A good source of current of information about who's online and what they do there is the Pew Internet and American Life Project, available at www.pewinternet.org. While the majority of the reports focus on adult use of technology, several do look at teenagers and college students, as well as other demographic groups and trends.

Of course, the best way to decide what's worth adding to a Web site is to ask the users themselves. A teen advisory board could choose from a list of marketing options, selecting the options they think would work best for them. A survey of teen library users, the students at a school, or the teachers and parents a librarian hopes to reach might help with decision making as well.

C: TEEN TECHNOLOGY SURVEY

Survey

Age:_____

School: _____

About how much time to do you spend using a computer on an average day?

___ None

___ One hour or less

___ 2–3 hours

___ 4 or more hours

How much of that time do you spend on the Internet (rather than, for example, using a world processor to write a paper)?

___ None of it

___ Less than half of it

___ More than half of it

Where do you go online?

___ School

___ Home

___ At a library

___ Other: _____

How fast is your Internet connection?
___ Dial-up
___ DSL or cable
___ Don't know

What three Web sites do you visit most often?

_____

_____

_____

What do you mainly use the Internet for?
___ School work and research
___ Socializing with friends
___ Online games
___ Shopping
___ Other: _____

Do you have a page on MySpace or another social networking site?
___ Yes—Which site(s)? _____
___ No

Do you have a blog?
___ Yes
___ No

Do you read other peoples' blogs regularly?
___ Yes
___ No

Do you use RSS feeds (or a site like Bloglines or MyYahoo!) to keep up with your news sites and blogs?
___ Yes
___ No

Do you use instant messaging services (IM)?
___ No
___ Yes, sometimes
___ Yes, every day

Which one do you use?
___ Yahoo!
___ AOL
___ Windows Live Messenger
___ Other: _____

Do you have an e-mail account?
___ Yes—How often do you check it? __ Daily __ Weekly __ Monthly
___ No

Do you watch video clips online?
___ No
___ Yes: What do you watch? ___ Music videos ___ Movie trailers
       Other: _____

Do you have a cell phone?
___ No
___ Yes: About how many calls do you make and receive per day? _____
How many text messages do you make and receive per day? _____

What's your favorite way to be contacted?
___ Phone
___ Text message
___ Instant Message
___ E-mail
___ Other:_____

Which of the following portable devices do you own, if any?
___ iPod or other MP3 player
___ PDA (personal digital assistant). What kind? _____
___ BlackBerry or other e-mail device
___ Laptop computer
___ Digital camera
___ Other:_____

Do you ever listen to podcasts?
___ No
___ Yes: List your favorites: _____

Do you share digital photos with your friends?
___ No
___ Yes: How? ___ Cell phone ___ E-mail ___ Instant Message
       ___ MySpace, Friendster, etc. ___ Flickr ___ Other:_____

What new technologies are you and your friends most excited about?

D: LIST OF PROJECTS BY TECHNOLOGY

Are you interested in starting a blog, but want to see how others are using them? Wondering about wikis, and how they might be incorporated into your library Web page? Curious about podcasting, but not sure how it relates to your work with teens? This list will help you figure out where to go in this book to find out more about each type of technology.

I have listed each idea under the most appropriate technology. Some ideas fall under more than one category, such as "Idea #76: Incorporate Audio/Video Booktalks," which is included under both the Audio and Video categories. Other ideas in the book depend on content rather than technology—such as including your collection development policy on your Web site, or posting teen book reviews—and these are not listed here. For each idea, I provide a brief summary. If you're intrigued, locate that idea in this book and read that section for much more detailed information.

AUDIO/PODCASTING

What it is: Audio is simply recorded sound files—music, voice, and so on—available online so that Web site users can listen on their computers or their portable devices. Podcasting (a term combining "iPod," the popular portable MP3 player, and "broadcasting") makes it possible for users to subscribe to a series of audio files. After users begin their subscription using iTunes or similar software, any new audio files in the series are automatically downloaded for their listening pleasure.

Idea #18: Add Some Audio

Find out more about audio in this general overview of the technology.

Idea #19: Consider Podcasting

Find out more about podcasting in this general overview of the technology.

Idea #32: Listen Up: Audio Files

Use audio files to get the word out about library and to publicize library services for teens.

Idea #33: Become a Podcaster

Start a library podcast for teens.

Idea #49: Give an Audio or Video Tour

Create an audio tour of your library or your teen area to add to your Web site.

Idea #51: Provide Downloadable Audio Books

Improve online access to library materials by adding downloadable audio books to your Web site.

Idea #69: Venture into Audio/Video Lectures and Lessons

Record audio files to provide lectures and lessons for your students to view anytime, accessible through your library Web site.

Idea #76: Incorporate Audio/Video Booktalks

Record audio booktalks that teens can listen to whenever they are online, or that they can download to their portable media players.

Idea #84: Use Audio to Give Teens a Voice

Let teens record their own poetry, music, and other creative efforts, then make their work available to the world by posting it to your Web site.

BLOGS

What it is: Short for "Web log," a blog is an online journal. Blog creators frequently use Web-based sites that make updating the blog very simple. Blogs usually consists of short entries that include links to other Web sites. Blogs are often chatty and opinionated in tone. They may have a "comments" link where readers can add their own opinions or suggestions.

Idea #13: Start Blogging

Find out more about blogging in this general overview of the technology.

Idea #14: Learn About Vlogs and Moblogs

Get ideas on how to enhance your blog by adding video or allowing teens to contribute their photos, video, or audio input using cell phones.

Idea #25: Build a Blog for Library News

Add a blog to your Web site that focuses on what's new at the library.

Idea #73: Blog about Books

Start a blog with a literary focus—new titles, book reviews, and more.

Idea #91: Begin a TAB Blog

Focus your blog on the activities of the library's teen advisory council, perhaps allowing teens to contribute the blog's content.

Idea #100: Start a Summer Reading Blog

Create a library blog just for the summer reading program, with news, book discussions, and so on.

Idea #104: Add a Game Blog

Bond online with your teen gamers by creating a blog about video games and the library.

DISCUSSION BOARDS/FORUMS

What it is: A discussion board is an online space where users can leave messages that other users then respond to. Discussion boards might also be called Web forums, message boards, discussion forums, discussion groups, or bulletin boards. A discussion board keeps a running record of what users have posted, so anyone joining can read the entire discussion from the beginning.

Idea #11: Start a Discussion

Find out more about discussion boards and forums in this general overview of the technology.

Idea #78: Promote an Online Forum

An online forum focused on book discussion is a great way to promote reading. Get your teens talking about books by creating one for your site.

Idea #92: Encourage Online Discussion

An online forum is a good way to help your teen advisory council members communicate with each other between in-person meetings.

Idea #101: Get Your Summer Readers Talking

Let the teens in your summer reading program share book suggestions, questions, and opinions by adding a discussion board to your Web site.

E-MAIL

What it is: Electronic mail. Messages, usually text, are sent via computer. Users may have free online accounts, such as Yahoo! Mail or Gmail, or use software such as Microsoft Outlook to read and respond to messages. Photos, files, video and audio can also be sent by e-mail.

Idea #27: Use E-mail to Keep in Touch

Use e-mail distribution lists and listservs to publicize programs and keep teens informed about library issues.

Idea #29: Send Program Reminders

Send e-mail program reminders to teens the day or week before a special program.

FEEDS/RSS

What it is: Feeds allow Web users to "subscribe" to a blog or any other Web site where content is added regularly. Users utilize either a desktop newsreader such as FeedReader, or more likely choose an online service such as Bloglines or MyYahoo!. They can then see the newest headlines all in one place, rather than checking their favorite blogs or Web sites every day. Feeds can also be integrated into a Web page so that new headlines and items are automatically displayed on a page.

Idea #15: Get to Know Feeds

Find out more about feeds and RSS in this general overview of the technology.

Idea #26: Offer Feeds to Keep Teens Current

Add RSS feeds to your blog or Web site so that teens can subscribe to your new content.

Idea #105: Feature Breaking News

Add news or entertainment headlines to your Web site, using a feed so that they update automatically.

FORMS

What they are: Forms are HTML (Hypertext Markup Language) documents that allow users to submit information directly from a Web page. Users may type in information, select checkboxes, or choose an option from a drop-down menu. Users then click on a submit button to send the information. Forms are a good way to get feedback from your Web site users, since they don't require that users log into an e-mail account first to send you their comments.

Idea #12: Make Use of Forms

Find out more about forms in this general overview of the technology.

Idea #35: Ask for Comments

Create a comment form so that teens can easily contact you and express their opinions.

Idea #36: Take a Survey

Use an online form to survey your teen Web site users about their favorite books, what programs they would like to attend, or any other topic.

Idea #37: Suggestion Form for Materials

Let teens use a Web form to suggest the books, movies, or music they would like the library to purchase.

Idea #53: Issue Library Cards Online

Allow teens to sign up online for library cards, then pick them up at their closest library or get them through the mail.

Idea #63: Ask for Assignment Alerts

Forms are an easy way for teachers to notify their public or school librarian about upcoming assignments, so that the librarian can prepare.

Idea #74: Solicit Teen Book Reviews

Teens are more likely to send in book reviews if they can simply type or cut and paste them into an online form.

Idea #87: Let Teens Apply Online

Have your teen advisory council hopefuls submit their applications using a Web form, rather than filling out a paper application.

Idea #97: Take Sign Ups Online

Encourage teens to sign up for your summer reading program using an online form.

Idea #98: Accept Online Book Review Submissions

Summer readers will also appreciate the chance to submit their book reviews online, instead of handwriting them and taking them to the closest library.

Idea #99: Allow Electronic Raffle Entries

Offer online chances at raffle prizes for your summer reading program—teens can fill out an online form and click "submit."

INSTANT MESSAGING/CHAT

What it is: Instant Messaging allows users to type text messages back and forth in real time. IM utilizes software or Web-based programs. Users can also send each other files, photos, video and audio. Chat is similar but usually involves groups of participants gathered together (as in a chat room) and all of the participants reading each message as part of a group conversation.

Idea #16: Embrace Instant Messaging

Find out more about Instant Messaging in this general overview of the technology.

Idea #30: Adopt Instant Messaging

Use Instant Messaging to get the word out about your programs and services. By communicating with teens using one of their favorite methods, you may find it easier to keep in touch.

Idea #54: Offer Online Reference

Reference services that answer questions over Instant Messaging software have great teen appeal, since teens so often already use IM for socializing.

Idea #55: Provide Live Homework Help

Homework help services often use Instant Messaging to provide assistance with assignments, perhaps in conjunction with an online "whiteboard."

Idea #77: Invite Authors for Virtual Visits

Popular YA authors can "visit" your library through online chats, interacting with teens and answering their questions.

SOCIAL NETWORKING

What it is: MySpace, Friendster, Tribe.net, Facebook, and other similar sites allow users to post profiles that may include photos and information on their interests. They can then "network" with other users who share their interests or link to them as a "friend of a friend." Social networking sites may allow users to exchange e-mail, post to a blog, and much more. Mobile social networking uses cell phones to help people connect with friends. Sites such as Flickr allow people to share photos, while social bookmarking sites such as del.icio.us let users trade favorite locations on the Web.

Idea #23: Expand Your Social Network

Find out more about social networks in this general overview of the technology.

TAGGING/FOLKSONOMIES

What it is: A tag is an informal keyword or descriptive phrase. Tagging allows users, rather than a central authority, to organize or "catalog" information on the Web. A folksonomy is a system of organization that depends on user-generated tags.

Idea #24: Discover Folksonomies, Tagging, and Bookmark Sharing

Find out more about folksonomies, tagging, and bookmark sharing in this general overview of the technology.

TEXT MESSAGING

What it is: Sending text messages using cell phones. As with Instant messaging, users often abbreviate words or use acronyms to keep messages short.

Idea #17: Try Text Messaging

Find out more about text messaging in this general overview of the technology.

Idea #31: Start Text Messaging

Use text messaging to contact teens on the go to make sure they know about library programs, new books, and much more.

VIDEO/VODCASTING

What it is: More and more Web sites are making video available online. Video clips and even longer videos can be accessed online by users, who watch them on their computers or on portable devices such the newest iPods. Like podcasting for audio, Vodcasting takes video one step further by allowing users to subscribe to a series of videos. Users subscribe to a Vodcast and then the video clips are downloaded automatically each time a new one is posted.

Idea #20: Discover Video and Vodcasting

Find out more about video and vodcasting in this general overview of the technology.

Idea #34: Include Video

Videotape your teen programs, create a library news show, make a library "commercial"—the possibilities are endless.

Idea #49: Give an Audio or Video Tour

Create a video tour of your library or your teen area to add to your Web site.

Idea #52: Present Downloadable Video

Make movies and nonfiction videos available for download in the same way many libraries do e-books and audio books.

Idea #69: Venture into Audio/Video Lectures and Lessons

Use video to provide lectures and lessons for your students to view anytime, accessible through your library Web site.

Idea #76: Incorporate Audio/Video Booktalks

Record video booktalks by librarians, teachers, or teens, and share them on your Web site or start a regular Vodcast (video broadcast) program.

Idea #85: Capture Creativity on Video

Catch your teens on video during talent shows, Battle of the Bands programs, poetry slams, etc., then share their performances with the world.

VOICE COMMUNICATION

What it is: VOIP (Voice Over Internet Protocol) allows users to talk to each other as if they are on the phone, but using their computers and a microphone instead of a telephone. Many of these services are free. Users can talk to each other at the same time that they use Instant Messaging or other online services to trade photos, files, Web site addresses, and more, making this a great way to provide reference services via the Internet.

Idea #22: Find Your Voice with VOIP

Find out more about VOIP in this general overview of the technology.

WIKIS

What it is: A wiki is a type of Web site that allows many authors to collaborate to create content. Any author can add, edit, or delete materials on the site. Wikipedia.com is probably the best known example of a wiki.

Idea #21: Experiment with Wikis

Find out more about wikis in this general overview of the technology.

Idea #40: Test Out a Wiki

A wiki is one possible way to get feedback from teen library users, by creating a file any visitor to your Web site can edit and change.

Idea #57: Try a Pathfinder Wiki

Let students create their own pathfinder by contributing the best links, books, and other resources to the project.

Idea #70: Initiate Faculty/Student Wikis

Create wikis for your school so that teachers and/or students can collaborate and share ideas.

Idea #79: Offer a Readers' Advisory Wiki

Use wikis to help teens create "Best Books" lists, add their favorite titles, and contribute their book reviews.

Part VI.   Help Pages: 101+ Great Ideas for Teen Library Web Sites

A: REVIEW OF THE LITERATURE

In the ten or so years since the Internet became part of our everyday life, librarians have also been writing about every aspect of teen library Web sites. I highlight a few articles from professional journals here because they raise some excellent points. They also provide insight into the history of library Web sites for teens, and the way the Web has grown and changed over the years.

YA librarian Patrick Jones, author of *Connecting Young Adults and Libraries* (Neal-Schuman, 1992), wrote what may well be one of the first articles on the "YA Web" in November, 1996 (Jones, 1996: 48). In *School Library Journal*, he wrote about the importance of evaluating sites before linking to them, and the necessary task of "weeding" online collections of links as they become outdated. He also addressed the fact that, when sending Web site visitors to outside links, it is impossible to guarantee that those sites will not lead to something "offensive" or "objectionable."

A year later, Jones followed up his first article with "A Cyber-Room of Their Own: How Libraries Use Web Pages to Attract Young Adults" (*School Library Journal*, November 1997, p. 34–37). He surveyed librarians across the country about their teen sites. Creating a successful YA area on the Web, he concluded, is similar to creating a physical library space: "Load it up with high-interest materials; make it attractive; involve YAs in the process, and most of all, make it distinct from other parts of the site by clearly defining its audience and giving it an identifiable appearance, content, and scope" (Jones, 1997: 34). Offering a young adult Web site signals a library's commitment to serving teens, he wrote; but, in his survey, Jones found that most public library Web sites did not yet have a separate area for teens. Jones mentions five elements generally found on YA Web pages: book reviews, links, resource lists, program information, and information on library services. At this point, several libraries were also soliciting teen book reviews and other writing, and about half involved teens in creating and maintaining the Web sites.

In March, 2000, Sara Ryan of Multnomah County Library in Portland, Oregon, wrote an article for *School Library Journal* called, "It's Hip to Be Square." Ryan suggested that librarians give up on attempts to offer "cool" Web sites and instead focus on creating sites that are useful. She provided a list of do's and don'ts, including:

Do allow teens to contribute their own reviews;
Don't just link to search engines—describe them and explain what each search engine is best for;
Do include links to local resources, and be sure to add crisis hotlines;
Don't use "glitzy Web animations and media files" if you want to reach a wide audience (Ryan, 2000: 138–41).

In 2003, Sandra Hughes-Hassell and Erika Thickman Miller of Drexel University published a very thorough, academic look at "Public library Web sites for young adults: Meeting the needs of today's teens online." This article examined the reasons why public libraries develop Web sites for young adults, how they promote them, and what the barriers are to the creation and maintenance of these sites. The authors found that the focus of teens on the Web is social activities, and concluded that:

If librarians want to attract young adults to their collections and services, they must become integral members of the online community. Furthermore, library Web pages must address the needs of young adults on many levels—academic, social, and recreational. Although finding useful information to complete a research paper for school may initiate a teenager's visit to a library Web page, the social and recreational aspects may be critical in assuring a return visit (Hughes-Hassell and Miller, 2003: 145).

The authors also surveyed libraries with teen Web pages and came up with some interesting findings. Teen involvement in Web site development was fairly high, with teens contributing creative content, suggesting links, submitting design ideas, or in a few cases creating the sites themselves. However, many libraries limited teen contributions because of library administration was concerned about site security and inappropriate or unapproved content.

Librarians reported that the major challenges involved in Web site creation included lack of time for updating pages, lack of training, and lack of staff. Another common complaint was about "the restraints imposed by library administration" on the design and content of the teen Web pages (Hughes-Hassell and Miller, 2003: 151).

The authors also pointed out that only three of the librarians who responded to the survey said that their sites offer interactive services, and that only 12.7 percent used their sites to help teens connect with their peers (Hughes-Hassell and Miller, 2003: 152). They conclude that teens need to be more involved in the creation of library Web sites. They also suggested that before librarians begin developing Web sites, they should assess the needs of their patrons and decide on a purpose for their site.

Another useful article comes from the Spring 2004 issue of *Young Adult Library Services*, written by Patrick Jones and Angela Pfeil, "Public Library YA Web Pages for the Twenty-First Century." In this article, the authors provide a list of suggestions for teen pages, including logical organizations, simple design, real-life help, annotations for each included site, language free of library jargon, and much more. Jones and Pfeil strongly emphasize the importance of involving teens in Web site development. Librarians also need to promote the Web page "at booktalks, school visit networking meetings, and so on. They need to brand it by putting the name and URL on every document" (Jones and Pfeil, 2004: 15). The article also proposes criteria for an award recognizing the best public library Web sites for teens, including how well the site meets teens' developmental needs and how well it incorporates youth participation. Twenty excellent public library Web sites are listed and briefly described, including many that I mention in this book.

In "A Case for Making Original Content Part of Your YA Web Page," published in the Winter 2005 issue of *Young Adult Library Services*, Paula Brehm-Heeger argues against emphasizing a collection of links. Instead, she believes that library Web sites for teens should be places where teens can access information created specifically for them. She includes photos, artwork, comments about a program, teen book reviews, and opinion articles as examples of good ideas for original content.

In the May 2006 issue of *School Library Journal*, Christopher Harris makes a passionate argument for adopting "School Library 2.0" ideas. Expanding on the Web 2.0 movement, Harris argues for a "digitally re-shifted" school library that uses technology to move outside of the library walls. In this model, media specialists encourage teachers and students to contribute content to blogs, podcasts, and other Web-based projects. Librarians would also use recent innovations to reach out to the school community, using, for example, Web-based bookmarking sites to build pathfinders.

While professional journals are good sources of information about library Web sites for teens, inspiration is also likely to come from online sources and personal connections. In reading some of the blogs of librarians who work with teens, I came across insightful and up-to-the-minute commentary about teens, technology, and libraries. One good source of information is the Alternative Teen Services Blog. For example, one of the bloggers on the site recently mused, on the topic of video podcasting, that "the use of podcast technology with teens should be fun and exciting. If I were using podcast technology to attract teens to the library, I would approach the Teen Advisory Board to create content for these videos. Teens would be the best source, presumably, to come up with creative skits that promote the library as a cool place to be" (Stephanie Librarian, "Podcasting & Teens," accessed April 29, 2006. http://yalibrarian.com/2006/01/podcasting-teens.html).

It's good to know that while libraries—perhaps inevitably—lag behind in implementing new ideas and technology, there are plenty of teen librarians thinking, talking, and writing about these ideas and how they might want to use them in the future to develop appealing Web sites.

B: JOURNAL ARTICLES ON LIBRARY WEB SITES FOR TEENS

Braun, Linda W. "Building a Better Web Site." *School Library Journal*. (July 1, 1998). Available: www.schoollibraryjournal.com/article/CA152995.html.

Brehm-Heeger, Paula. 2005. "A Case for Making Original Content Part of Your YA Web Page." *Young Adult Library Services* 3 no. 2 (Winter): 32–34.

Farmer, Lesley S. 2005. "Virtual Reference Service for K–12 Students." *Knowledge Quest* 33, no. 3 (January/February): 22–24.

Harris, Christopher. "School Library 2.0." *School Library Journal*. (May 1, 2006). Available: www.schoollibraryjournal.com/article/CA6330755.html.

Jones, Patrick. 1997. "A Cyber-room of Their Own: How Libraries Use Web Pages to Attract Young Adults." *School Library Journal* 43, no. 11 (November): 34–37.

———. 1996. "A Page of Our Own." *School Library Journal* 42, no. 11 (November): 48.

Jones, Patrick, and Angel Pfeil. 2004. "Public Library YA Web Pages for the Twenty-first Century." *YALS: Young Adult Library Services* 2, no. 2: 14–19.

Ryan, Sara. 2000. "It's Hip to Be Square: Designing a Teen-Friendly Library Web Site." *School Library Journal* 46, no. 3 (March): 138–41.

Sandra Hughes-Hassell, and Erika Thickman Miller. 2003. "Public Library Web Sites for Young Adults: Meeting the Needs of Today's Teens On-line." *Library & Information Science Research* 25, no. 2: 143–56.

C: BOOKS RELATED TO LIBRARY WEB SITES

Blowers, Helene, and Robin Bryan. 2004. *Weaving a Library Web: A Guide to Developing Children's Web Sites.* Chicago, IL: ALA.

Braun, Linda W. 2003. *Hooking Teens with the Net.* New York: Neal-Schuman.

———. 2003. *Technically Involved: Technology-Based Youth Participation Activities for Your Library.* Chicago, IL: ALA.

———. 2002. *Teens.library: Developing Internet Services for Young Adults.* Chicago, IL: ALA.

Champelli, Lisa. 2002. *The Youth Cybrarian's Guide to Developing Instructional, Curriculum-Related, Summer Reading, and Recreational Programs.* New York: Neal-Schuman.

Crane, Beverly E. 2003. *Internet Workshops: 10 Ready-To-Go Workshops for K–12 Educators.* New York: Neal-Schuman.

Craver, Kathleen W. 2002. *Creating Cyber Libraries: An Instructional Guide for School Library Media Specialists.* Greenwood Village, CO: Libraries Unlimited.

Fisher, Julieta Dias, and Ann Hill. 2003. *Tooting Your Own Horn: Web-Based Public Relations for the 21st Century Librarian.* Worthington, OH: Linworth.

Junion-Metz, Gail, and Derrek L. Metz. 2002. *Instant Web Forms and Surveys for Children's/YA Services and School Libraries.* New York: Neal-Schuman.

———. 2001. *Instant Web Forms and Surveys for Public Libraries.* New York: Neal-Schuman.

Logan, Debra Kay, and Cynthia Beuselinck. 2001. *K–12 Web Pages: Planning & Publishing Excellent School Web Sites.* Worthington, OH: Linworth.

McCorkle, Sandra K. 2003. *Web Pages For Your Classroom: The EASY Way.* Westport, CT: Libraries Unlimited.

Minkel, Walter, and Roxanne Hsu Feldman. 1998. *Delivering Web Reference Services to Young People.* Chicago, IL: ALA.

Richardson, Will. 2006. *Blogs, Wikis, Podcasts and Other Powerful Web Tools for Classrooms.* Thousand Oaks, CA: Corwin Press.

Song, Yuwu. 2003. *Building Better Web Pages: A How-to-Do-It Manual for Librarians.* New York: Neal-Schuman.

D: GENERAL WEB DESIGN BOOKS

Cohen, June. 2003. *Unusually Useful Web Book*. Indianapolis, IN: New Riders.

Flanders, Vincent, and Dean Peters. 2002. *Son of Web Pages That Suck: Learn Good Design by Looking at Bad Design*. San Francisco, CA: Sybex.

Krug, Steve. 2005. *Don't Make Me Think: A Common Sense Approach to Web Usability*, 2nd ed. Berkeley, CA: New Riders Press.

Lynch, Patrick J., and Sarah Horton. 2002. *Web Style Guide: Basic Design Principles for Creating Web Sites*, 2nd ed. New Haven, CT: Yale University Press.

MacDonald, Matthew. 2005. *Creating Web Sites: The Missing Manual*. Sebastopol, CA: O'Reilly.

Nielsen, Jakob. 2000. *Designing Web Usability: The Practice of Simplicity*. Indianapolis, IN: New Riders.

Nielsen, Jakob, and Marie Tahir. 2001. *Homepage Usability: 50 Web Sites Deconstructed*. Indianapolis, IN: New Riders.

Robbins, Jennifer Niederst. 2003. *Learning Web Design: A Beginner's Guide to HTML, Graphics, and Beyond*, 2nd ed. Sebastopol, CA: O'Reilly.

———. 2006. *Web Design in a Nutshell: A Desktop Quick Reference*, 3rd ed. Sebastopol, CA: O'Reilly.

Williams, Robin, and John Tollett. 2006. *The Non-Designer's Design Book*, 2nd ed. Berkeley, CA: Peachpit.

E: DIRECTORIES OF PUBLIC LIBRARY TEEN WEB SITES AND SCHOOL LIBRARY WEB SITES

Public Libraries with Young Adult Home Pages
Available at: http://yahelp.suffolk.lib.ny.us/virtual.html

Web Pages Created by School Librarians
Available at: www.school-libraries.net

F: LINKS FOR LIBRARY WEBMASTERS

Creating a Web Page for Your School Library
Available at: www.iasl-slo.org/creatingWeb.html
Useful links from the International Association of School Librarians, including directories, tutorials, and other resources.

Designing School Web sites to Deliver
Available at: http://fno.org/Webdesign.html

Writer and consultant Jamie McKenzie offers information on site design, legal issues, HTML, and links to other resources.

Library Webmaster Links
Available at: www.librarysupportstaff.com/4libWebmasters.html
General resources, news, articles, legal information, design, links to tutorials and more, from Mary Niederlander at LibrarySupportStaff .com.

"So You Would Like to Be a Library Web Master"
Available at: www.greece.k12.ny.us/ath/library/Webworkshop/default .htm
In this slide presentation from a workshop, school librarian Will Haines covers design fundamentals, planning, and technology tools.

Writing School Library Web Pages
Available at: www.sldirectory.com/libsf/resf/wpages.html
Part of the Resources or School Librarians Web site, links on this page include design ideas, a book list, sample sites, information on writing for the Web, and more.

Writing Your Own Web Page
Available at: www.sldirectory.com/compf/write.html#top
Part of the Virtual Middle School Library, this site has links to useful resources such as tutorials, clip art, link validation services, HTML guides, and more.

G: KEEPING CURRENT:
BLOGS FOR LIBRARY WEBMASTERS

Alt Teen Services Blog
Available at: http://yalibrarian.com
Two teen librarians who work for the Kansas City Public Library blog about young adult services, with many posts about technology and teenagers.

Blog Without A Library
www.blogwithoutalibrary.net/
"Libraries, technology, and everything in between," from librarian Amanda Etches-Johnson.

Free Range Librarian
Available at: http://freerangelibrarian.com
Writer, speaker, and librarian K. G. Schneider, who works at the Librarian's
     Index to the Internet and is a representative for ALA's Library and
     Information Technology Association, frequently writes about tech-
     nology and libraries.

Infomancy
Available at: http://schoolof.info/infomancy/
Christopher Harris writes about school libraries and technology.

Information Wants to Be Free
http://meredith.wolfwater.com/wordpress/
Librarian Meredith Farkas, creator of the Library Success wiki, blogs
     about technology, especially social networking tools.

Librarian in Black
http://librarianinblack.typepad.com/
Librarian Sarah Houghton blogs about "web design, technology news,
     library world news, reference stuff, funky gadgets, and other useful
     (or simply amusing) sites and posts" on this informative site.

Librarian in the Middle
Available at: www.beiffert.net/wordpress/
Resources and news for middle school librarians, including musing about
     technology and links to great resources.

Librarian.net
www.librarian.net/
Librarian Jessamyn West often blogs about technology, including the newest
     trends, the Digital Divide, and how libraries can stay up to date.

Library Clips
http://libraryclips.blogsome.com/
A librarian with a particular interest in current awareness tools blogs about
     RSS, social bookmarks, wikis, and more.

Library Stuff
www.librarystuff.net/
Steven M. Cohen blogs about libraries and technology.

Library Web Chic
www.librarywebchic.net/wordpress/
Web design and technology resources from librarian Karen A. Coombs.

Open Stacks
Available at: http://openstacks.net/os/
Librarian Greg Schwartz blogs about technology, with an emphasis on
  podcasting. His podcast feed is: http://feeds.feedburner.com/open-
  stacks.

Pop Goes the Library
www.popgoesthelibrary.com/
Librarians Sophie Brookover, Liz Burns, and Melissa Rabey write about
  pop culture in the library, with plenty of posts about the Web and
  technology tools.

RSS4Lib
http://blogs.fletcher.tufts.edu/rss4lib/
A blog dedicated to how libraries are using RSS feeds.

The Shifted Librarian
Available at: www.theshiftedlibrarian.com
Librarian Jenny Levine writes about libraries and technology, including
  Web 2.0 tools.

Tame the Web
http://tametheweb.com/
Librarian Michael Stephens, who has presented at many conferences and
  workshops, writes about technology in libraries, especially social
  software and gaming.

Weblogg-ed
Available at: www.Weblogg-ed.com/
Will Richardson blogs about "Weblogs, wikis, RSS, audiocasts and other
  Read/Write Web related technologies in the K–12 realm."

YALSA Blog: Technology category
Available at: http://blogs.ala.org/yalsa.php?cat=20
See the latest posts on technology on the Young Adult Library Association's
  blog by viewing the technology category.

H: LINKS TO INNOVATIVE LIBRARY WEB SITE PROJECTS

Blogging Libraries
Available at: www.blogwithoutalibrary.net/?page_id=94

The Elite Project
Available at: www.le.ac.uk/li/distance/eliteproject/index.htm

Innovative Internet Applications in Libraries
Available at: www.wiltonlibrary.org/innovate.html

Libraries Using IM Reference
Available at: www.libsuccess.org/index.php?title=Online_Reference#
    Libraries_Using_IM_Reference

Index

About the Author

Miranda Doyle is the library media teacher at Martin Luther King Jr. Academic Middle School in San Francisco, California. She received an undergraduate degree in Political Science from Stanford University, then attended San Jose State University for her Masters in Library and Information Science. She also received a multiple-subject teaching credential from San Francisco State and completed her School Library Media certification. She has worked as a teen librarian for the Venice Branch of Los Angeles Public Library, as an assistant librarian at Notre Dame High School in Belmont, California, and as a volunteer children's librarian in the Philippines. In her six years with San Francisco Public Library, Miranda worked at several branches as a teen, adult, and children's librarian. She has reviewed teen books for *School Library Journal* for the past ten years, as well as writing articles for both *School Library Journal* and *Voice of Youth Advocates*. She also designed and maintains the Teenlibrarian Web site at www.teenlibrarian.com. She can be contacted at mirandadoyle@yahoo.com.

6207　85